D1473096

CLAUDEL

Nicolas Poussin, *The Triumph of Flora.* Oil, 165 × 241 cm, 1630. *(Courtesy of Cliché des Musées Nationaux, Louvre, Paris.)*

CLAUDEL

Beauty and Grace

Angelo Caranfa

Lewisburg
Bucknell University Press
London and Toronto: Associated University Presses

Associated University Presses
440 Forsgate Drive
Cranbury, NJ 08512

Associated University Presses
25 Sicilian Avenue
London WC1A 2QH, England

Associated University Presses
P.O. Box 488, Port Credit
Mississauga, Ontario
Canada L5G 4M2

The paper used in this publication meets the requirements
of the American National Standard for Permanence of Paper
for Printed Library Materials Z39.48-1984.

LIBRARY OF CONGRESS
Library of Congress Cataloging-in-Publication Data

Caranfa, Angelo.
    Claudel: beauty and grace/Angelo Caranfa.
        p. cm.
    Bibliography: p.
    Includes index.
    ISBN 0-8387-5134-2 (alk. paper)
    1. Claudel, Paul, 1868-1955—Criticism and interpretation.
    2. Claudel, Paul, 1868-1955—Aesthetics.   3. Aesthetics,
    Modern—20th century.   4. Aesthetics, French.   5. Grace (Aesthetics)
    I. Title.
    PQ2605.L2Z5968 1989
    848'.91209—dc19   87-47982
                                                                    CIP

PRINTED IN THE UNITED STATES OF AMERICA

Per i miei genitori
Pour la reine de mai

Faites que je sois comme un semeur de solitude et que
celui qui entend ma parole
Rentre chez lui inquiet et lourd (*CGO*, 99).

Make me to be like a sower of solitude, and make the one
who hears my words
Enter within himself restless and heavy [with thought].

Ah, ce n'est point le bonheur que je t'apporte, mais ta
mort, et la mienne avec elle,
Mais qu'est-ce que cela me fait à moi que je te fasse
mourir,
Et moi, et tout, et tant pis! pourvu qu'à ce prix qui est
toi et moi,
Donnés, jetés, arrachés, lacérés, consumés,
Je sente ton âme, un moment qui est toute l'éternité,
toucher,
Prendre
La mienne comme la chaux astreint le sable brûlant
et en sifflant! (*PM*, 1030).

Ah, it is not happiness I bring you, but
death, and mine with it.
But what does it matter to me if I make you
die,
And myself, and everything, provided that at that price
which is you and me,
Surrendered, thrown down, torn, lacerated, consumed,
I feel your soul, for a moment which is all eternity,
touching,
Taking
Mine as lime seizes the sand, burning and hissing!

Mais, alors, nous serons les *poëtes*, les faiseurs de nous-mêmes
(*OP*, 203).

After death we shall be the *poets*, the makers of ourselves.

Contents

Preface   9
Note on the Translations   11
References   13

Introduction   17
1 Claudel and Proust on Beauty   23
2 Claudel and Merleau-Ponty on Perception   42
3 Claudel and Weil on Grace   59
4 Claudel and Sartre: The Grace of Creation and the
   Beauty of Nothingness   79
5 Claudel and Gide: Beauty and Grace in Baroque Art   97
6 Claudel and Redon: The Image of Beauty and Grace   119
7 Claudel and van Gogh: Expressiveness of Beauty and
   Grace   135
Conclusion   157

Notes   161
Select Bibliography   179
Index   187

Preface

This work attempts to reveal Paul Claudel's vision of beauty and grace, showing Claudel's centrality in modern French aesthetics by relating his vision to that of Marcel Proust, Merleau-Ponty, Simone Weil, André Gide, Jean-Paul Sartre, Odilon Redon, and Vincent van Gogh. It is not the intent of this work to yield to a Catholic approach to literary criticism and aesthetics, but rather to help the reader experience Claudel's mental anguish, torn as he was between artistic realization and the beauty and grace of objective and spiritual realities. By linking Claudel with some of the most fascinating creative figures of modern French art (literary, poetic, and visual), I hope to point out to the reader the ambiguity between the subjective and objective evidence of beauty and grace in modern French aesthetics.

This work relies exclusively on the use of key texts, which have been selected to represent the *opera* of each author and to facilitate the organization and development of the thesis in a logical, clear, and simple way without being obscured by countless footnotes and cross-references. Also, the work will not make use of secondary sources, because they would render it more voluminous but not necessarily more conclusive and more convincing. An expanded bibliography of secondary sources is included for serious scholars who wish to explore further the manifold aspects of the various creative figures analyzed here. All italics in the quoted texts belong to the authors themselves, unless otherwise indicated.

There is hardly an aspect of modern French literary, philosophic, and visual influences that I did not discuss with friends and colleagues. My deepest thanks go to them, especially Professors Michael Ewbank and Gregg De Young. Professor Constance Gosselin Schick has been an unselfish and authoritative source of information. She has helped me to see more clearly the various influences, affinities, and coincidences permeating modern French literary and artistic criticism. At each step of the way I have been fortunate enough to have had her advice on everything from the selection and pairing of the various authors, to the removal from the text of mistakes and awkward expressions, to the checking of my own translations. In fact, in the process of revising the manuscript, Professor Schick not only restructured it, but took it upon herself to rewrite the chapters on Redon and Gide.

I am particularly grateful to Bucknell University Press and its readers. My thanks also go to Beth Gianfagna and Paula Wissing of Associated University Presses for their outstanding work on copyediting the manuscript. But my deepest appreciation must go to my parents and my sister.

Note on the Translations

Throughout the text, English translations for all quotations in French have been provided in the form of endnotes. I have made use of published translations where these were available. I myself have provided translations for the following works by Paul Claudel: *Présence et prophétie, Cinq grandes odes*; and *Partage de midi*. I have also provided translations for André Gide's *Poussin*, Jean-Paul Sartre's *L'imaginaire*, and Vincent van Gogh's *Lettres à Emile Bernard*.

Excerpts from the following works are reprinted by permission of Editions Gallimard: *Oeuvre poétique*, by Paul Claudel (trans. as *Poetic Art*, by Renée Spodheim and reprinted by permission of Philosophical Library Inc., 1969); *L'oeil écoute*, by Paul Claudel (trans. as *The Eye Listens*, by Elsie Pell and reprinted by permission of Philosophical Library Inc., 1950); *Présence et prophétie*, by Paul Claudel; *Cinq grandes odes*, by Paul Claudel; *Partage de midi*, by Paul Claudel; *Phénoménologie de la perception*, by Maurice Merleau-Ponty (trans. as *The Phenomenology of Perception*, by Colin Smith and reprinted by permission of Routledge & Kegan Paul and the Humanities Press International Inc., 1962); *A la recherche du temps perdu*, by Marcel Proust (trans. as *Remembrance of Things Past*, by C. K. Scott Moncrieff and Terence Kilmartic and reprinted by permission of Random House Inc., 1981); *La nausée,* by Jean-Paul Sartre (trans. as *Nausea* by Lloyd Alexander, and reprinted by permission of New Directions and Hamish Hamitton Ltd., 1964); and *L'imaginaire*, by Jean-Paul Sartre. Excerpts from *La pesanteur et la grâce*, by Simone Weil, are reprinted by permission of Librairie Plon (trans. as *Gravity and Grace*, by Emma Granfurd and reprinted by permission of Routledge & Kegan Paul and Putnam Publishing Group, 1952). *The Jerusalem Bible* is reprinted by permission of Darton, Longman & Todd, and by permission of Doubleday. Excerpts from *The Letters of Vincent van Gogh*, ed. Mark Roskin, are reprinted by Permissions of Constable & Co. Ltd., and Atheneum Publishers, a division of Macmillan Inc. Excerpts from *Poussin*, by André Gide, are reprinted by permission of © le Divan^M^Succession André Gide.

References

References to the following works appear parenthetically in the text, and are abbreviated as follows:

Works by Claudel

CGO Cinq grandes odes. Paris: Gallimard, 1957.
OE L'oeil écoute. Paris: Gallimard, 1946.
OP Oeuvre poétique. Paris: Gallimard, 1957.
PM Partage de midi, first version in *Théâtre,* vol. 1. Paris: Gallimard, 1956.
PP Présence et prophétie. Fribourg, Suisse: Librairie de l'Université Fribourg, 1942.

Other Works

P Gide, *Poussin.* [Paris]: Au Divan, [1945]. Pagination is mine.
JB The Jerusalem Bible. New York: Doubleday, 1966.
OR André Mellerio, *Odilon Redon.* New York: Da Capo Press, 1968.
PhP Merleau-Ponty, *Phénoménologie de la perception.* Paris: Gallimard, 1945.
R Proust, *A la recherche du temps perdu*, vol. 1. Paris: Gallimard, 1954.
I Sartre, *L'imaginaire.* Paris: Gallimard, 1940.
N _____, *La nausée.* Paris: Gallimard, 1938.
LG Van Gogh, *The Letters of Vincent van Gogh.* Edited by Mark Roskill. New York: Atheneum, 1972.
LB _____, *Lettres à Emile Bernard.* Paris: A. Vollard, 1911.
PG Weil, *La pesanteur et la grâce.* Paris: Plon, 1948.

CLAUDEL

Introduction

A distinguishing characteristic in much of twentieth-century French literary, artistic, and philosophical expression is a yearning for the sublime rather than a longing for wisdom. The human person is shown living in anticipation of a mystical ecstasy here on earth, longing to dissolve totally in the infinite, the eternal. The function of the creative spirit in twentieth-century French culture is to reveal not so much the physical reality of forms as the splendor of their inner beauty, their hidden essence, their spiritual transcendence. Fullness of being is attained in the light of a creative power that is conscious of both the nothingness of the human spirit and the divinity of the human self. In their paintings and literary and philosophical works, many twentieth-century French artists, writers, and philosophers contemplate themselves as the creators of beautiful forms. These created forms become not only the sign of yearning, but even the instrument of salvation, that is, of a mystical communion. For the twentieth-century French creative artist, the beauty of created forms is a metamorphosis of the phenomenal world into its unseen form; the phenomenal world becomes beautiful because it is seen from inside out, from the spiritual to the phenomenal.

By penetrating deeply into the hidden form of the phenomenal, creative artists perceive an inner luminosity, that is, they encounter grace without going beyond or outside the phenomenal world. The invisible world must be heard speaking the language of grace, must be seen as the image of the Form, must be comprehended as the mystery of the Idea, the essence of Being, and not pure nothingness, pure sensations, pure created forms, pure dreams. In order to grasp and express the world of Beauty, the creative artist, therefore, must have an awareness of the luminosity shining from within things. Otherwise the artist is driven to create alternate modes of beauty, beauty that is only dreams, appearances.

The poetry of Paul Claudel (1868–1955) offers a particularly apt example of this interplay between beauty and grace, between phenomenal forms and their unseen form, between visible and invisible worlds. In his poetic expression, Claudel achieves a seemingly balanced fusion of the two; his thought and art give evidence of subjective beauty or created art and also objective beauty or grace. His work testifies to the possible unity of created forms and revealed essences, the harmony of artistic imagination with the existence of grace as beauty within phenomenal forms. In Claudel's vision, beauty belongs not only to the physical senses or even to the mind's eye, but also to the form of Being where it finds its objective ground. This Being, for Claudel the Word of God, is incarnated, an incarnation that took place in Mary's womb. In Mary, all phenomenal beauties pass over into grace just as, in her, grace takes on bodily forms; in Mary, grace becomes incarnate in the body, and the body becomes filled with the light of grace; in Mary, human beings are conceived anew from grace, which reveals to them the path that opens up toward the mysterious splendor of the hidden form, Being, God. Claudel's poetic beauty, in sum, bears witness to the passionate longing of the human person to recapture the lyricism of this created universe, a lyricism that has been muffled by humanity's turning away from the path of objective, created beauties. For Claudel, the worlds of grace and beauty are inseparable, so much so that by abandoning the former the latter is also abandoned, resulting either in an altered, false vision of the world and the beautiful or in a painful, anguished awareness of their absence.

The juxtaposition of the thought of Claudel and of Marcel Proust (1871–1922) reveals an interesting articulation of the problem of beauty and grace in twentieth-century French culture. While beauty can be said to deal with ontology, with the form of Being, with the whatness of things irrespective of how the subject perceives and grasps that whatness, grace on the other hand refers to a primordial source of truth and goodness that shines in all phenomenal forms by virtue of an incarnation. Claudel and Proust face a problem that every creative artist confronts: the creation of forms that reveal both the beauty of the phenomenal world as well as its mystery, the unseen and unknown source of its splendor. In Proust, grace no longer speaks through the phenomenal; the beauty of the world is hidden, impenetrable. Consequently, nature pales beside the lights of "immaterial equivalents," which are self-created artistic forms. In Claudel on the other hand, phenomenal forms achieve their ultimate luminosity in the realm of grace, which, for him, is God's creative Word revealed in the word of Scripture. For Claudel, the human person is the image and likeness of God, as is creation: this is the conclusion of Claudel's poetic art, the poem of creation, the *magnificat*.

Perception of the beautiful comes from the person's encounter with the world, with phenomenal forms, and Merleau-Ponty (1908–61) reinstitutes the beautiful within the "milieu of existence." Unlike Proust, whose aesthetic rests on the notion that, since things are in a constant state of dissolution, their beauty cannot be grasped but must be created through the artist's thought, for Merleau-Ponty, the human person, in encountering phenomenal forms, perceives the "primordial bed" of all thing—their idea, their form, their eternal origin. This "primordial bed" can be seen as Merleau-Ponty's grace, since it is what opens up human existence to the Source. However, in Merleau-Ponty's vision, the beautiful remains forever within the circle of subjectivity, the "visual field" of the beholder, and, therefore, of ambiguity and doubt. Claudel's grace transcends the "I" of the perceiver, just as it transcends the "I" of the artist. While Claudel agrees with Merleau-Ponty that perception of the beautiful comes from within the human person, from his or her being-in-the-world, at the same time Claudel admits, like Proust, that this "milieu of existence" has been covered with a veil of darkness (Proust's "evaporation zone" and Claudel's original sin). Ambiguity and doubt become the very channel by which the Claudelian self is led to see the light of grace, a grace that originates not within the perceiver, but in the very source of Being, Beauty itself.

As form, the beautiful can be materially grasped. The phenomenal would not be beautiful unless it were an image of what Merleau-Ponty calls the "primordial bed" and therefore beyond human vision. Beauty as hidden form manifests itself in the world as a sense of gracefulness, a concealed delight, a hidden idea, an ordered harmony. In a still more hidden and more harmonious way than the beautiful, grace reveals itself in phenomenal forms and in the realm of salvation, making possible the perception of the beautiful from truth and goodness, or from Being itself. The beautiful is based on the fact that truth and goodness manifest themselves to the perceiver as being gracious, noble, and meritorious. The appearance of grace in the beautiful is the presence in the visible forms of the goodness of creation, which, in turn, points beyond itself. Both Claudel and Simone Weil (1904–43) see the beautiful as a harmony of the phenomenal and the good; both conceive of beauty as a unity of the sensible and the mental world; for them beauty reveals that which human beings desire but cannot attain. However, they differ in that, whereas for Weil the human person beholds beauty as detached form, as a renunciation of the physical senses, for Claudel the human person beholds beauty in its sensory and mental unity with God's incarnation in the world. For Claudel, the human person does not leave the sensory forms of beauty behind in order to behold the depths of grace, as is true for Weil; rather, grace reveals beauty to be the manifestation, the testimony, of God's splendor on earth. In this sense, the testimony of the world is a testimony of beauty and grace.

Jean-Paul Sartre (1905–1980) too abandons the phenomenal as "nothingness," a total concealment of the Form, of Being, of Beauty. For him, the nothingness of creation is the place where the absolute beauty of created forms shines forth; the beautiful is identical with the artist's own act of being. This means that to reveal the beautiful is to separate it from the form of Being, from the luminosity shining within things, from grace, and to make it exclusively the domain of existence. In revealing existence, the artist is the creator of essence, of form. Behind the nothingness of this existence, the artist finds its transcendence. There the beautiful is made manifest to the artist as icons expressing the truth that existence precedes essence, since existence is a testimony to the person's creative will or power. For Claudel, of course, the nothingness or the hiddenness of the world unveils the very Being, the very image of what God has created out of nothing: the artist perceives Being by gazing on nothingness. Being itself proceeds from God whose grace (light) shines only in the eyes that perceive the invisible depth of Being, a depth that is filled creatively from the grace of the Word made flesh.

André Gide's (1869–1951) analysis of Poussin's art also emphasizes the mysticism of an aesthetic "for itself." Ignoring the sacralizing effects of mythologies and the spiritualizing images of Christianity, Gide considers only the mystical effects of the artist's own inner world and thought, finding grace, so to speak, in the purely sensual and aesthetic beauty of Poussin's work. In fact, Gide's interpretation of Poussin removes that spiritual eros by which artistic creation transports the beholder into the world of creation, revelation, and incarnation where the beautiful dwells. Claudel, on the other hand, in his study of Flemish art of the baroque period, discovers in art the grace that once again transcends the subjective evidence of the artist and that, while incarnated in aesthetic forms, points beyond them to the revelation of a splendor within the phenomenal world.

The testimony of art as grace itself is expressed by Odilon Redon (1840–1916). His paintings are pleasing forms created by the mind, the artist's thought and imagination, and, therefore, cut off from any connection with the phenomenal world and the objective evidence of grace. Redon places the perceiver in the world of dreams, in the realm of the indeterminate, in a sphere of pure fantasy. Phenomenal forms are lost, floating in undefined space, in the abyss of a metamorphosed world. As the image that makes visible the primordial image, thought uses phenomenal things as pure symbols mirroring itself. In Claudel's image, thought mediates between the phenomenal world and the primordial image; it mirrors not itself but the juxtaposition of visible/invisible, known/unknown; it provides a form that is synthetic of both the seen and the unseen.

Vincent van Gogh (1853–90) typifies the struggle of the modern artist to express a grace and beauty consonant with the phenomenal world. Engulfed in the dark clouds of existence, in the violent storm of the human person's creative desire, in the depths of human sorrow, if not despair, van Gogh must retreat from the phenomenal world. Failing to achieve a synthesis between beauty and grace of his own source of pure forms and phenomena, a union of art and reality, van Gogh releases his own colorful and expressive creations, producing discord between his grace and the phenomena. He, like Claudel, tells us that nothing is complete in itself; all phenomenal forms are drawn from within, and all fit into a more harmonious whole, into a more general form, into a picture. The artist's task is to capture the vibrations of reality, to reveal the human person's longing together with the beauty of the world through the grace of expressed forms and the rhythms of colors. For both Claudel and van Gogh, all that exists strives in the direction of a more truthful and complete form; that is, reality, life itself, moves toward an idea, a truth, a source, in which beauty reveals itself with gracefulness, mystery, silence, and gravity. They differ in that while Claudel's expression of grace moves art and the world of phenomena continually closer to consonance with the truth and goodness of Being, van Gogh's art, which is his grace, moves continually toward distortion and distance (alienation) from the world.

1

Claudel and Proust on Beauty

L'idée d'éternité se réduit à celle d'une *fermeture* par elle-même infrangible. Or, toute *forme* se déduit de cette même idée d'une enceinte *fermée* sur elle-même, et nous avons vu que rien en ce monde n'échappe à la nécessité de la forme. (*OP*, 203)[1]

... je ne pus plus voir sans plaisir Mme Elstir, et son corps perdit de sa lourdeur, car je le remplis d'une idée, l'idée qu'elle était une créature immatérielle, un portrait d'Elstir.... On sent bien, à voir les uns à côté des autres dix portraits de personnes différentes peintes par Elstir, que ce sont avant tout des Elstir. (*R*, 851)[2]

Beauty is both the inner form of things and its exterior manifestation. As long as this inner form is seen, objects are illumined by the light of beauty, thereby transcending their phenomenal existence. If we are to encounter the beautiful, we must first see this interior form; we must possess both physical and spiritual senses by which we penetrate deep into this form in order to behold the beautiful. The inner form of things, then, must be seen as the expression of Being whose image is that primal form of beauty that captivates the perceiver, transporting us into the realm of Beauty itself where this inner form attains a mysterious splendor, a transcendence, an eternal moment.

Beauty thus is the being of things, a being, which, while identical with phenomenal existence, also contains an inner objective form. This being, however, can be covered either when we deny its existence or when our senses are unable to grasp it. In either case, beauty is hidden, immersed in the darkness of material reality or in the mental ground of the perceiver. This is the moment when our own desire may replace the objective inner form of things with created forms, thereby annihilating the boundary between reality and art, subjective and objective form. In this way, the beautiful, instead of guiding the perceiver from phenomenal beauty into the world of Being proper, transports us into the created forms of the artist's inner world.

It is from this viewpoint that we approach Claudel and Proust, who provide us with a clear contrast between beauty as form of Being (Claudel) and beauty as created forms (Proust). Unlike Proust, whose sense of the beautiful is found in the categories of "pure phenomenalism" and "the idea," or "subjective idealism," Claudel locates beauty in God's form, a form that transfigures the phenomenal world by assuring that God remains present, though hidden in things. While Proust's aesthetic leads the artist to make manifest "the immaterial equivalents" of the inner form of things, Claudel's aesthetic demands that the artist reflect and express the inner form in a language of images that maintains the hiddenness of the beauty of Being. For Claudel, to see the beautiful as "subjective idealism," as "pure idea," without an objective ground, is to remove the beautiful from its ultimate inner form, its source.

Claudel: Beauty as Form

According to Claudel, all objects have motion in common. This motion is not a temporary state of matter; it is not a mere property, a force that cannot be separated from matter; it is its permanent act and the very instrument of its existence.

> Toute chose créée acquiert de ce fait qu'elle ne vient pas d'elle-même un *sens*. De quoi la transcription générale est le mouvement, la fuite. Elle désigne son origine en s'en écartant. Le mouvement ... est le premier sens que l'élément possède de lui-même, en n'étant pas *de* lui-même. (*OP*, 185)[3]

Being the condition of all that exists, motion belongs to the order of forms, and all forms, whether they imply change or permanency, belong to the order of self-determining or existential activity. Each object moves to know itself, and since the universe, in its inorganic, organic, psychic, and spiritual activities, is part of a homogeneous whole, each object is connected to all that which is nature and knows itself by constructing its own boundaries, its own limits, its own state of equilibrium.

> Cet équilibre, dans le domaine de la matière, que ce soit organisée ou brute, ne se trouve que dans l'établissement d'une forme ou figure de composition. Tout ce qui est travaille à être d'une manière plus complète; c'est-à-dire à construire l'idée en qui il puisse s'agréger à ses différences organiques. (*OP*, 155)[4]

Form, therefore, reveals what exists by revealing what it is not: "The universe...cannot cease to be present, to represent before that which is that which is not" (*OP*, 186).

On the basis of the "primary sense," human beings too know themselves through movement, that is, by sensing the world. Movement is the essence of the senses, which are in a state of constant vibration. "Vibration is movement held in check by form" (*OP*, 155). This vibratory character of the senses shows how it is possible for the human person to be born together with the world, and to know the self in relation to nonbeing. For this reason, Claudel says that the senses create the self. Touch (and next to it, taste and smell) is "a measured reduction of ourselves" in that it gives the self the first measure, the first sense, by which what is (exists) feels itself by touching other things. The higher senses of sight and hearing allow the human person to be totally present in the world through images: "Sight gives us images of space; hearing draws their duration. From these images, one builds itself on difference, the other on variation" (*OP*, 168). The eye, which Claudel calls a sort of "portable, smaller sun," is wholly in contact with the object touched, and, while the other senses give the human person impressions in succession, sight is "the homologue of contrasting and simultaneous impressions" (*OP*, 168). Hearing, finally, is the center of vibratory oscillations, because within its open space of silence it computes the vibrations of sound. The ear is the instrument by which the self appreciates the rhythms of the movement that animates it, using its own sensations as a continuous wave.

Or, la personne informée auditivement devient son, c'est-à-dire modifiée par le son, de même que, selon la vue, elle devient couleur, c'est-à-dire modifiée par la couleur dans ses racines vibratoires. (*OP*, 169)[5]

People thus feel what we are not; we touch, we smell, we taste, we see, and we hear by means of a movement that does not come from ourselves: "Within the world, we feel outside God" (*OP*, 184). Hence, at a deeper level, our sensibility reveals the infinite Being, which is nothing other than God. God exists, the world "flees," that is, the world at any moment is identical to oblivion. Everything, then, acquires its movement, its sense, its image, from God from whose first movement all things proceeded.

Dieu, étant toute l'existence, ne peut permettre à rien d'exister aussi, qu'à la condition de s'exclure à sa mode de Lui. L'homme, ce témoin vertical, ne peut constater, en fin d'analyse de la matière, que le fait pur mathématique, le mouvement. Tout *périt*. L'univers n'est qu'une manière totale de ne pas être ce qui est. Que disent donc les sceptiques et quelle n'est pas la sécurité de notre connaissance! Certes, et nous avec, le monde existe; certes, il est, puisqu'il est ce qui n'est pas. (*OP*, 184)[6]

By virtue of our existence, we feel ourselves in relation to the world primarily because we are outside God; that is, we are what God is not since we know that God is, that is, he is pure existence. The human being, this "vertical witness," possesses in the senses a feeling for transcendence; with each sensation we call ourselves into being, into becoming a conscious body.

Tout passe, et, rien n'étant présent, tout doit être *représenté*. Je fais acte de présence. Je constitue. Je me maintiens dans la forme et la figure. Je me fais connaître. Je réponds à l'appel. (*OP*, 186)[7]

The form, the figure, the image, is thus the place where there occurs a discourse between knowledge and the world, subject and object. The image, however, may be understood as the figure of both the sensing subject and the world stamped with form. In other words, through the one image the sensing subject is capable of representing its inner being and that of the world. Existence for the human person is knowing the world, which becomes defined inwardly. This means that the sensing subject and the world form, as it were, a closed circuit, a circle, and coexist internally; and it is because of this inner sense that there can be an image that brings together what exists scattered about the world. "If we cannot produce the object, we can produce within ourselves a state which is the equivalent of knowledge and the sign which we give it as expression" (*OP*, 178). Sensation becomes a sign, and "the word" is that equivalent of knowledge by which the sensing subject perceives itself, knows itself, and determines itself. In "the word," the only thing left of the object is its intention, its form, its sense. Furthermore, "the word is not merely the formula of the object. It is the image of myself as informed by this object" (*OP*, 179). The sensing subject adapts this sensation to its own; it assimilates this image, which becomes the subject of comprehension. And comprehension is the act by which the sensing subject substitutes itself for the object it comprehends; it takes within itself the idea, the form, the sign, by which it evaluates the tension between itself and all existing things.

Le mot, en effet, nous l'avons vu, n'est pas seulement le signe d'un certain

état de notre sensibilité, il est l'évaluation de l'effort qui nous a été
nécessaire pour le former, ou plutôt pour nous former en lui. (*OP*, 203)[8]

Consequently, "the word" is the object that has entered the sphere
of freedom and stands at the subject's disposal. "With the word I
become master of the object it represents; I can carry it with me
wherever I please, I can act as if it were there" (*OP*, 178). People are
free to use at will the thing represented by the word that they have
provided; they are free to utilize its services for the satisfaction of
their own needs; they are free to carry the word around as the instrument of comparison and discovery in order that they may create their
own existences.

Nous lui [le mot] empruntons sa force créatrice, c'est-à-dire la force par
quoi elle est créée. Nous connaissons ce qu'elle est et nous comprenons
ce qu'elle fait. (*OP*, 181)[9]

The word thus brings into being this "creative force"; it is the accomplishment, as well as the act, of our creative power; it is that
which constitutes the form by furnishing intentionality to the object.
The word and knowledge are two terms of a single phenomenon.
Knowledge implies that we have found the "objective formula" that
makes the word concrete. This means that the word is not the sign
of knowledge, but its very presence, its living being, its creative
vibration, its permanent movement, by which we recover what we
have received from the world, since the world is prior to us. The
word is the bringing into light of Being itself; it causes all things to
be born through and with it; it is the common symbol of the world
itself.

L'être vivant a à se connaître, c'est-à-dire à connaître autour de lui le
monde dont il se fait une image. Mais cette image n'est point seulement
le moulage inerte du vide que laissent entre eux des termes irréduc-
tibles.... D'elle, des séries de mobiles attendent leur déclenchement.
(*OP*, 186–87)[10]

Like painting, in which a particular color has meaning only in relation to other colors and the picture itself, the word too has meaning
only in its relation to the world. Just as in the picture the end of the
work is not found in each color taken separately, but in their propor-
tions, their harmony, within the form of the whole, so too the word
is harmonious in its mutual relationship with other words to the images of the universe. Poetic art, concludes Claudel, is the source and
foundation of knowledge; it strives for clarity and brilliancy of ex-

pression by capturing the intentionality of the "irreducible terms" of things. Its goal is "to stir us to a state of harmonious and intense, precise and strong intelligence" (*OP*, 203) by means of the exquisite charm of an integrated arrangement of words, and, consequently, to produce artistic pleasure, as well as a "feeling." A given expression is but "the evaluation of effort" that has to do with its use and the creative act.

L'image, une fois trouvée à son tour, détermine notre action. En un mot, il nous faut créer, par la jointure de ses différents éléments, la figure, le milieu selon lequel nous sommes aptes à co-naître. (*OP*, 180)[11]

The words of the poet are the words of the "creator's vibrations," of the rhythms of the universe, and the poet, "who is the master of all words," is in contact with the visible and invisible circle of signs, and, therefore, through the poet's art, words realize their intention. In order to convey this harmonious and intense, right and strong feeling, the poet must create "by a wise use of objects [that is, words]," a new circle of signs whose testimony is proportional with that of the end or purpose it confirms. In this way, the poet uses words so that the available images link themselves up in accordance with an almost musical idea, the vibration of which is included in them and elaborated according to the rhythmic law of motion and the intention for which words are created. Knowledge, intentionality, existence, and birth can thus be experienced as the beauty of a "three-voice cantata," the sonority of words, images, and rhythms.

Mais, tandis que notre existence ici-bas est pareille à un langage barbare et rompu, notre vie en Dieu sera comme un vers de la justesse la plus exquise.... Mais, alors, nous serons les *poëtes*, les faiseurs de nous-mêmes. (*OP*, 203)[12]

The poet, and to a lesser degree, we ourselves as speaking subjects, can bring into being a form, an idea, through our art by organizing the relations between words themselves, since what the words express is nothing other than that which does not exist, their hidden intention or meaning. The poet follows the order of nature as the reality of nonbeing; for nothing can be defined or represented in terms of origin or end. The world around us is but a fixed frame, a closed circuit filled with matter and movement, and its parts are harmonious to each other; each part complies with the necessity of being felt, seen, known, and represented not by and of itself, but as part of a whole. Parts exist not only on the condition that they should not become the whole, but also on the condition that the whole realizes its intention, its form; otherwise the poet's words, and words in general, violate the circuital form of the world, as well as the state of equilibrium between representation and valuation. But as long as the poet's words keep this intentionality, this circuital form, the poet attests to the permanence of things.

L'acte par lequel l'homme atteste la permanence des choses, par lequel, en dehors du temps, en dehors des circonstances et causes secondes, il formule l'ensemble des conditions permanentes dont la réunion donne à chaque chose son droit de devenir présente à l'esprit, par lequel il la conçoit dans son coeur et répète l'ordre qui l'a créée, s'appelle la parole. Pour désigner cette parole nous nous servons de trois termes: le verbe, le mot, le nom. Le verbe désigne la vertu de celui qui parle; le mot, le mouvement particulier qui est le motif de chaque être et dont l'émotion de celui qui l'énonce est l'image; le nom...la différence en ce que chaque individu n'est pas l'autre. (*OP*, 194–95)[13]

In expression, knowledge does not precede speech; it results from it at the moment the verb, the word, and the noun achieve their intention, which impels the poet to consolidate things in their quality of images. "The Word does not imply death; or, the word is one of my states" (*OP*, 196).

Behind the word there indeed lies an image, "one of my states," an expression of the self as an existing body in a state of permanent vibration. The body considered physiologically is a body that does not exist by itself; at each moment of its vibration it is in relation with itself as verb (creative force), as word (vibration or image), and as name (reason or cause) and the world. Indeed, to say that the body knows itself and responds to the call is to say that the body does not simply occupy a space or does not simply exist as an extended substance. The body, concludes Claudel, teaches what space is, because it is itself the creator, the continuous possibility of knowledge and birth. It is the body that teaches both the effects of the world on it and its attention on the world. For this reason,

De longtemps sans doute il ne sera permis d'aller plus loin, de remonter à la source même de la sensation, au tableau de distribution, à ce poste central où l'onde destinée à alimenter les différents organes de la périphérie reçoit sa première élaboration. (*OP*, 170)[14]

But beyond this biological existence, the body, which is the circuit for the transformation of that initial current, is the work of an inner source of energy, its expression, and its extension in the world. This source is the soul, and it is this power that confers upon the body its word, its name, its intention, and its completion. The soul is the form through which the body is what it is, its act, its particular existence. And through the body, the soul comes to experience the world by "the wave," which redirects the senses only after they have been created themselves. Accordingly, the sensing body is not merely a physiological organism, but also a unity of "signification," and, therefore, it has a "sense." By its own vibration or wave, the soul invades the senses and thus makes itself the instrument of the body's intention, "the call" to the "first elaboration" of images, which both the world and we incarnate. In other words, the soul makes itself the center of knowledge, of consciousness, of creative action, by converting sensory vibrations into conscious and permanent images that harmonize with the form, the end, of things.

> La conscience donc est cette faculté par quoi l'homme sait ce qu'il fait, et, par conséquent, s'il fait bien ou mal. Bien ou mal, c'est-à-dire conformément ou non à ses fins prochaines ou foncières, réelles ou imaginaires, à sa fantaisie ou à son *devoir*. Les choses ne naissant pas seules sont reliées par une obligation mutuelle....Sa conscience lui apprend s'il a contrevenu ou non à son dessein et à sa nature. (*OP*, 191)[15]

Hence, the body is a human body only insofar as it is the visible expression of the mutual obligation between itself and the soul that completes the body's circuit. "Man has been created to be the witness and the interpreter of a certain performance, to determine its sense within himself" (*OP*, 190). Every human person, in fact, is a particular expression (name) and image (word) of God's creative sense (verb), which directs the body's attention and the soul's intention toward his gaze. God sees humanity in himself, and, therefore, as being that is seen, God calls the soul to see its form, to be born with a specific name, and, in order to respond, the soul uses the word that is appropriate to its nature, "the intention of the soul, this attention of God directed toward the end to which it is destined" (*OP*, 198). The orders of created things vary according to the form, the intention, they are to carry out; similarly, people vary because of their knowledge of bodily things, and each one, in turn, is unlike the others in the moment of birth, in the moment of creating for the self a sensory, conscious, and spiritual body, a witness to God's Word.

> De même qu'un mot est formé de voyelles et de consonnes, notre âme, à chaque aspiration, puise en Dieu la plénitude de sa sonorité. Naître alors pour elle sera le même acte que connaître, d'une conscience pleinement illuminée. (*OP*, 199)[16]

It is this "fully illuminated consciousness," this inner sensibility, this connaturality with things, that has been sown in our souls and presents the infallible promise of being born. It is the "breath of God," which spreads through the bodily senses; it is the "total energy" of God's Light, which continually irradiates the body through the life-giving rays of the soul; it is "the sonorous wave" of the spiritual world, which is governed by immutable relationships but reflected in the material world, where it produces the sonorous harmony of things, the poetic beauty arising from the vibratory rhythm of the phenomenal world and of words.

> Nous verrons alors, comme le nombre manifeste l'unité, le rythme essen-tiel de ce mouvement qui constitue mon âme, cette mesure qui est ma personne; nous ne le verrons pas seulement, nous le serons, nous nous produirons nous-mêmes dans la perfection de la liberté et de la vision et dans la pureté d'un amour sans défaut. (*OP*, 199)[17]

To love corresponds birth, that is, conscience combined with vi-sion, which, through the eyes of the soul, turns the body's attention in the direction of its living form, its source. When the soul becomes God-like through the "purity of love without fault," the exterior senses follow the movement of the intellect, and, in turn, the soul overflows with visions that fill it with the joy of seeing perfect love, as well as with the joy of creating itself in its image. But the joy of seeing pure love and the gratifying pleasure of creating oneself in-terpenetrate, and senses, intellect, conscience, and love dissolve in the unity of ecstasy where the soul is consumed in the "depth of the abyss" according to the silence of transfigured and resplendent darkness, in naked and simple unity.

> Dans cette amère vie mortelle, les plus poignantes délices révélées à notre nature sont celles qui accompagnent la création d'une âme par la jonction de deux corps. Hélas! elles ne sont que l'image humiliée de cette étreinte substantielle où l'âme, apprenant son nom et l'intention qu'elle satisfait, se proférera pour se livrer, s'aspirera, s'expirera tour à tour. O continua-tion de notre coeur! ô parole incommunicable! ô acte dans le Ciel futur! Toute possession charnelle est incomplète dans son empan et dans sa durée et qu'en sont les transports auprès de ces noces opimes! O mon Dieu, tu nous as montré des choses dures, tu nous as abreuvés du vin de la pénitence! (*OP*, 199)[18]

When the soul comes to this creation, this union with Divine Being, this vision of love, then its knowledge will be complete as its being. The soul is carried out of itself in ecstasy and flows into the nonbeing of the primal ground, the source, which is God and the abyss. In this way, it achieves the highest creation possible to it. In the abyss, it is absorbed into "the unspoken lamentation of love," which envelops it and transforms its "carnal possession" into the beatitude of divine rapture. This abyss is the pure love in which absolute movement flows forth from the eternal permanency of the divine circle, which is this blissful birth comprehending its vibratory rhythm, its form, its intention, as luminosity of God's existence.

> Lors le Temps sera fermé sur nous et le Présent en sera le centre éternel. Le *temps* établi, voici qu'éclate de toutes parts le choeur! Quoi de mieux fait que ce qui est achevé?... Quoi de plus fini que ce qui ne peut plus finir?...De même que le jour répète, jamais le même, le jour, et l'an l'an- née, comme à des intervalles réguliers, l'écrou des astres se relâche ou se resserre, et que sans jamais rompre la ronde les enfants de la Nuit l'ouvrent ou la rétrécissent comme une bouche...notre occupation pour l'éternité sera l'accomplissement de notre part dans la perpétration de l'Office, le maintien de notre équilibre toujours nouveau dans un im- mense tact amoureux de tous nos frères, l'élévation de notre voix dans l'inénarrable gémissement de l'Amour! (*OP*, 203–204)[19]

In the eternal present, God, the divine stirring within the ground, the abyss, vibrates and utters the word, the signification, the intention, the meaning of the "infallible promise" of God's mystery, which is God, who sees himself in his Word, and the Word elevates the soul to behold the Divine Poet, God himself, who speaks "a most ex- quisitely just verse."

Proust: Beauty as Dream

Proust's aesthetic crystallizes around an original moment when the regret of the past is brought to consciousness and an influx of creative power emerges. It is from the interplay of the dream-awake paradox that Proust apprehends beauty. And when this paradox is most intense, the mysteries of birth, death, and resurrection, the sacramental moment of self-transformation, and the origin itself ap- pear before the eyes objectively; that is, they come to life. This aesthetic orientation is found in Proust as early as the first page of *A la recherche du temps perdu*.

> Quelquefois, comme Ève naquit d'une côte d'Adam, une femme naissait pendant mon sommeil...Formée du plaisir que j'étais sur le point de goûter, je m'imaginais que c'était elle qui me l'offrait. Mon corps qui sen- tait dans le sien ma propre chaleur voulait s'y rejoindre, je m'éveillais. (*R*, 4)[20]

This movement to oneness with the object of love and consummation of the subject itself refers to that complete world wherein we respond to (awaken to) beauty's revelatory delights. In dreams, then,
the hidden and the indescribable begin to be revealed and described.
And what is revealed and described is another, quite different reality
(the ideal, the sublime, the objective, the form), which, like material
reality (phenomenon), is an appearance, a mere dream, a fleeting
sensation.

The conversion to oneness with the object of love out of the consummation of the subject raises a most fundamental problem. On
the one hand, oneness with the form as an objective reality cannot
be achieved without the dissolution of the self; on the other hand,
extinction of the self means that nothing is; that is, existence is pure
phenomenon, absolutely changeable. But if nothing is, and yet we
feel something, then we remain forever bound to the chains of terror
and anguish. The yearning for a complete unity with the object of
love brings forth the need to perish; through death, love is revealed
in its divine aspect.

Peut-être est-ce le néant qui est le vrai et tout notre rêve est-il inexistant,
mais alors nous sentons qu'il faudra que ces phrases musicales, ces no-
tions qui existent par rapport à lui, ne soient rien non plus. Nous
périrons, mais nous avons pour otages ces captives divines qui suivront
notre chance. Et la mort avec elles a quelque chose de moins amer, de
moins inglorieux, peut-être de moins probable. (*R*, 350)[21]

These conceptions, these divine captives (impressions, images,
pure forms), are for Proust the immediate transformation of a longing; the aesthetic moment converts the most inflamed desire into an
image possessed by the imagination, which itself stands between the
phenomenal and the objective, between body and thought, between
the awakened life and dreams. Proust emphasizes this underlying
connection when he writes:

Mais dès que j'eus terminé la lettre, je pensai à elle, elle devint un objet
de rêverie, elle devint, elle aussi, *cosa mentale* et je l'aimais déjà tant que
toutes les cinq minutes il me fallait la relire, l'embrasser. Alors, je connus
mon bonheur. (*R*, 500)[22]

As in this letter from Gilberte, so too in the music of Vinteuil, in the
painting of Elstir, in the theater of Berma, in the literature of
Bergotte, in the love for Albertine and Madame Guermantes, in the
visits to the countryside and to the various cities—heavenly
moments spring up within a feeling, and the whole sensory system

at once crystallizes in the form of an ecstatic experience that reveals the intimate connection between subjective (sensory) and objective (thought). Of his visit to Florence, Venice, Pisa, and Parma, the narrator explains:

> ...je ne cessai pas de croire qu'elles correspondaient à une réalité indépendante de moi, et elles me firent connaître une aussi belle espérance que pouvait en nourrir un chrétien des premiers âges à la veille d'entrer dans le paradis....Et, bien que mon exaltation eût pour motif un désir de jouissances artistiques....(*R*, 391)[23]

To experience aesthetic enjoyment is thus the same thing as to have an objective form present before the eyes. And when this form becomes *cosa mentale* (enters the mind), it acts as an intoxicant, a stimulant, a force, because the form itself cannot be possessed (apprehended) as anything other than an image, an impression, a sensation, a flash of reality. In the artistic mind, images are forms expressing sentiments that are one with the lovable and the beautiful, understood not as an abstract unity, but as concrete and living forms emanating and abstracted as *cosa mentale* from the world of experience, which provides the a priori power for the artistic mind in the sense that experience is the fundamental structure of knowledge.

> Dans la Sonate de Vinteuil, les beautés qu'on découvre le plus tôt sont aussi celles dont on se fatigue le plus vite, et pour la même raison sans doute, qui est qu'elles diffèrent moins de ce qu'on connaissait déjà. Mais quand celles-là se sont éloignées, il nous reste à aimer telle phrase que son ordre, trop nouveau pour offrir à notre esprit rien que confusion, nous avait rendue indiscernable et gardée intacte; alors, elle devant qui nous passions tous les jours sans le savoir et qui s'était réservée, qui par le pouvoir de sa seule beauté était devenue invisible et restée inconnue, elle vient à nous la dernière. Mais nous la quitterons aussi en dernier. Et nous l'aimerons plus longtemps que les autres, parce que nous aurons mis plus longtemps à l'aimer. (*R*, 531)[24]

What is most beautiful in itself, then, is the least immediately accessible to the mind, and the most immediately accessible is the least beautiful in the sense that it has no lasting duration, no permanency. The aesthetic act stands in direct relationship to the perceiver's and the object's reserve, since the object to be apprehended depends on the receiver's capacity to apprehend. It is this mental commitment on the part of the artist that allows the deeper and higher form of the self-disclosing Beauty, the secret of Truth, to shine from the invisible and unknowable, or the reserve of things. It is in the ultimate depth of the reserve that the mind confronts the still deeper intensity of meaning and truth. And truth arises solely from the mind's agreement that what it yearns for is present in the aesthetic moment, the moment when the mind is caught between the unsatisfied longing to see, hear, touch, smell, and taste Beauty, on the one hand, and the fear of extinction, on the other; between the endless change of reality and the reserve of things; between despair and exaltation, grief and joy. This is the moment when the mind strives to apprehend the hidden, the permanent essence of things, that immaterial love whose luminous form reveals the mystery of both the self and the world as in a mirror. If only the mind could bring out the reserve of things, if only the mind could recapture the lost past, then, and only then, we would experience that mystery of beauty, that divine thing (love), living out that hour of intoxication (a state of subjective idealism) in which the experiential world would exist in the mind (memory). No love, no beauty, Proust tells us, fills us that is not already there in the reserve, "but displaced, no longer weighing upon us, satisfied by the sensation which the present affords it, a sensation that is sufficient for us, since for what is not the here and now we take no thought" (*R*, 816).

Beauty, then, takes form in these pleasant moments, in the here and now, when the self transcends the phenomenal world, the life of habit, for the sake of that Beauty which constitutes the joy beyond all joys and comes to live in the authentic world of impression, which is the world of the artist whose knowledge includes the unsatisfied longing to apprehend the hidden forms of things and to express them truthfully; that is, in the paradoxical tension between subjective and objective reality, inner life and outer form, work of art and living forms. Speaking of Elstir's paintings and his beautiful wife, Gabrielle, Proust writes:

> Ce qu'un tel idéal inspirait à Elstir, c'était vraiment un culte si grave, si exigeant, qu'il ne lui permettait jamais d'être content; cet idéal, c'était la partie la plus intime de lui-même: aussi n'avait-il pu le considérer avec détachement, en tirer des émotions, jusqu'au jour où il le rencontra, réalisé au dehors, dans le corps d'une femme...qui était par la suite devenue madame Elstir et chez qui il avait pu — comme cela ne nous est possible que pour ce qui n'est pas nous-mêmes — le trouver méritoire, attendrissant, divin. Quel repos, d'ailleurs, de poser ses lèvres sur ce Beau que jusqu'ici il fallait avec tant de peine extraire de soi, et qui maintenant, mystérieusement incarné, s'offrait à lui pour une suite de communions efficaces! (*R*, 850–51)[25]

Beauty and the encounter between the subject's and the object's reserve and its manifestation are the most incarnate yet, at the same time, the most mysterious reality: Beauty as grace—meritorious, divine, and solemn—as communion in love. And the grace of Beauty becomes the source of inebriation, of ecstasy, and communion or dialogue with Beauty becomes the source of inspiration, of truth.

In the beautiful, however, what the artist (Elstir) extracts from within himself and what is there as the outer form (the object's reserve) are one only for a moment. Reflecting power makes known (manifests) something, which is so exacting and yet ever new it never allows Elstir to be satisfied, and which intensifies continuously, so that even in the moment of intoxication (the moment of realization) Beauty still remains unfathomable, hidden from the artist. And the artist's expression of Beauty in the idea (reserve) is intimately related to the offering, to the surrendering of the self, to the sacrifice, which, in turn, is intrinsically connected to the act of contemplation that ascribes to the object of beauty its worth and loves it as an implacable divinity, an immaterial essence, an invisible form. Through the reflecting power, Elstir sees the form, the soul of things, in its movements, expressions, thoughts, and actions; indeed, he sees (imagines) it even more clearly and consistently than the real, and the body exists only in the lovely form, in the beautiful itself.

> Depuis que j'avais vu Albertine, j'avais fait chaque jour à son sujet des milliers de réflexions, j'avais poursuivi, avec ce que j'appelais elle, tout un entretien intérieur où je la faisais questionner, répondre, penser, agir, et dans la série indéfinie d'Albertines imaginées qui se succédaient en moi heure par heure, l'Albertine réelle... ne paraît, dans une longue série de représentations, que dans les toutes premières. (R, 858)[26]

Thus, on the one hand, when Elstir perceives objects, he encounters their reserve, which demands either total surrender or resistance. On the other hand, in and of himself, the artist, in his perceiving, desires either to serve love unconditionally or to conquer it, dominate it. The artist approaches this paradox under the guidance of what Proust calls "the inward eye," "the eyes of the memory," "the eye of the soul," with which, from first sight, things are apprehended; that is, the eyes see first the outer or material form, then the eyes of the memory see the inner form or the reserve and, through the imagination, penetrate the saving grace of the idea, the immaterial equivalent of Beauty.

> Mes regards se posaient sur sa peau, et mes lèvres à la rigueur pouvaient croire qu'elles avaient suivi mes regards. Mais ce n'est pas seulement son corps que j'aurais voulu atteindre, c'était aussi la personne qui vivait en lui et avec laquelle il n'est qu'une sorte d'attouchement, qui est d'attirer son attention, qu'une sorte de pénétration, y éveiller une idée. (R, 716)[27]

But the more one apprehends, the deeper the penetration of being, the more it is possible to grasp being as immaterial form. "The novelist's happy discovery was to think of substituting for those opaque sections, impenetrable to the human soul, their equivalent in immaterial sections, things, that is, which one's soul can assimilate" (*R*, 85). What appears is beautiful to the extent that these "immaterial sections" unify the visible world into a mystical painting, extracting and rearranging the images of the unseen, the reserve of things, into what is seen. The immaterial equivalents allow the artist (Elstir), who is this "awake sleeper," to express his original form, and to see and portray phenomenal forms as the outward expression of his reserve, of his thought, of his remembrance.

> Cette Albertine-là n'était guère qu'une silhouette, tout ce qui s'y était superposé était de mon cru, tant dans l'amour les apports qui viennent de nous l'emportent—à ne se placer même qu'au point de vue de la quantité—sur ceux qui nous viennent de l'être aimé. Et cela est vrai des amours les plus effectifs. (*R*, 858)[28]

On his entrance into Elstir's studio, Proust remarks:

> ...je me sentis parfaitement heureux, car par toutes les études qui étaient autour de moi, je sentais la possibilité de m'élever à une connaissance poétique, féconde en joies, de maintes formes que je n'avais pas isolées jusque-là du spectacle total de la réalité. (*R*, 834)[29]

The poetic knowledge invoked by Proust with respect to Elstir's artistic forms again implies the "formula of the unconscious gift" of the artist, a gift that allows him, Elstir, to isolate from the total spectacle of reality new forms, new impressions, new images, thereby constantly recreating nature. Elstir's paintings, then, delight Proust because they reveal the thought, the reserve, the idea, the immaterial equivalent of material objects without which they would not exist distinctly and/or poetically. But in revealing the idea, Elstir realizes his aesthetic feeling at the same time, his memories, which serve as basis for "a poetic knowledge." But this does not mean every memory, of course; the memories that Proust alludes to are those of poetic knowledge, which are capable of joining together what in natural forms is incompatible; the memories that join material forms with pure forms, thought itself, not the memories of habitual life. The revelation of thought as "the feminine and pictorial ideal" is this "poetic knowledge" of the artist, which is the world of the "profound sleep." In this way material forms, too, are revealed as having an interior form likewise based on thought. For once material forms are transformed completely into ideas in paintings, they become pure dreams. It is the world of dreams that brushes aside everything that conceals phenomena from the inner feeling of the artist, who is then brought face to face with the hidden form, the idea, the reserve, thought, of phenomenal forms. In other words, the artist must forget the visible representation of objects in the attempt to penetrate beneath material forms (appearances) to the inner reality of the objects themselves. The desire to express the inner form, to make reality as it is poetically, leads the artist to a perception of the (static) forms within the material world; "I tried to find beauty there where I had never imagined before that it could exist, in the most ordinary things, in the profundities of 'still life'" (R, 869).

Beauty, then, proceeds from "the profound sleep," from the idea, from the mental process of the artist, from a dream that organizes phenomenal forms into a luminous grace within which another world of another order begins to take shape in the interplay between contemplation, penetration, apprehension and the objects of apprehension; between reality and ideality, art and living forms, body and soul (reserve). It is "the pure subjective creations" that the artist proposes to make visible. The artist uses the eye of the memory to perceive the phenomenal world, because the world of nature is filled with an "evaporation zone," a field of "immaterial sensations," a number of different impressions, fleeting memories, "memories joined to one another," which the bodily senses cannot link with precision to the "feminine and artistic ideal." The phenomenal world, however, can be unified around the artist's archaic images, the "vital milieu," which are seen in the remembrance of things past, in the imagination, the world of images impressed on the mind, in dreams. In dreams, the eye of the memory sees by looking away (in the memory) from that which is visible to the senses, by closing off bodily senses to the objective elements of the phenomena.

S'il est vrai que la mer ait été autrefois notre milieu vital où il faille replonger notre sang pour retrouver nos forces, il en est de même de l'oubli, du néant mental; on semble alors absent du temps pendant quelques heures; mais les forces qui se sont rangées pendant ce temps-là sans être dépensées, le mesurent par leur quantité aussi exactement que les poids de l'horloge ou les croulants monticules du sablier. On ne sort pas, d'ailleurs, plus aisément d'un tel sommeil que de la veille prolongée, tant toutes choses tendent à durer et, s'il est vrai que certains narcotiques font dormir, dormir longtemps est un narcotique plus puissant encore, après lequel on a bien de le peine à se réveiller. (R, 821)[30]

Sleep, then, opens the inner self to a reality that the eyes cannot see, the ears cannot hear, smell cannot scent, touch cannot embrace, taste cannot savor, and the mind (intellect) cannot grasp; this awakens, deepens, and sweetens the feeling of delight, directing the eye of the memory to behold beauty, which reflects the radiance, the saving grace of the Beauty that can be expressed only in images. These images emanate from the penetration of the reserve of things into the perceiver (artist), on the one hand, and the exteriorization of the perceiver's thought, idea, on the other hand. From this dynamic process the beheld image and experienced reality enter the self, and both intimately encounter each other in the dream, which is the remembered depth, "the eyes of memory," of Beauty in its dialectical tension with the world of habit. "For beauty is a sequence of hypotheses which ugliness cuts short when it bars the way that we could already see opening into the unknown" (R, 713). Ugliness is what forbids the eyes specifically, and the senses in general, to penetrate any further the wellsprings of ecstatic enjoyments, the reserve of things, from which the wave of violent intoxication rises to the horizon of the mind's eye in which the eyes of memory see themselves in that mysterious light of the form, the idea, of Beauty. It is the Idea — Beauty, Love, Truth — that organizes darkness (non-being) around itself into a luminous form, a saving grace, within which a world begins to take shape in the interplay between the perceiver's power to grasp the reserve of things and the "evaporation zone" which prevents contact with it.

> Quand il [Swann] avait regardé longtemps ce Botticelli, il pensait à son Botticelli à lui qu'il trouvait plus beau encore et, approchant de lui la photographie de Zéphora, il croyait serrer Odette contre son coeur. (R, 225)[31]

The figure of Odette thus possesses a lovelier form in the encounter with the idea of beauty, in its coexistence with the likeness of Botticelli's images, or in the emergence of Beauty itself.

> Il [Swann] n'estima plus le visage d'Odette selon la plus ou moins bonne qualité de ses joues et d'après la douceur purement carnée qu'il supposait devoir leur trouver en les touchant avec ses lèvres si jamais il osait l'embrasser, mais comme un écheveau de lignes subtiles et belles que ses regards dévidèrent, poursuivant la courbe de leur enroulement, rejoignant la cadence de la nuque à l'effusion des cheveux et à la flexion des paupières, comme en un portrait d'elle en lequel son type devenait intelligible et clair. (R, 223–24)[32]

The fact that the artist makes intelligible an archetypal form is rooted in the power of the eyes to penetrate Beauty. But when artists have made Beauty visible, their eyes will see nothing other than the reflection, the "mark of a particular being." For the artist is called to represent, in one being or another, absolute Being, which is the hidden form of the self and the world. So that what the artist makes real in a particular being is always, at the same time, that inconceivable image, that immaterial equivalent, which illuminates living forms, unveiling them in their unique beauty. It is this image that the artist wants to fashion and to make worthy of perceiving. And it is for this reason, Proust claims, that artists both reveal and conceal themselves in their work, creating (expression) images from their being-in-between the light of night (dreams) and the darkness of day (phenomena); between the light of Being and the abyss of non-Being, the ugliness that forbids the eyes to enter into communion with the reserve of the beloved object. For non-Being is like the surface of a mirror that prevents the perceiver from grasping the reflected images (objects) within the mirror. And this is the source of the artist's suffering; to be powerless to turn the eyes, the eyes of the memory, the mind's eye, and reason toward Beauty, Being or Love.

Je pose la tasse et me tourne vers mon esprit. C'est à lui de trouver la vérité. Mais comment? Grave incertitude, toutes les fois que l'esprit se sent dépassé par lui-même; quand lui, le chercheur, est tout ensemble le pays obscur où il doit chercher et où tout son bagage ne lui sera de rien. Chercher? pas seulement: créer. Il est en face de quelque chose qui n'est pas encore et que seul il peut réaliser, puis faire entrer dans sa lumière. (R, 45)[33]

Conclusion: Poetic Beauty

L'art poétique evoked by Claudel and the "poetic remembrance" described by Proust have this is common: the recognition, by means of the soul or the inner sense or the reserve, of the transcendence, the mystery, the rapture and the abyss, the source, within phenomena and the need for the artist to create forms that will express this. They differ as to what those forms are and how they are created. For Claudel, the poetic form is an intelligible image revealing, on the one hand, the circular, permanent movement (structure) of all things where all parts obey the vibratory rhythm that regulates them and directs them to their end; and, on the other hand, the original form, God's Word. For Proust, the aesthetic form is the memory, the thought of this "awakened sleeper" actually made real (objectified) as a substitute for what exists in reality. For Proust, there is no objective verification of the inner form, the reserve of things, the vital image: "The feminine and pictorial ideal" is essentially a matter of a "profound sleep."

Whereas Proust regards consciousness as the inability of the senses and reason to grasp the image of things, Claudel views consciousness as a "knowledge," as a creation that proceeds from existence as the affirmation of not being God, from the knowledge of Being perceived through one's own limits, from the sense of being oneself with the world. Proust's artist is confronted with the "evaporation zone," which prevents him from ever sensing the reserve hidden in things; Claudel's artist discovers the one circular form, the verb, the word, the name, made manifest in all things and images. For Proust, beauty is a form of dream that can be expressed only through immaterial equivalents provided by the sensing subject's own inner self and substituted for the lost forms offered by reality. For Claudel, beauty must be grasped and expressed as it exists in the world in accordance with the laws of vibrations, movements, equilibrium, rhythms, form, proportion, and intentionality and as an affirmation of what is not. For Claudel, the word attests to the permanency of things, to the image of the Divine Word; for Proust, the word creates the only possible permanency, the only source of Beauty.

2

Claudel and Merleau-Ponty on Perception

La vue ne résulte point d'une image qui se peint sur notre cervelle, mais d'un contact réel avec l'objet que le regard attouche et circonscrit. (*OP*, 168)[1]

C'est dans mon rapport avec des "choses"que je me connais, la perception intérieure vient après, et elle ne serait pas possible si je n'avais pas pris contact avec mon doute en le vivant jusque dans son objet. (*PhP*, 439)[2]

The agreement on perception that emerges from Claudel and Merleau-Ponty is remarkable, especially when we consider that Claudel was a poet and a convert to the Catholic faith and Merleau-Ponty was a philosopher who attempted to produce a bridge between philosophical anthropology and a phenomenological approach to ontology. Both regard perception as an encounter, a contact with the world as it exists; by seeing the world we feel it, know it, live it, and become conscious of its form, its transcendence, so that we can create our own existence. For both of them "knowledge" speaks of the human being as existent, as being born in relation to the world. "Each sensation is a birth; each birth is a simultaneous birth-knowledge" (*OP*, 173), writes Claudel; and, in the words of Merleau-Ponty, "The subject of sensation is ... a power which is born into, and simultaneously with, a certain existential environment, or is synchronized with it"(*PhP*, 245).

For this reason, perception means to Claudel and Merleau-Ponty "to understand the rapport" of phenomena and consciousness, the objective and the subjective, the exterior and the interior, the visible and the invisible, the impersonal and the personal. Through perception the self makes contact with phenomenal Being, with a preobjective Form. "And it is this pre-objective realm that we have to explore in ourselves if we wish to understand sense experience" (*PhP*, 19). This preobjective domain makes possible the "birth" within the self so that it may come to feel being, to know and experience it. In the words of Claudel, it is "*to be born* (with the negative initial), that is to say, to be that which is not, that is, the image of that which is, the ending and the ended image of that which has no beginning" (*OP*, 185).

As "creative action," as "creative vibration," the self is an active form in the movement of Being; "I cannot escape being except in being" (Merleau-Ponty). This Being manifests and realizes itself through *connaissance*, which makes possible the understanding of Being by way of *naissance*, and so *naître* must be conceived as an image of Being. This image has a hidden aspect because it stems from Being itself, from that which allows things to be born continuously. In this way, form is the language of consciousness that is acquired by the self's contact with the primal form, the preobjective world or archetype itself. This is the point where Claudel and Merleau-Ponty differ. For Claudel, form is God's witness in the world, and in the incarnate Word God reveals himself to the world so that the world in turn perceives and grasps the living and personal presence of God's image, which has been hidden as a result of sin. Sin makes possible the actual temporal descent and manifestation of God's form through the body of Christ, which restores both the eternal and the temporal form to sight.

A vous de faire. A vous d'accomplir dans le Temps ce qu'au fond de vous-mêmes Je témoigne en ces paroles qui sont incapables de passer....Entre le Temps et la Cause, est-ce que le Coeur de Jésus ne se fera pas pour nous l'interprète de l'Eternité et l'instrument de notre résurrection sans cesse renouvelée dans l'instant? (*PP*, 40)[3]

For Merleau-Ponty, on the other hand, the central focus is upon the existential and the thinking subject itself as incarnate thought or consciousness, and the perceptual act conceives of itself as the infinite and the transcendent. By maintaining that the human person connects *connaître* with *naître* through "doubt," Merleau-Ponty introduces into the phenomenology of perception an original past, an archaic form, which is "God as the rational author of our *de facto* situation" (*PhP*, 232). Any recourse to Claudel's notion of eternity and Christ's form is hypocritical because, for Merleau-Ponty, "eternity feeds on time," and consequently it is only "in the ambiguity of time" that human beings are born and know themselves.

L'éternité est le temps du rêve et le rêve renvoie à la veille, à laquelle il emprunte toutes ses structures. Quel est donc ce temps éveillé où l'éternité prend racine? C'est le champ de présence au sens large, avec son double horizon de passé et d'avenir originaires et l'infinité ouverte des champs de présence révolus ou possibles. (*PhP*, 484)[4]

Here, then, are the varied contrasting elements seen in the figures of Claudel and Merleau-Ponty. On the immanent horizon, "to understand the rapport" carries the necessity of distance from the form (what Claudel calls "the flight") as well as nearness to the form (what Merleau-Ponty calls "point of maturity"); for the proper distance makes known what exists as hidden, as invisible, as mysterious, and as an experience of Being. However, Claudel's reference to eternity and the Christ's form is displaced by Merleau-Ponty's notion of eternity as an horizon of an infinite "field of presence" that opens to the invisible world or Being itself. Furthermore, whereas Merleau-Ponty believes that Being can be perceived and experienced from the vision of humanity being-in-the-world, Claudel, on the other hand, believes that Being can shine only in the illumination of God. In God's form all things integrate into a universal intentionality, which is Being or the "sense of the divine" in creation made visible through the body of Christ.

Claudel: The Divine Image

As we have seen, the basic structure of *L'art poétique* is simple. All that is born, body or spirit, exists and knows at the same time, according to its own world. There is form, movement, vibration, equilibrium, proportion, and harmony in all creation. And all creation is natural as to its end, but eternal as to its sense. The world is seen via sensation as the "unspoken lamentation of love," the primal ground, and the enrapturing work of poetic art. In poetic art, human beings bear some witness to their primal experience of creating themselves in the image and likeness of what they are not. Poetic art calls the self to know, represent, and experience Being in the world, a Being that lends the world its total harmony and comprehensibility, a center to which all things must converge if they are to be seen, understood, and experienced.

> Dieu est touours au présent et c'est au présent qu'Il est présent à toutes choses. C'est dans ce présent en Lui que toutes choses puisent leur commencement et leur fin. Il est...le compas et le cercle....(*PP*, 11)[5]

Just as poetic art weaves all words into an exquisite sentence, endowing it with a musical tone, so too all things constitute themselves around the *connaissance* of God and, consequently, create a beautiful sight to behold. The form of creation possesses a vibratory movement only in its coexistence with other essential images or in its birth from Being.

From this we can understand how, by referring to Genesis, Claudel requires that the eyes and senses see God as the form of light. In fact, implanted in the depth of all beings there is "a luminous spark which one calls rhythmic theme, or form, or life, or soul" (*PP*, 87). And the task of this spark, Claudel goes on to explain, is to give form and proportion to the darkness. "It is necessary that the Light shine in perfect darkness, and that the one who does not further its reception, furthers its reflection" (*PP*, 11–12). Color results from the relationship between the double (exterior and interior) rhythmic and vibratory movement of light, "one free, the other constrained and enclosed."

> Moi aussi, je suis. . . un foyer de lumière et d'énergie. Et l'onde lumineuse dans son expansion ne rencontre, nulle part, de corps inertes, mais partout des systèmes de forces en travail, plus ou moins compacts ou compliqués. Elle est obligée de composer avec cet obstacle, de modifier sur lui son rythme et son allure. C'est cette réaction, cet *allumage* de l'objet sous le choc solaire que nous appelons couleur. . . . La couleur est le héraut de la flamme. Or, soit un cercle dont le foyer lumineux est le centre. (*OP*, 167)[6]

From this logic, it follows that the "luminous speck" is the relationship of all things to God by the descent of the light into the darkness, into our being. Indeed, light gives form to darkness, and light existed prior to, or finds itself anterior to, the senses. In fact, it is at the heart of "the darkness which the filial sentiment, the desire for the origin, the sense of God" (*PP*, 60) places the soul in a proper viewing point so as to perceive God himself, or the Origin, which has become accessible to bodily organs. That is, God has come over to the side of darkness, nonbeing, in order that the human person may be called into being: "It is not enough to say that we look at the world existing, we cause it to exist by seeing it" (*PP*, 96). The senses, however, are not only the instruments that place us in contact with the world; they are also the product and external form of our internal faculties and of that "insatiable sentiment" which shapes the depth of our being in conformity with the form that exists outside us so that we might perceive it and receive its impress, its image. In this way, the world that is (exists) is defined in relation to the perceiver's inner form and the sensible world.

> L'invitation extérieure s'adresse par le moyen de l'organe approprié à tout ce qui constitue l'individu. Lequel organe est ici notre oeil appelé, délégué, préposé, au nom de notre corps et de toute la personne, à la tâche de voir. C'est l'appel de Dieu au dehors et de toute l'oeuvre immense de Dieu autour de Lui-même auquel l'homme a répondu par. . . ce

double soleil réceptif par lequel il communie avec tout ce qui est au dehors lumière. (*PP*, 80)[7]

Such then is the perceived world and the perceiving subject: light, as an invitation from God speaking to an appropriate organ. In order to respond to the invitation from God, the soul uses the light outside so that it may come to know and feel existence by seeing the world as it exists. Claudel insists that it is as if the need to see the world makes the eye, and the eye sees the world to verify and execute all sensory tasks of the body, which "the sight shows it" (*PP*, 81). The exterior world enters our inner self through sensory perception, and its image comes to paint itself "in the depths of the eye," which is not a raw material but an active power, a profound oscillation, a busy workshop where the luminous image from the outside comes to bind itself by means of a fine thread to our physiological body, which opens and closes itself to the world. Thus it is within perception, within the contact of the sensing subject and the world, that Claudel discovers the breath of life, the form, the light, "the harp in the depths of our eye," which give existence to both the perceiving subject and the world. The senses are "the creative vibrations" by which we come to realize our unique existence.

Ainsi la lumière, avec toutes ces choses au dehors qu'elle contouche et manifeste, a été introduite à l'homme pour lui apprendre à voir, pour lui montrer où il est, pour l'amener de la puissance à l'acte, pour réaliser au fond de lui-même toutes ces possibilités de différence qui constituent l'expression de la personne, et lui apprendre à promener cette différence essentielle comme un instrument de connaissance (co-naissance) sur tous les êtres qui l'entourent. (*PP*, 97–98)[8]

The world we recreate or rediscover, through sensory perception, is a world we have experienced through our bodies, and the body is the instrument of *connaissance*, the way of coming to know the soul, precisely because the soul is the possibility of action. Perception thus expresses the possibility of birth; the perceived world is structured according to the body's way of looking. "Everything which is called by the gaze has a right to see" (*PP*, 100). The perceived world is thus a reply to the body's sensations, and the body does not exist as other things exist. Rather, it exists as a center from which the soul radiates and around which all things arrange themselves according to the order of their particular form. For Claudel, the body and the world form, as it were, a closed circuit and coexist internally; and it is because of this internal existence that there can be a possibility for knowledge, for birth.

Il suit que le principe de son existence et de sa forme est aussi l'ouvrier de sa connaissance. Celle de l'homme peut se définir *une naissance consciente qualifiée par l'objet qui en limite l'expansion.* (*OP*, 165)[9]

This "conscious birth" is nothing but the knowing body; the experience that the body has of itself thus teaches the perceiving or sensing body that it is not the various things that surround it but a new mode of existence, of being — that is, a body that sees, hears, smells, tastes, and touches the world with the depth of sensibility, reason, and conscience. For this reason, "conscious birth" is an existing body externally and internally conscious of itself and the world.

Tout être, en effet, est une traduction autonome de ce regard créateur et la réalisation dans le temps de la forme prescrite à son obéissance, c'est-à-dire à son opération, et du signe nécessaire à sa signification. Cette forme est l'expression concrète, en même temps que le moyen, de la connaissance qu'il a du général en tant que particulier. La connaissance est l'instrument qui permet à tout être de co-naître. Cette co-naissance...se couronne chez l'homme d'une action volontaire, consciente et intelligente. (*PP*, 100)[10]

This is to say that with the emergence of *co-naître*, the self is not only a general being, but a particular person whose vision now must be directed at the source of light, and of Being itself. The self is a particular "signification," a concrete expression, of God's creative gaze. And this further means that the human person is no longer a being, but a son/daughter. "God has created him profoundly confident of the secrets He has reserved for His Word. He is His son with a particular name" (*PP*, 101). From this observation it follows that the self's whole existence must be perceived from inside out, from the particular call that God issued when he created it: "Return, return ceaselessly to your source" (*PP*, 73). This source, however, can be perceived only through his begotten Son, Christ, who reopens the path "in the depths of the eye" toward seeing God's form, a form that has been veiled by sin. Through the body of Christ, the self's external senses are redirected by way of the faculties of the soul toward the interior senses, where they become the soul's eyes, which behold the source, the primal ground, the light, God.

Et nous, au fond de notre demeure abîmée, nous avons des yeux pour boire à ces coupes débordantes que nous tend, tour à tour, la générosité de notre Dieu. Des yeux dirigés non seulement vers l'extérieur, mais vers l'intérieur, pareils à ces animaux symboliques dont parle saint Jean, qui sont *pleins d'yeux au dedans et au dehors*, un regard vers Dieu dont le péché seul altère la limpidité. (*PP*, 79)[11]

The paintings of Rubens and Perugino, continues Claudel, teach us the very relation the interior senses have with the exterior senses. By bringing to expression the visible world from inside out through the use of red and blue colors, for example, these two masters illustrate that "to the outer ray there corresponds deep within ourselves a palette of sensibility" (*PP*, 77–78). The paintings penetrate and inform the inner senses to awaken "a wave as vibrant as the most pure sound" (*PP*, 76). Accordingly, the painted world of Rubens and Perugino, insists Claudel, is a vision that, paradoxically, sees the form, the light, of both the subjective and the objective aspect of perception.

> L'exercice des quatre autres sens fait appel en nous...le champ du subjectif....La Vue au contraire, semble-t-il, est entièrement tournée vers l'objet, elle me transporte tout au dehors, je suis tellement requis à regarder que j'oublie pour le moment d'exister, l'objet m'occupe, il se substitue à moi, il travaille au dedans de moi à ma place. (*PP*, 75)[12]

In their paintings, Rubens and Perugino thus attest to the correspondence between seeing the world and being taken over by it; by seeing the world they are enraptured by its light, which shines in the depth of their being and guides their inner eyes on the path to the light, God, who is the Divine Artist making himself visible from his relationship with the world.

Vision is seeing from "the depths of the eye," which preserves in itself God's images from the "knowledge" of its original birth. The exterior senses are essentially the soul's interior eyes; they are the paths on which the perceiving subject confronts God's light in the world and thus comes to an act of birth (*co-naissance*). Sight, explains Claudel, sees pure light; sound hears the "words of Love"; taste savors the bread of the Eucharist, the intoxicating cup of the crucified Christ, the salt of wisdom, and the tears of Mary who communicates to the self the taste of God himself; and odor scents the aromatic perfumes of "the gold of intelligence," "the incense of desire," and the "inalterable myrrh of charity" (*PP*, 68). So it is that with all the bodily senses the human being is born inwardly with the heart; and this inner vision, concludes Claudel, does not demand more of the world than what the world is.

> C'est au coeur seul qu'il demande le secret de notre filiation. Il nous respire pour savoir l'odeur que nous avons....Alors nous connaîtrons avec Lui des ténèbres si grandes que l'Ecriture...ne trouve d'autre comparaison que la lumière de Midi. (*PP*, 43)[13]

The more God wills to be touched or perceived, the more he advances from the darkness of the abyss, through his work and the Patriarchs of the Old Testament, to the incarnate Word on which "theology has based the sublime theory of the transforming or deified Vision" (*PP*, 13). This vision, which is the secret of our filiation, is not seeing the image from the order of the senses and the light of the intellect. Rather, it is perceiving in the order of grace and the "rhythmic theme" of time, which confirm God's presence in the world and in human beings. This vision sees the "inalterable myrrh of charity," which alone is capable of conceiving.

C'est alors, dit l'âme sanctifiée, *que je connaîtrai comme je suis connue*, dit cette image pure au fond de nous, dit cette Conception en qui elle a été rendue capable d'invoquer le Père. (*PP*, 37–38)[14]

And this birth is simply "I am" in a perceptual contact with the absolute, the primal ground, the One, Being, the triune God who shines "in the deep night," in the image of "the seventh day," where the soul comes to rest in the womb of eternity. There the soul is consumed by the "blessed nothingness" of the ground, which is God and the abyss. There the soul is consumed by the flaming fire of "the light of Noon" of God's creative light in the yet brighter light of the Son who is the Divine Lover. "Under the exigency of its lover, suddenly the soul is snatched from the shadows" (*PP*, 27). In the soul's return to the ground, the darkness, the source, it tastes the beloved and desires him fully; it recognizes itself in perfect nakedness with the Beloved. But this "being snatched from the shadows" is precisely the soul's return to nonbeing, or a birth in the total way of being one with the light, the origin, or an experience of the sense of God.

This vision of God's sense implies that the human being is the concrete expression of light, of God the Father. According to Claudel, the self is not merely a body existing as other bodies exist in their relationship to God the Creator. Rather, the self is a creature that God calls into being by virtue of its contact with his image. This image, which is the secret of "our filiation," does not signify a sonship with God as much as it indicates an analogy: like the light of this personal and living God, the self is not only a body (phenomenon), it also manifests, radiates, and bears witness to God's light. But the self cannot make visible God's form without the interior senses by which it perceives God from its inner eyes. This "devouring sentiment," this "incense of desire" is forever waiting to conceive in the depth of the dark night and through the essential form of absolute

Being — that is, of God, the world, and self. Conception takes place when this Being is received in the night of all births, in the image of all images. Then, and only then,

> Tout en nous devient simultané, transcrit une fois pour toutes le "bleu" de l'Eternité. Nous nous sommes apportés nuptialement. La vision nouvelle n'est que le développement de cette bienheureuse nuit en nous de la Foi. C'est alors que l'âme, prêtant l'oreille, et oublieuse des parois de sa maison, entendra cette parole qui lui a été promise: *Sponsabo te in sempiternum.* (*PP*, 46)[15]

There is a moment, an instant, when the interior light of this "new vision of Faith" becomes one with the exterior light of the "blue Eternity" that shines from Christ. And this occurs because "the incense of desire" and the "devouring sentiment" of the self are quenched as the soul finds repose in the revealed form of the Divine Lover, the Son. "It is on this that the Sky fixes itself before our eyes. The proportion of their moments is no longer susceptible to change. Time has become Ecstasy" (*PP*, 306). The soul is thus transformed into its eternal form and becomes as radiant as the light; it becomes clothed with the white garments of resurrection and transfiguration through which the whole universe is born with Christ.

In this state of ecstasy, of absolute bliss, the soul knows (*connaissance*) God as Absolute Being, and at the same time it is born into, and simultaneously with (*connaître*) what it was not prior to its phenomenal birth or existence (*naissance*), which is precisely this divine light. In this state, the soul bears witness to what it knows consciously (*connaissance*) or unconsciously (*naissance*); the soul uses the light that shines in the darkness, in the heart, and in the mind. This light without change sees, speaks, acts, lives, and gives life; it transforms into light the darkness of the world. This is indeed the eternal now, the instant, when the soul returns to its source "in the bosom of the Trinity" where it sees the unending and unbeginning mystery of the divine sensation, the creative vibrations, which are the "Permanence danced by Movement, Eternity scattered by Time" of the "Point developed by the Circle," of "the Act interpreted by Action," of "Unity across Many" (*PP*, 307). This is the Divine Presence, which the soul knows and realizes while seeing; this is the moment when it says: "I am [like God] a place of light and energy." Here Claudel is not being poetic; what he is trying to express is the inner vision of the soul's divine nature, which is based on the notion that God is "Permanence danced by Movement" within the Trinity, which accounts for the knowledge that God is existence and that he is also love. For it is his energy, his light, his love, that direct the perceiver's eyes toward his image, the Son, revealing the splendor of the Holy Spirit in the very intention of God, the Father, who is the very act of feeling, knowing and being born with: He is "the Unity across Many." It is pure divine sight; for he is the eye of the self's vision. "Our entire religious life is our attention to the particular intention that God had in calling us into being" (*PP*, 100).

Merleau-Ponty: The Temporal Image

Like Claudel, Merleau-Ponty insists that the self's relationship with the world requires conscious attentive acts. "Attention is therefore a general and unconditioned power in the sense that at any moment it can be applied indifferently to any content of consciousness" (*PhP*, 34). As a "general power," attention is a mere possibility, an intentionality that explicates and thematizes the world as indeterminate horizons while it transforms them into figures. Like Claudel, Merleau-Ponty conceives of attention as the means by which the self comes to know itself in confronting the world. "This passage from the indeterminate to the determinate, this recasting at every moment of its own history in the unity of a new meaning, is thought itself" (*PhP*, 39). Again, with Claudel, Merleau-Ponty says that through attention the self encounters the world in what is a perceptual act, a birth, which both unites the self interiorly with the outside world, a world which has a prehistoric origin, a primordial form. But whereas Claudel identifies this primordial form with absolute Being, with the light of God, which can be perceived from the proper use of the external senses, Merleau-Ponty does not admit this absolute Being. For him the domain of experiences or temporality is the only ground from which the eternal can be seen.

> Dire que j'ai un champ visuel, c'est dire que par position j'ai accès et ouverture à un système d'êtres, les êtres visibles, qu'ils sont à la disposition de mon regard en vertu d'une sorte de contrat primordial et par un don de la nature, sans aucun effort de ma part; c'est donc dire que la vision est prépersonnelle; — et c'est dire en même temps qu'elle est toujours limitée, qu'il y a toujours autour de ma vision actuelle un horizon de choses non vues ou même non visibles. La vision est *une pensée assujettie à un certain champ* et c'est là ce qu'on appelle un *sens*. (*PhP*, 250–51)[16]

Perception is thought opening itself up to reality. It is not merely an inward consciousness, a language known only by the self and that expresses thought itself. "Man is of the world," and it is from concrete existence that his "sense" appropriates what is there and makes it visible to the self, although this vision always contains a horizon that is not seen. Nor is perception merely a momentary sensation, a certain "nothingness" of consciousness: "The perception of being is for someone who is able to step back from it and thus stand wholly outside being" (*PhP*, 246). The visible reality or being can be perceived only when the perceiving subject looks at it from a distance, from a domain that is beyond or invisible; only when the subject's look grasps Being, not as pure interiority but as an encounter with the world of things, an encounter that is prepersonal, since it occurs "by virtue of a sort of primordial contract and by a gift of nature"; transpersonal, since it occurs within a "milieu of existence"; and transcendent, since it reveals a horizon of things "not seen or even not visible."

> Dans chaque mouvement de fixation, mon corps noue ensemble un présent, un passé et un avenir, il sécrète du temps, ou plutôt il devient ce lieu de la nature où, pour la première fois, les événements, au lieu de se pousser l'un l'autre dans l'être, projettent autour du présent un double horizon de passé et d'avenir et reçoivent une orientation historique. (*PhP*, 277)[17]

Standing outside Being because of possessing time, the perceiving subject experiences that "sense" which is a union of the subjective and the objective, history and perceptual moment. The revelation of Being as an invisible horizon is possible only when the subject's gaze renews its primordial contract with the world. In this way, invisible things, too, are revealed as having a temporal horizon, a historical orientation likewise founded on Being. Being offers itself to the visible world only within a historical context that, for the "sense" of vision, is not separable from the perceptual moment, since being stands in a "presumptive unity" with time. Perception thus cannot be separated from the place, "this place in nature," in space and time in which it takes place.

> La perception est toujours dan le monde du "On." Ce n'est pas un acte personnel par lequel je donnerais moi-même un sens neuf à ma vie. Celui qui, dans l'exploration sensorielle, donne un passé au présent et l'oriente vers un avenir, ce n'est pas moi comme sujet autonome, c'est moi en tant que j'ai un corps et que je sais "regarder." Plutôt qu'elle n'est une histoire véritable, la perception atteste et renouvelle en nous une "préhistoire." (*PhP*, 277)[18]

In this prehistorical horizon, the individual does not stand before the world as "autonomous subject" but rather as an impersonal "one," a body perceiving the phenomenal world and in this process ratifying and renewing the invisible world of a prehistory as well as of a primordial contract with being. Rather than being "a true history," perception is the self coming to understand itself within its experience of time and space.

La constitution d'un niveau spatial n'est qu'un des moyens de la constitution d'un monde plein: mon corps est en prise sur le monde quand ma perception m'offre un spectacle aussi varié et aussi clairement articulé que possible et quand mes intentions motrices en se déployant reçoivent du monde les réponses qu'elles attendent. (*PhP*, 289–90)[19]

In the body, the perceiver sees the "spectacle as varied and as clearly articulated as possible" that constitutes an integral whole by the very fact that the perceptual is the "depth" of "the impersonal One" incarnating itself as a "general milieu" in the world, which contains the body. The body, then, is "a meaning which clings to certain contents" (*PhP*, 172), in which sense is perceived and received as the image of a certain depth of the "milieu of existence." Moreover, in view of the condition that the self is-in-the-world, the perceiver is brought to this "maximum of clarity" through the body serving as the "common texture of all objects and...at least as regards the perceived world, the general instrument of my 'comprehension'" (*PhP*, 272). The body thus provides unity and comprehensibility to perception and insures that the "motor intentions" receive the expected and understandable responses from the world. Such clarity and comprehensibility are present when the phenomenal, which human beings encounter, is visible only because the image by which the world communicates with them emerges from "the impersonal One," from the "milieu of existence," from the body as the "depth" of existence. The self, by virtue of its being-in-the-world, is that norm, that total comprehensibility, harmony, and coherence around which phenomenal things come together in order to reveal themselves. The human person is that norm because he or she is the "contents" of the dispersed and indeterminate horizons, of the general context of things.

In its perceptual encounter, the perceiving subject must find an opening that discloses the visibility of the whole spectacle from which the perceptual act derives its maximum illumination.

Pour chaque objet...il y a une distance optimale d'où il demande à être vu...elle est obtenue par un certain équilibre de l'horizon intérieur et de l'horizon extérieur....La distance de moi à l'objet n'est pas une grandeur qui croît ou décroît, mais une tension qui oscille autour d'une norme.... (*PhP*, 348–49)[20]

What is involved here is not, as in the individual sciences, the mere technical adjustment of the sensory and mental apparatus to the visual field; rather, it is the proper correspondence of an impersonal existence to its living existence, of an individual background to a universal horizon. Not only sensory, intellectual, cultural, and historical distances must be brought into optimum focus, but also existential prerequisites must be met in order that the different and clearly perceived images that make their claim on the individual's "milieu of existence" may also find a maximum of visibility, a sense, in the existence of a natural world; the body, instrument of comprehension vis-à-vis the perceived world, is not the subjective condition of the possibility of seeing an object, for what it is ought not to intrude upon the object's objective existence or to substitute itself for phenomenal reality.

If the perceiving subject can commune with the world, it is not because it constitutes the world from thought or inner consciousness; rather, it is because the subject submerges itself in the thickness and density of the world by the perceptual experience. The object, the body, and the world are connected in a living manner, and the self finds itself in a world that continuously demolishes and remakes its existence.

> Nous avons réappris à sentir notre corps, nous avons retrouvé sous le savoir objectif et distant du corps cet autre savoir que nous en avons parce qu'il est toujours avec nous et que nous sommes corps. Il va falloir de la même manière réveiller l'expérience du monde tel qu'il nous apparaît en tant que nous sommes au monde par notre corps, en tant que nous percevons le monde avec notre corps. (*PhP*, 239)[21]

By contact with the body and the world, by learning to feel our bodies, we rediscover ourselves, we renew ourselves, we awaken in ourselves that primal source of existence, that objective and transcendent ground in our own subjectivity. If this totality of things is fragmented, then, not only is the perceptual encounter disrupted, but everything about phenomenal reality becomes incomprehensible. Or, if this projection by which we open ourselves to a knowledge of the wholeness of the image is excluded from our encounter with the world, then, again, everything becomes incomprehensible: the world, the body, and thought are no longer related to each other with respect to their "presumed unity."

Perception as the unity of and oscillating tension between the body and the world, the objective and the subjective, the personal and the impersonal, thought and things, is also consciousness of self.

Toute pensée de quelque chose est en même temps conscience de soi, faute de quoi elle ne pourrait pas avoir d'objet. A la racine de toutes nos expériences et de toutes nos réflexions, nous trouvons donc un être qui se reconnaît lui-même immédiatement, parce qu'il est son savoir de soi et de toutes choses, et qui connaît sa propre existence non pas par constatation et comme un fait donné, ou par inférence à partir d'une idée de lui-même, mais par un contact direct avec elle. La conscience de soi est l'être même de l'esprit en exercice. (*PhP*, 426)[22]

This self-consciousness makes the self the norm of its own existence, as well as of all things. In the self, the tension between its body and all bodies, its thought and all thoughts, its existence and general or historical existence, its being and Being itself, is fully experienced. In this tension, perceptive Being is not simply a "material mass"; rather, it is filled with ambiguities, since, on the one hand, it reveals itself to an individual self, and, on the other hand, it is still the same Being that is the object of perception by all individuals. "There is always around my actual vision a horizon of things not seen or invisible" (*PhP*, 251). This Being cannot be divorced from subjective existence, yet it reveals itself as "the impersonal One" and, therefore, as independent of the perceiver as subject. It gives its perceivers the root of all their experiences and their reflections; however, in itself it is presumptive and primordial. In fact,

Comme...je n'ai pas d'autre témoignage sur mon passé que ces témoignages présents et que, cependant j'ai l'idée d'un passé, je n'ai pas de raison d'opposer l'irréfléchi comme un inconnaissable à la réflexion que je fais porter sur lui. Mais ma confiance dans la réflexion revient finalement à assumer le fait de la temporalité et le fait du monde comme cadre invariable de toute illusion et de toute désillusion: je ne me connais que dans mon inhérence au temps et au monde, c'est-à-dire dans l'ambiguïté. (*PhP*, 397)[23]

The dynamic tension between ambiguity and certainty, doubt and confidence, the known and the unknown, while operating simultaneously, is not reciprocal:

Chaque perception...ne disparaît que pour laisser place à une autre perception qui la corrige. Chaque chose peut bien, après coup, apparaître incertaine, mais du moins il est certain pour nous qu'il y a des choses, c'est-à-dire un monde. Se demander si le monde est réel, c'est ne pas entendre ce qu'on dit, puisque le monde est justement, non pas une somme de choses que l'on pourrait toujours révoquer en doute, mais le réservoir inépuisable d'où les choses sont tirées. (*PhP*, 396)[24]

And as the self emerges from this "inexhaustible reservoir," it witnesses a deepening of its perceptual field, of its consciousness; it becomes present to its world and to the general world in that the self coexists with all other perceptual visual experiences, "and all these perspectives together form a single temporal wave, one of the world's instants" (*PhP*, 381). At the same time, the self communicates what it sees by means of its body to others; and it is this communication that constitutes the self's unique consciousness, its body, its grounds of existence. Within this temporal horizon, human beings must see that they are not thought over body, intellect over senses, idea over phenomenon. Neither must they think of themselves as absolute selves with freedom to bestow upon themselves and others a certain image; because "the form of objects is not their geometrical shape, it stands in a certain relation to their specific nature, and appeals to all our other senses as well as sight" (*PhP*, 265). As body, the human being is a being whose total existence is found in an encounter; as body among other bodies, this human being perceives self in perceiving the world. Through perception, "the senses intercommunicate by opening onto the structure of the thing" (*PhP*, 265).

This opening up to the image or form of things, this projection to the world, makes it possible for the perceiving subject to see what it has never sensed. This opening up to the image is the consciousness of the mystery of the form, which is this "inexhaustible reservoir" of things and can never be fully exposed by the perceiver. The perceiving subject does not possess a gaze capable of grasping the sphere of the general; the subject is itself perceptible reality, and its body is one among perceptible things. Things preserve their own thickness, their own density of being; they never become completely visible.

> Si la chose même était atteinte, elle serait désormais étalée devant nous et sans mystère. Elle cesserait d'exister comme chose au moment même où nous croirions la posséder. Ce qui fait la "réalité" de la chose est donc justement ce qui la dérobe à notre possession. (*PhP*, 270)[25]

For this reason, the perceptual synthesis no more unveils the mystery of the object than it does that of one's own body. Because of this, the perceived object presents itself as invisible, and the perceptual synthesis is indeed achieved in the world and not at the metaphysical point occupied by the thinking subject. Thus, if the self is a being-in-the-world, then it must root its experiences in the form; it must see within the world the image that transcends the world. This is for Merleau-Ponty the "mystery of the world and of reason" (*PhP*, xvi).

L'ipséité n'est, bien entendu, jamais *atteinte*: chaque aspect de la chose qui tombe sous notre perception n'est encore qu'une invitation à percevoir au delà et qu'un arrêt momentané dans le processus perceptif. (*PhP*, 269–70)[26]

The mystery, the ground for perceiving beyond the world, the invitation the world extends to people to open themselves up to the invisible, the "series of my experiences" conceived as a call to experience the ambiguity of time, to discover the Being which is forever, are for Merleau-Ponty the eternal and the infinite.

Mais si nous retrouvons le temps sous le sujet et si nous rattachons au paradoxe du temps ceux du corps, du monde, de la chose et d'autrui, nous comprendrons qu'il n'y a rien à comprendre au-delà. (*PhP*, 419)[27]

In recovering its own history by discovering the "prepersonal" domain, the preobjective sphere, the self can indeed have a glimpse of eternity, of the life of perception, which is the experience of "God as the rational author of our *de facto* situation" (*PhP*, 232). It is only from the "*de facto* situation" of being-in-the-world that the individual can see God as "the mystery of reason"; then it is in time that some sort of eternity is felt, for beyond the here and now, "being [is] that which appears, and consciousness as a universal fact" (*PhP*, 455). This is the view of eternity, of transcendence, of Being, for Merleau-Ponty: eternity is in time, and time is subjectivity itself. And time is constant without being eternal; it is in motion, making explicit the actual field of the perceiving subject's situation in its past, present, and future dimensions, as well as the Origin of the world.

Nous sommes au monde, c'est-à-dire: des choses se dessinent, un immense individu s'affirme, chaque existence se comprend et comprend les autres. Il n'y a qu'à reconnaître ces phénomènes qui fondent toutes nos certitudes. La croyance en un esprit absolu ou en un monde en soi détaché de nous n'est qu'une rationalisation de cette foi primordiale. (*PhP*, 468)[28]

Conclusion: The Unseen Image

The conclusion to be drawn from Merleau-Ponty's observations is that "we are in the world" and must not confuse "absolute spirit" with temporal or incarnate subjectivity. According to Merleau-Ponty, the human person is all that he or she sees, and to claim a world "in itself detached from us" is to fail to see that God cannot be known, or be apart, from the self's de facto situation. Faith is a recognition of this being-in-the-world and anything beyond this situation is rationalization. For Claudel, the self sees the world, and by seeing it the self lives the world. This temporality awakens in the human person consciousness of the light, which is the manifestation of the hidden form in things, which in turn is the manifestation of Christ's body as the form, the light; this harmonizes and blends all forms into a brilliant unity, into a proportioned whole, into a circle. Seen from the eyes of faith, this gift of the Triune God causes both the human person and the world to transcend themselves.

Despite this difference, Claudel and Merleau-Ponty do not want the mystery, the hiddenness, the form, to be dissolved into perfect clarity; for clarity of the form would destroy the mystery of the world and of Reason itself or Being. In his own way, each sees the human person as a body-soul unity, and each understands the self's perceptual act from a vital center in which the self stands in a relationship of real contact with the Origin, the One, the Ground, Being. Both of them justify sensory knowledge from the interior to the exterior senses, and both of them regard the senses as the pathway to *connaissance* and *connaître*. Both stress the self's relationship with the phenomenal world, with nature. The most natural reality is for human persons to create a conscious existence for themselves. Consciousness and perception go together, and even if people do not consciously open themselves up to the world, the image, they cannot escape the fact that the form of things still unfolds itself in virtue of the visible universe and for the sake of the invisible, the constant, and the transcendent.

For Merleau-Ponty, the image radiates from certainty as well as from doubt, from the infinite openings as well as from the limitations of the human person's own "visual field." For Claudel, however, the image radiates from the human person's own darkness: in the darkness of sin God's form makes visible the Light of creativity, of redemption, in Christ who transforms the human person into a new vision. From Christ's sense the soul comes to know and is born with the eyes of faith that will lead it in time from phenomenal vision to the spiritual sight of God when it beholds the light, the form, the image, of its likeness. Then it is the incarnation, the birth, of the Word, which for Claudel is the poetic art and pure light; it is the rebirth of the world and the splendor of an eternal form. This is the unseen image for Claudel, an image that can be perceived and known.

3

Claudel and Weil on Grace

Toute notre vie religieuse est l'attention à l'intention particulière
que Dieu a eue en nous appelant à l'existence.... (*PP*, 100)[1]

L'attention, à son plus haut degré, est la même chose que la
prière. Elle suppose la foi et l'amour. (*PG*, 135)[2]

To discuss the notion of grace theologically is immediately to raise
the problem of image, of knowledge, of freedom, of the relationship
between God and the human person. Although created in the image
and likeness of the Creator, the human person is seen in the Judeo-
Christian context as still steeped in evil, unable to hear the voice of
God and see his splendor in the world in and of himself or herself.
While both Claudel and Weil describe the self's absolute freedom as
the pinnacle of grace, as the summit of mystical union in the divine
Word, sole and perfect image of God, they differ from each other as
to its mediation.

Claudel's view of grace is that of a "theology of vision" that does
not destroy the phenomenal relationship between God and the
human person. In fact, for Claudel, the phenomenal reality of this
theological vision allows the human person to make real contact with
"the unspoken lamentation of love," which is the life of grace by
which the person is transformed corporeally and mentally into the
image of God's only begotten Son in order to become a living splendor, a witness of God's light in the world, just as the Word made
flesh is the radiance of his love and the form of his being. Claudel's
theological vision focuses on the knowledge of divine sensations by
means of external senses, which, through the inner faculties of the
soul, awaken in the human person a sense for God, which is a sense
of filiation to God. Through the Incarnation, God gave his image
(Son) and infused the spirit of filiation within human beings so that
the mystery of the Trinity shines in them.

Celui qui Est ce qui a toujours été, c'est le Père; celui qui est ce qui Est,
la ressemblance qui fixe l'identité, le verbe qui traduit la substance, c'est

le Fils; et celui qui Est ce qui sera, ce trait de l'amour qui épuise d'un seul coup entre les deux participants toute possibilité d'être ailleurs que dans l'immédiat, c'est l'Esprit. (*PP*, 11)[3]

It is this filiation that truly defines the human person; it gives that person a divinized substance, a similitude that regenerates the self and makes it participate in God's spirit. Such a filiation communicates to the human person the possibility of the life of grace, a life that may be lived existentially as one of the children of God called forth from the darkness to participate in his eternal light "at the center of the hour of Noon."

Besides this experiential mediation of the theological vision, Claudel sees the Church also as the phenomenal form of God's grace.

Elle...est l'exaltation de l'humilité, elle est la componction dans la gloire! Elle est suave et une, elle est bien recueillie sur le baume. Vaisseau honorable, récipient de l'orthodoxie, secret spirituel, vase de prudence, sanctuaire insigne de la dévotion! Pleine de grâce.... (*OP*, 215)[4]

As "penitence in glory" the Church is the "honorable vessel" of the spiritual mysteries, of God's form of revelation in Christ. Her members participate in God's glory through the Eucharist, the very embodiment of that grace which brings the whole being (body and soul) to sense God's divine sensations. The Eucharist "impregnates, illumines, accents, flavors, inflames, vivifies" (*PP*, 55) the bodily senses and the internal faculties, thereby making sensations and knowledge a salvific means and a mediation. With the Eucharist, Claudel sees human existence opening up to the divine touch; the human person learns to "wait for the sound of His voice, His impulses, His prohibitions" (*PP*, 55).

By contrast, Weil sees grace as a force beyond the phenomenal manifestation of God's image, beyond the self's natural faculties, beyond the Church. According to her, the human condition is to confront the law of gravity, which separates all things, and grace only serves to sharpen the gap between the world and the self, the self and God. "Grace fills empty spaces, but it can only enter where there is a void to receive it, and it is grace itself which makes this void" (*PG*, 12). Indeed, by conceiving the world as empty spaces in which light and gravity rule, Weil arrives at an unmediated unity of creation and God, of the corporeal realm of nature and the moral realm of grace. "To lower oneself is to rise in the domain of moral gravity. Moral gravity makes us fall toward the heights" (*PG*, 5).

Although humanity is in the image and likeness of God, Weil sees it closed off in the darkness of the body and in the impotency of mental powers. "We must renounce everything which is not grace, and not even desire grace" (*PG*, 15). To give up everything means the total separation of the human person from phenomenal existence so that God may be perceived and known through the unseen and the unknown.

L'attention seule, cette attention si pleine que le "je" disparaît, est requise de moi. Priver tout ce que je nomme "je" de la lumière de l'attention et la reporter sur l'inconcevable. (*PG*, 137)[5]

To Weil, the way of seeing and of conceiving God is an upward movement of the attention that strips all perceptual attributes from itself in order to arrive at a kind of knowledge by way of the void. "If we love God while thinking that he does not exist, he will manifest his existence" (*PG*, 18). In fact, knowledge of God as one who surpasses all that can be felt, seen, and known, as one who is totally inconceivable, corresponds to the failure of the perceptual act and to the inability of the creative act to penetrate the beauty of God's form hidden in things. For Weil, the beautiful lies beyond the summit of phenomenological perception in that she refuses to admit any manifestation of God's image in the world and in humanity. The beautiful, consequently, is also hidden and unknowable; for as long as the person goes on conceiving, wishing, and longing, the beautiful cannot be perceived or grasped.

"Experience of the transcendent: This seems contradictory, and yet the transcendent can be known only through contact, since our faculties are unable to invent it" (*PG*, 140). It is contact with the void in human sensibility and internal faculties that carries one beyond sensibility and knowledge to God, the Unconceived One. But this void, concludes Weil, is precisely the experience of the Incarnation as noncontact with God: "In order that we should realize the distance between ourselves and God, it was necessary that God should be a crucified slave" (*PG*, 105). Thus, this crucified Slave is stripped of all sensible forms, even of the knowledge and love of God insofar as they can be felt, perceived, and known. At the furthest distance from God, the self sees by unseeing and knows by unknowing that this Slave became flesh for its sake in order that it in turn may grow into the likeness of his death and resurrection. "He has descended, he descends in the act of creation, and also in the Incarnation, the Eucharist, Inspiration, etc." (*PG*, 54). With such a belief, grace loses the phenomenological mediation of the form; it becomes essentially an unmediated contact.

For Claudel, then, grace is a form of the beautiful to which the self opens in its perceptual encounter with the world and the Word, the Form, the Eucharist. The Eucharist reveals a harmony of phenomenal forms and God's promise of fulfillment, of birth. For Weil, grace is also the beautiful, but it demands a refusal of phenomenal mediation, since what must be realized is the Unconceived One in the wretchedness of the self stripped of senses and mental faculties, denied the ritual of the Church and any medium by which it makes contact with God's hidden image.

Claudel: The Phenomenal Mediation of Grace

L'art poétique instructs that God reveals himself as Creator, as Divine Poet, as "Permanence danced by the Movement," as "the unspoken lamentation of Love." If indeed the world is such a manifestation of God's love, it follows that this manifestation takes its shape from the image of the world itself. It is the form of things, their word, that is the revelation of God's eternal Being. According to Claudel, whatever can be known about God can be perceived and known in the world, since it is God himself who has revealed it to the world.

> La masse muette *somme* Dieu de l'ensemencer d'une parole, de lui donner cela par quoi en lui elle soit capable de finir, d'expirer, de rendre ce qu'elle a reçu. Et voici que la vie a tressailli dans son sein. (*OP*, 186)[6]

This word or seed by which all things spring into life allows Claudel to perceive and know absolute Being, which, although different from phenomenal beings, is nevertheless made visible through them. This word, which shines in the visibleness of phenomenal forms, is simply the mystery, the eternal transcendent glory, the sublime rapture, grace itself.

> C'est un paradis à la fois et c'est une horloge, c'est la distance sanctifiée par la figure, c'est le temps consolidé par le rapport, c'est l'Infini aménagé par le nombre, c'est la liberté absolue dans la clôture infrangible, c'est la sécurité dans l'inépuisable, c'est l'évidence dans le mystère, c'est la spontanéité dans la fascination de la Loi...c'est une vigilance inextinguible...c'est la Danse des Lanternes, c'est un chiffre dont la clef est partout, c'est une insurrection et c'est un choeur, c'est une cité et c'est une équation. (*PP*, 246–47)[7]

This "distance sanctified by the figure," this "phenomenal in the mystery," this "time made permanent by proportion" is simply the

Word of God by which the self can come to know both the transitory form of the many images in the world and his mystery, his beauty, his infinite kingdom in the world. According to Claudel, when Christ "appeared in full light," then "by a unity of grace and nature" (*PP*, 154), the mystery, the ineffable or Unknown One, is made visible through the world in the Church, whose radiant form is prefigured in the law of the Old Testament: "But Christ did not come from Nations, he came from Israel" (*PP*, 184). In this way, all phenomenal forms, by the inheritance of Old Testament figures, are elevated by the Church to the form of God himself. "I see before me the Catholic Church who is the entire universe!" (*CGO*, 105). Integrally dependent on God in its very existence yet possessing its own being or form, the world is thereby made one through the Church by its participation in the likeness of absolute Being, of God's splendor, by its reception of the grace-given life of Christ. For the Church is "an always visible God, an always present people; the exaltation of the bread, the display of the secret heart" (*OP*, 217). The Church thus represents a perfect correspondence between the exterior and the interior verbal image of God.

In fact, even the architectural development of the Catholic temple serves as Claudelian testimony that the Church is the "real contact" between an always invisible God and an always visible people.

> Car voici que la Croix qui, selon la promesse sacrée, devait tout "tirer à elle," avait été plantée dans le fond de l'édifice, selon ce geste des deux bras écartés qui montre, qui déploie, qui appelle et qui arrête.... Seuls autour de l'autel des officiants dans le choeur reçoivent siège et disposition; la foule par son arrêt même fait paraître en s'y figeant le mouvement qui l'a attirée, déterminé par un acte précis, son assistance subordonnée à la perpétration du drame liturgique où elle communie, à la perfection de l'Heure. La travée médiane barrée par les mystères impénétrables guide jusque-là les yeux, les bas-côtés mènent et ramènent dans leur circuit le pas. (*OP*, 210)[8]

Like the word, the architectural form of the church is a liturgical drama, a means of communion to "the perfection of the Hour," an instrument for the knowledge of God. By its "impenetrable mystery," revealing the relationship between the creator and the human being, the Gothic church embodies the celebration of the Divine Office. Everything—stained glass windows, vaults, flying buttresses, steeples—carries the subject along the path to spiritualization and reveals that God is light. For Claudel, the Gothic form is a contemplative poem, a prayer, a kind of symphony more eternal than human and offering the structure for transcendence. Churches such as those of Rheims, Rouen, and Notre Dame have given France the entire stage for its liturgical drama, writes Claudel, bestowing upon it the "silence of the 'Good News.'" Chartres in particular makes "the exaltation of the bread" visible as a concordance between Old and New Testaments, two modalities of the same visible Word. "The seed, here too, is the grain of mystic black mustard! Go in and you shall be able to venerate the little statue found, in times of old, beneath the ground, like a black kernel" (*OP*, 216).

In the sixteenth, seventeeth, and eighteenth centuries, the Catholic church becomes a theatrical spectacle, its faithful an audience, as God's visible image has to be made ever more obvious, since his verbal form, obscured by the "Protestant blasphemy," which denied the power of the priest to sanctify this "grain of mystic black mustard," cannot penetrate the liturgical drama. The sign of the cross now plays itself out in the baroque expression, transformed by the spatial and temporal discoveries of the Renaissance. "Henceforth, on the steady stone, Rome erected the enormous dome" (*OP*, 216–17). The human being again communicates with God through everything that is corporeal; the human being sees in the full daylight of the senses the altar in all its liturgical adornments, the closed tabernacle, and the cross. In the baroque form, the liturgical drama finds itself flooded with the light of the natural world. Consequently,

si la présence du Christ sous les espèces consacrées n'était point seulement...une sorte de luxe alimentaire, un mystère réservé au contact du palais avec la langue, il importait maintenant que le culte rendu ne fût point limité à l'acte liturgique, mais que l'Eucharistie reçût parmi nous une résidence et un honneur continuels. (*OP*, 216)[9]

For Christ, the meal is the consecration of his corporeal death: the flesh that is consumed, the blood that is spilled, the thirst and the hunger that are felt, the sweat that is poured, and the weight of the cross. Hence, neither the relationship between God and the self, nor between Christ and the Church, can be understood in a purely spiritual sense. What is visible in the baroque form is always this meal, this sacramental cult, this liturgical drama as a spiritual-corporeal form in the permanent and concrete reality of the Eucharist. The meal and the cross constitute for all times the perfection of the hour, the mystery, the liturgical act, for which Christ came. "Even today the birth Christ in time has begun. He has received a name. A mother was given to Him" (*PP*, 151). The introduction of a mother into the eucharistic cult is a visible sign of an always visible God, since the eucharistic form is Christ's act intended to constitute the interior form of the Church. For this reason, concludes Claudel, while it may be true that the Gothic form of the Middle Ages is more revealing of the mystery of the Word than the baroque form of the seventeenth and eighteenth centuries, it is equally true that the baroque Church consummates all cultic meals of the world that have realized their essential communion with divinity through eating and drinking. The baroque form thus preserves in full the impregnation of the image of the mother by the Spirit of God, handing over the fruits of nourishment from Sarah to Mary to the Catholic Church to the person. This, according to Claudel, is what the prophet Isaiah means when he says that Zion has given birth in pain.

Paroles vraiment *pleines de grâce* et qui ne s'adressent pas seulement aux enfants d'Abraham, ni même à la Colombe de Nazareth; mais à nous-mêmes au travers de tous les siècles! Car en enfantant le Christ, c'est nous-mêmes, qui faisons partie de Sa chair et de Son âme dans l'unité de l'Église, à qui une Vierge a donné le jour. Déjà l'oeuvre de notre rédemption a commencé....C'est elle qui nous a enfantés et nourris, c'est cette Vierge, notre mère, au sein de qui nous avons puisé *le beurre et le miel jusqu'à ce que nous sachions* réprouver le mal et choisir le bien. (*PP*, 146–47)[10]

As "at the breast of this Virgin" humanity becomes one with Christ, so after the Incarnation, Death, and Resurrection, the Church becomes consubstantial with Mary, being her image, equal in splendor and in grace. Insofar as this birth of Christ is the express image of the Old Testament, it is a remembering of a people in exile and thus a meal commemorating a death. But since Christ, unlike Old Testament figures, has risen from the dead, this banquet transforms death into an eternal communion of joy. Since Christ makes visible the cultic meal of the past, what had once occurred in Mary's womb now becomes present in the sacramental meal of the Eucharist in the Mother Church.

Le Christ fut un homme public et dès le commencement il choisit les lieux publics pour séjour. De même que si nous le cherchons aux jours de son passage, nous le trouvons dans la maison de Simon et dans l'auberge d'Emmaüs, au puits de Sichem et à la table de Cana, et toujours, selon le reproche pharisien, "avec ceux qui boivent et qui mangent," de même l'Église.... (*OP*, 209)[11]

The meal of the Church, whereby the Church comes to be interiorly—"it is the bread which makes the Church" (*PP*, 30)—is the same as the meal of crucifixion whereby Christ obediently accepted death; but it is also the same as the banquet of resurrection veiled under the sacramental form.

This, according to Claudel, is what the architectural form of the Church has revealed in the past and still reveals:

Car, depuis le Paradis...l'homme toujours a eu pour gardien de sa prière et pour protecteur de ses eaux l'arbre qui, pousse et végétation de l'unité, est l'expression de l'Attente dans le témoignage; assis, agenouillé sous l'ombre. Mais cependant que le païen, impuissant à maîtriser l'arcane, en recherchait les ténèbres obreptices pour y cacher ses poupées, l'Église chrétienne a absorbé le bois mystique adaptant intérieurement à la congrégation humaine ses avenues et son choeur. (*OP*, 207)[12]

Corresponding with the inner state of the human congregation, of its sanctification by uncreated light, the artistic form of the Christian Church absorbs, or assimilates, the "mystic forest" of the external manifestation of God and thus becomes spiritualized from within. In other words, the world, of which the Christian Church is a manifestation, is drawn interiorly towards the Creator by "a persistent will to exist, a certain metaphysical look at the present where our being finds the nourishment of its continuity" (*PP*, 14). This means that when mankind reaches a state in which the act of seeing the form is replaced by a "metaphysical look at the present," the whole being of the world becomes one in a total vision of God; the "mystic forest" becomes illumined by the form of grace, by his Presence, by his light: "For the shadows are exterior, the light is within. / You can see only with the sun and know only with God in you" (*CGO*, 100). Transmitted in the artistic form of the Church, this internal illumination of both the phenomenal world and the person is the visible expression of the exaltation of the sacramental form, of the Eucharist.

La table est mise, il n'y a qu'à se servir. Dieu se donne à nous, à perte de vue, montagnes et plaines, cirques et vallées, pâturages et déserts, et ces perspectives triomphales à l'infini! Il n'y a qu'à rentrer dedans!...Ce n'est pas le pain que nous voulons, c'est l'essence du pain...cette monnaie de l'éternité, ce rond lumineux et clandestin que le prêtre à chaque aurore fait glisser entre nos lèvres. (*PP*, 33–34)[13]

It is the essence of the meal—this "money of eternity," this "mystical grain"—that has become sensibly perceptible, because "the body is the work of the soul," and, as such, the body makes God's form visible. The "black spot in the depths of our eye" no longer sees darkness, because it is now under the light of grace; it hears the sounds of the "mystic forest" of the phenomenal world, but now savors it with "divine sonority" in the soul. This essence not only fills the soul, but the body too is filled with spiritual delights in the presence of the body of Christ.

> Il est venu non pas pour Se faire comprendre, mais pour Se faire constater. Dans Ses premières démarches au regard de notre âme, Il ne S'adresse pas à notre intelligence, Il S'adresse à notre constatation. Il S'adresse à nos *sens*, c'est-à-dire aux différentes formes de notre *sens* intime, à notre sens du sens. (*PP*, 62)[14]

In addressing himself to the "sens du sens," God has put on, so to speak, interior bodily senses. However, bodily senses no longer constitute an obstacle to redemption; instead they are a mediation, a way of coming to know God, because they are the expression of the soul. It is the soul that changes, "in the depths of our eye," bodily sensations for the spiritual touches of grace. This does not mean that the body no longer has a tendency to lose itself in the corporeal world, to move away from divine sensations; what it means instead is that "we try to fashion God's Wisdom, but it is God's Wisdom that fashions us" (*PP*, 52). In the light of divine wisdom, of grace, the "look of our soul" pierces the outer form of the body and the Claudelian believer is able to see the correspondence between the divine advances of grace, on the one hand, and the body's disposition to grace, on the other. "By means of His all-seeing eye, God solicits the finest threads of our will. Such is the accomplishment of Grace as it works on our disposition" (*PP*, 89–90).

The will is free to choose the good when it sees through "the all-seeing eye" of grace, when it is nourished by the essence of the bread of the Divine Word, incarnate "at the breast of the Virgin Mary," and thereby visible and tangible, both sensually and spiritually. Indeed, according to Claudel, the good Form, to which the will conforms in its good dispostion, came down from on high to be felt, while still remaining perfect Sense:

> C'est lui qui tire de toutes choses pour moi la moralité et l'action de grâces et qui fait que tout à ma droite et à ma gauche devient rythme, idée, ressemblance, proposition, tempérament et hymne. (*PP*, 262)[15]

In this relationship of similitude, correspondence, and rhythm between Christ and the human person, only one choice exists: the good. This choice is performed by the will, "a spontaneous movement of desire," and by the unifying action of grace.

As for the faculties of reason and imagination, continues Claudel, one has but to open "the metaphysical eye" to see the senses unite themselves with reason and imagination in such a way as to constitute "the ideas and the images" in reference to an "abstract spectacle," without the abstract spectacle ever destroying the senses, however. Ideas and images are good when, in place of merely accepting empirically the thing that is, a correspondence, a relationship, a resemblance, or a proportion to this "abstract spectacle" or divine idea is seen. In this sense, the good is what is; but this whatness is not the changing physical appearance of things; rather, it is their substance, their being or form, their measure, in which they participate and strive to become. But whereas reason and imagination work in the domain of the temporary, of the changeable, the good has its natural place on the plane of the eternal. This is why for Claudel a good choice supposes an appropriate illumination of the mind by grace whereby sensation, reason, imagination, and will are harmonized in the "idea, resemblance, proposition, temperament and hymn" of the one Good, God.

> La Grâce attire, provoque, invite à la manifestation cette surface, cette enveloppe à qui tout le reste est attaché, sur qui elle puisse exercer son action et qui soit idoine à la qualifier, en même temps qu'au-dessous se construit l'engin propre aux profondes entreprises de la connaissance....C'est d'abord un éclat léger et pur qu'enrichit bientôt la sortie des trésors les plus profonds, tous ces métaux spiritualisés. (*PP*, 88)[16]

It is God who inseminates human actions by his Word; he is not only the interior eye that sees deep into the soul, but also the "light and pure ray" by which the soul sees; moreover, he is the soul's food in that he is the living bread that opens the womb of the senses, the reason, the imagination, and desires so that they strive in one harmonious movement towards the good: everything must be felt according to the divine good pleasure. This is the good disposition of the will of God, and such is the sensation of the divine.

> Elève-toi donc vers Dieu au sommet du candélabre, ô langue ardente et intelligente, arme acérée de l'esprit, organe de la jouissance, de la parole et du désir! (*PP*, 130)[17]

Grace and desire thus are both necessary for the transfiguration of existence. Within this rhythmic movement of the senses, reason, and will on the one hand, and of divine grace on the other hand, and by an "affectionate accord" of the two, the will is illuminated so that it may choose the good. Grace thereby is able to awaken the soul "sleeping in us, or rather it watches while we sleep" (*PP*, 14) and thus fills the soul with divine splendor. Once the equilibrium between grace and human nature is achieved, the soul then directs the eyes to see with pure pleasure; the ears to listen in silence to "the unspoken lamentation of love"; the "flaming tongue" to savor with delight what is gracious and good; the hands to be raised in prayer so that ideas, images, memories, reason, will, and sensations may be elevated toward grace; and the feet may follow the way of the cross in humility, faith, and hope. In this way, God is witnessed in and by existence; he is experienced and known in the world through good actions. God becomes truly incarnate in the world as light, as the form of all that the world is, as well as what it is not; for, in the words of Claudel, every void attests God's fullness, as every number manifests the rhythmic law of the harmonious whole. "Let it be either a formless void or a continuous number, both are to the measure of my desire" (*PP*, 245). In its earthly pilgrimage, as it looks at the world illumined by God's splendor, "the soul, kneeling at the feet of its Master, is at one and the same time the theatre and the witness to this epiphany of colors" (*PP*, 90). This is the liturgical drama, the soul's theater, which the development of the Church teaches; and although it is true that the source of joy lies in Paradise, in the beatific vision of God where the "Wisdom of God is before you like a tower of glory and a crowned queen" (*CGO*, 52), it is equally true that grace can be enjoyed here on earth through the sacramental form of the Eucharist.

Grace then is love in the act of self-giving. By this sublime act God knows the human person as bride and bridegroom know each other when the time has come to consummate their love. God, the bride and bridegroom of the soul, possesses the divine flame, the "ardent tongue of desire" that is pure love, for he is love. Yet he is powerless to bestow his "tongue of fire" in the soul if he finds the soul cold, without longing, without waiting, and without proper disposition. But when the soul comes to understand that the divine Lover calls on it by its proper name, with words that enchant it, the soul cannot fail but to open itself up to the divine touches of the Lover: "The Soul knows what it needs to know" (*PP*, 16). What the soul needs to know is to dispose itself, to respond and consent to the advances of the Lover. Such is the mystery of human actions; such is the mystery of the Trinity that abides within the soul in the state of grace; and such is the consummation of the world by the senses, of the body by the soul, and of the soul by the grace of divine love.

Dépouillée de ses sens, l'âme séparée n'a plus le moyen de s'informer extérieurement; mais elle n'est point privée de ce sens premier constitué de son rapport mouvant au seul point fixe. L'impulsion, qui naguère mettait en branle les différents appareils des sens et qui par eux lui procurait la perception de son image, l'âme à présent directe en épouse le coup et la visée. En son "temps" de tension elle se réalise dans toute sa puissance;

elle n'a plus le moyen de se former d'image avec ses sens; mais la disposition par laquelle elle les mettait en mouvement constitue à elle seule une
certaine image. Elle se compose dans un certain équilibre...Cette image
est le don qu'elle fait à son créateur par le second temps de sa respiration,
et la matière de sa joie ou de sa torture. (OP, 201–202)[18]

Weil: Unmediated Grace

Unlike Claudel, who accepts and lauds humanity for its "ardent
tongue of desire," for its ability to will that which is good in the world,
a world that truly manifests the light that is God, Weil rejects this
natural desire. "The intelligence has nothing to discover, it has only
to clear the ground. It is only good for servile tasks" (PG, 15). Accordingly, the intellect deludes itself about what it knows; for what
it knows is nothing other than the reflected servitude, the darkness,
the void, of existence.

Accepter un vide en soi-même, cela est surnaturel. Où trouver l'énergie
pour un acte sans contrepartie? L'énergie doit venir d'ailleurs. Mais pourtant, il faut d'abord un arrachement, quelque chose de désespéré, que
d'abord un vide se produise. Vide: nuit obscure. (PG, 13)[19]

The void, therefore, is not true nothingness, because the intellect
in itself cannot know it. The void is revealed by and reveals the existence of an outside force. In fact, for Weil the world as a whole
must be seen as having a void in order that it may need this outside
energy, grace. Grace is that outside force by which the human person
comes to know the void as good. To desire the good means to endure
the void; further, it means to love being nothing, for love itself is a
nothingness. Thus, while the self thinks it loves nothingness, it really
loves something other than what the intellect knows; what the individual comes to love is the good, which presupposes the void and
evil.

Si je pensais que Dieu m'envoie la douleur par un acte de sa volonté et
pour mon bien, je croirais être quelque chose, et je négligerais l'usage
principal de la douleur, qui est de m'apprendre que je ne suis rien. Il ne
faut donc rien penser de semblable. Mais il faut aimer Dieu à travers la
douleur. (PG, 129)[20]

What the intellect must recognize by verification and demonstration
is the preeminence of evil, and, at the same time, it must be in-
different to the good. "There lies the essential grace. And it is the
definition, the criterion of good" (PG, 137).

The intellect thus can never penetrate the good, but it can judge those actions which express it. For this reason, it needs to be keen, discerning, and precise, while, at the same time, it must turn its attention away from the world.

> Dans la perception sensible, si on n'est pas sûr de ce qu'on voit, on se déplace en regardant, et le réel apparaît. Dans la vie intérieure, le temps tient lieu d'espace. Avec le temps on est modifié et si, à travers les modifications, on garde le regard orienté vers la même chose, en fin de compte l'illusion se dissipe et le réel apparaît. La condition est que l'attention soit un regard et non un attachement. (*PG*, 139)[21]

In looking at the void, at nothingness, at suffering, the only real knowledge possessed by the intellect is that of truth, beauty, and goodness, which are the result of one and the same manner or gaze: detachment. Looking at what does not exist, the individual sees what really is, which is not the human person thinking or seeking or desiring; rather, it is the human person suffering in the void. The capacity of the intellect to drive away a thought, a desire, once and for all, is the gateway to the good.

Weil regards knowledge as a look, not a longing or a penetrating thought. Moreover, when the intellect succeeds in driving away its thoughts, it reconciles all contradictions unto itself. Its logic derives and depends on the knowledge of the void, of the descending movement of necessity or gravity; for grace makes itself necessity, an outside force. Even if we desire nothing but the good, of necessity we must accept the fact that we cannot choose the good: "It is after long, fruitless effort which ends in despair, when we no longer expect anything, that, from outside ourselves, the gift comes as a marvelous surprise" (*PG*, 53). Not to affirm that its effort must be destroyed in order for the good to be obtained is for the intellect to deceive itself, because an attachment to a particular good can only be illusion and can only be destroyed by a detachment or by an attachment that is incompatible with it. Far from demanding that human beings passionately desire, think, and imagine that which is good, the rule of contraries demands that they turn toward evil, because the latter is equivalent to the former, just as destruction of the self and detachment from the world are equivalent to attaching oneself to the world. "We do not become detached, we change our attachment. We must attach ourselves to all" (*PG*, 161). Not to embrace the all is tantamount to replacing the law of gravity, of necessity, by the operations of the mind, to think that the human person is free to choose the good. "Our will is forever sent from one means to another like a billiard ball" (*PG*, 167).

But, according to Weil, to say that the self in its natural state cannot understand that its will is forever sent from one place to another, from one means to another means, is true only inasmuch as it is also false. This is so because the self must first accept the given; that is, it must first destroy the will for the sake of the world, or destroy the world for the sake of the self, or destroy the self for the sake of the good. If the self realizes this, the will, in being sent from one means to another, will soon discover the good as something other than the world, as something other than the self. "To strip ourselves of the imaginary royalty of the world. Absolute solitude. Then we possess the truth of the world" (*PG*, 14). For in solitude, the self faces itself in the void, in its wretchedness, in things that can be of no value to the will. The truth of this solitude lies in the greater possibility of the intellect to cultivate within itself the moral gravity of detachment.

> L'usage de la raison rend les choses transparentes à l'esprit. Mais on ne voit pas le transparent. On voit l'opaque à travers le transparent, l'opaque qui était caché quand le transparent n'était pas transparent.... L'incompris cache l'incompréhensible, et pour ce motif doit être éliminé. (*PG*, 152)[22]

What Weil points out is that knowing is unknowing, and willing is a negation of all will, since reason, the power to choose the good, merely hides the reality of human nothingness, the supreme actualization of desire and lack. "Evil is the form which God's mercy takes in this world" (*PG*, 166). Without evil, that which is truly absolute, truly good, and truly boundless cannot be desired. "The soul transports itself outside the actual body into something else. Let it therefore transport itself into the whole universe" (*PG*, 160). The whole universe, the all, is the incomprehensible One, and reason should be used only to lead us to see this undemonstrable truth. "The role of the intelligence... is merely to submit. All that I conceive of as true is less true than those things of which I cannot conceive the truth, but which I love" (*PG*, 150). Accordingly, the self cannot have a desire for the truth until it has reached the realm where it can neither desire the good nor achieve it by its own efforts, where the self recognizes that truth pases through evil into goodness. Such a state comes about when the self submits or gives itself up to the solitude of a self-consuming mental dialectic.

> La contradiction est le critérium. On ne peut pas se procurer par suggestion des choses incompatibles. La grâce seule le peut.... La grâce seule peut donner du courage en laissant la tendresse intacte ou de la tendresse en laissant le courage intact. (*PG*, 117)[23]

If indeed evil is the form by which God's grace reveals itself in the world, then, true contradiction is revealed at its fullest with Christ on the cross: "For it is both a free-will offering and a punishment which he endured in spite of himself" (*PG*, 120). According to Weil, Christ's Incarnation is true only insofar as the contraries, free-will and punishment, are assumed, are submitted to in spite of reason. This is grace; it is the simultaneous existence of contrary things in the soul, the imitation of the order of the world. "Creation is composed of the descending movement of gravity, the ascending movement of grace, and the descending movement of the second degree of grace" (*PG*, 4). Christ is this descending movement of grace. His desire to redeem mankind is at the same time a desire to suffer. He experienced all human misery, except sin. Yet, Christ submitted himself to everything that makes the person capable of sin. All sins are attempts to fill the void, the nothingness, which is the human condition. Hence, only the complete annihilation of the self can be offered to God, just as he freely offered Christ to humanity. "There is absolutely no other free act which it is given us to accomplish, only the destruction of the 'I'" (*PG*, 29).

When the illusions of corporeality, sense perception, and understanding have been destroyed; when the self is aware of no desire, not even that of grace, other than the free act to destroy itself, and is no longer the subject of any image or thought, its condition is that of contemplation or prayer. "Attention, taken to its highest degree, is the same thing as prayer. It presupposes faith and love" (*PG*, 135). In this state of attention, the self becomes one with all being, without differentiation and distinction; by faith and love, the self identifies itself with Christ, who loves in it the acceptance of its nonbeing so that he may freely give the self his being.

Renoncement. Imitation du renoncement de Dieu dans la création. Dieu renonce—en un sens—à être tout. Nous devons renoncer à être quelque chose. C'est le seul bien pour nous. (*PG*, 37)[24]

From the lowest point of moral gravity, but no longer identified with it since the contradictions of all reality have been resolved in Christ, this only good that the human person desires is located within the eternal contradiction of the Word, and, by inversion, the self is elevated to unconditioned Being. "May I disappear in order that those things that I see may become perfect in their beauty from the very fact that they are no longer things that I see" (*PG*, 48). For existence is now beyond and above sensation, perception, and comprehension; it is an "equilibrium in Action" (*PG*, 203).

That there are degrees of attention or prayer is clear from the fact that as long as there remains memory, understanding, and will, prayer is not yet pure; this equilibrium in action has not yet been fully achieved. However, so long as the human person moves with grace, prayer still remains as faith and love, and God can be known from afar. "We have to place God at an infinite distance in order to conceive of him as innocent of evil; reciprocally, evil implies that we have to place God at an infinite distance" (*PG*, 126). In a state of prayer, in a state of pure detachment, in a state of suffering, the human person is not this particular being; the human person does not have a name, is free of all objects, and exists as all humanity. But in Christ, according to Weil, humanity is one Man, and that One is God whom the self must become. "I have to know that as a thinking, finite being I am God crucified" (*PG*, 104).

Thus, when attention is pure, the self creates itself: "Extreme attention is what constitutes the creative faculty in man and the only extreme attention is religious" (*PG*, 135). By creative faculty Weil means an act of uninterrupted interior prayer, as a descending movement of necessity and ascending movement of grace by which it is impossible to choose evil. In this state of extreme attention, God's presence in the world is seen, not as a perceptual and cognitive encounter between the perceiver and God's form hidden in things but as a gift. "There is, as it were, an incarnation of God in the world, of which beauty is the trademark" (*PG*, 173). Beauty, like the good, however, can only be encountered in the absolute solitude of suffering and/or contemplation, of praying. Without the void there is no beauty: "Distance is the soul of the beautiful" (*PG*, 172). But if the beautiful is the real presence of God in the world, there is, according to Weil, demonic art, which interrupts the melody of the universe by destroying the equilibrium of action that alone makes beauty acceptable to prayer. Beauty too must remain object- and even subject-free: that which is looked at, yet never approached. Poetry must be absence, nostalgia: a joy that is painful; a pain that soothes. Music must echo the double descending movement of gravity and grace.

> La montée des notes est montée purement sensible. La descente est à la fois descente sensible et montée spirituelle. C'est là le paradis que tout être désire: que la pente de la nature fasse monter vers le bien. (*PG*, 173)[25]

An art that ascends is illusory because sensorial rising cannot redeem; rather, it is beauty taken to its extreme point of suffering, namely, death or complete detachment, that saves. The beautiful must be on the side of evil, on the side of extreme suffering, if it is to proclaim God's presence in the world, and "the beautiful is the experimental proof that the incarnation is possible" (*PG*, 173).

The slope of nature, the slope of beauty, the slope that religious art mirrors is the suffering and the dying that calls into action grace, which alone can redeem from the void. Revelation, undiluted by the teaching of the Church, must be set up over and against death.

Le mal est infini au sens de l'indéterminé: matière, espace, temps. Sur ce genre d'infini, seul le véritable infini l'emporte. C'est pourquoi la croix est une balance où un corps frêle et léger, mais qui était Dieu, a soulevé le poids du monde entier. (*PG*, 109–110)[26]

In the balance of the cross, the self encounters something definitive, and this is why the teaching of the Gospels, constituted by God's Word and human suffering, remains for Weil this definite point of interaction between the self's nothingness and the divine, between the world and that which is not the world. For indeed nothing can bridge this infinite distance separating being and nonbeing, except the most concrete unintelligibility of God's impossible descent, the crucified Christ. "Consciousness of this impossibility forces us to long continually to grasp what cannot be grasped in all that we desire, know, and will" (*PG*, 113). The very consciousness of this impossibility transports the self to the threshold of the good, where it is "another which opens the door" of the good: dying and rising with Christ; for death alone redeems existence.

Comme Dieu est présent dans la perception sensible d'un morceau de pain par la consécration eucharistique, il est présent dans le mal extrême par la douleur rédemptrice, par la croix. (*PG*, 106)[27]

The Eucharist thus proclaims the extreme evil that the believer must adopt, since by gazing at evil and eventually death, he or she sees the supreme good, which is the complete destruction of the self. For, if we find joy in the thought that God is present, we must find the same joy in the knowledge that "we ourselves are not, for it is the same thought" (*PG*, 42). This knowledge is extended to the human person's sensibility through suffering and death. Death is the ultimate knowledge, which fills the void within the self; and, just as eternity transcends time and the unintelligible the intelligible, so death transcends both God's presence and absence in the world and in the self. Just as the law of contraries leads to the annulment of the phenomenal being, so the same law leads to the unifying grasp of opposites in the approach to God, who is the self destroyed.

It is in the knowledge and awareness of death and joy, of finite and infinite selfhood, the beatitude resides. Eternity is the identity of contraries where the soul and the other are distinct from and alien to each other yet are one. In this identity of contraries, the self grasps God; for his presence is the very contradiction of human existence.

> L'innocence et le mal. Que le mal lui-même soit pur. Il ne peut être pur que sous la forme de la souffrance d'un innocent. Un innocent qui souffre répand sur le mal la lumière du salut. Il est l'image visible du Dieu innocent. C'est pourquoi un Dieu qui aime l'homme, un homme qui aime Dieu, doivent souffrir. (*PG*, 107)[28]

God's revelation is finally known within a reverse order, and as long as "eternal beatitude is a state where to look is to eat" (*PG*, 117), it matters little whether the eucharistic meal finds its manifestation in the testimony of history or the Old Testament, and in the Church as the bride of God. "The mysteries of faith are degraded if they are made into an object of affirmation and negation, when in reality they should be an object of contemplation" (*PG*, 149). Contemplation, or extreme attention, or prayer, is not at liberty to degrade the mysteries of faith or to err with respect to what is the ultimate good, but the intellect can degrade faith, the will can do evil, and the Church can lead the self away from God; that is, from the mysteries of the Trinity, Incarnation, and Redemption. It is only in the purity of one's own heart where the intellect and the will conform to the slope of nature that they effect an equilibrium of action whereby they negate their desire and their ability to choose the ultimate good: detachment, void, suffering, and evil.

> Dieu ne peut aimer en nous que ce consentement à nous retirer pour le laisser passer, comme lui-même, créateur, s'est retiré pour nous laisser être.... Dieu qui n'est pas autre chose qu'amour n'a pas créé autre chose que de l'amour. (*PG*, 47)[29]

Love and detachment, however, are merely two sides of one and the same reality. It is by detachment that the self is united to God, and it is by suffering that it experiences divine love, which is attained in the contemplation of the contradiction between God and the self within the contradiction of the cross. "In contemplation, the right relationship with God is love, in action it is slavery. This distinction must be kept. We must act as becomes a slave while contemplating with love" (*PG*, 57). Love is in itself grace by its right relationship with both God and the world. As such, love is efficacious in its mode of detachment from all active willing, knowing, and having, from all that is not an act of suffering, from all that is not an inversion of the natural order.

> Nous naissons et vivons à contresens, car nous naissons et vivons dans

le péché qui est un renversement de la hiérarchie. La première opération est le retournement. La conversion. (*PG*, 39)[30]

In other words, whereas God's love creates by filling the void, human love creates by detachment, by exposing evil, by experiencing the void. In this sense, the self truly loves when it contemplates death, when it sees that its existence is sinful: "For it is the desire for a life which is finished that can no longer give anything new" (*PG*, 76).

Accordingly, formal doctrines of grace fall short of this aspect of inversion, of the slope of nature, of equilibrium in action, of the indeterminate as the ultimate contact with God, and of the absence and nonaction of God here on earth. Indeed, Weil insists that it is not within the Catholic or the Protestant vision to combine the contrary aspects of the unconditional reality in the right relationship with God, with the good, and with the knowledge of the void, of suffering.

Les mystères de la foi catholique ne sont pas faits pour être crus par toutes les parties de l'âme....L'Eucharistie ne doit donc pas être un objet de croyance pour la partie de moi-même qui appréhende les faits. Là est la part de vérité du protestantisme. Mais cette présence du Christ dans l'Hostie n'est pas un symbole, car un symbole est la combinaison d'une abstraction et d'une image, c'est quelque chose de représentable pour l'intelligence humaine, ce n'est pas surnaturel. En cela les catholiques ont raison, non les protestants. Seule la partie de soi-même qui est faite pour le surnaturel doit adhérer à ces mystères. (*PG*, 149–50)[31]

Hence, both Catholics and Protestants in different ways fail to attest to grace, because both in their own way fail to see that God's mysteries consist in the self's becoming all things, in its being completely detached from itself and the world, yet totally attached to itself and the world as a structure of the void, of nothingness, of evil.

To the extent that human beings deny this inversion, to the extent that they knowingly and willingly refuse to submit their actions to the "Father who is in secret and who sees in secret" (*PG*, 56), and to the extent that they refuse to see that love is a sign of their wretchedness — to that extent, human beings are separated from truth, the good, and the beautiful. To be one with the true, the good, and the beautiful is to renounce the end of all things, to renounce the belief that things have intentionality; it is to transform finality into necessity, necessity into suffering, and suffering into a means, which is the end of human existence. "It is the temporal seen as a bridge, a *metaxu*" (*PG*, 169). This implies that the phenomenal and the aesthetic cannot be a positive manifestation of God's grace; that the temporal world cannot be spiritualized by humanity's capacity to choose the good, to see God's form or image within the subjective and the phenomenal worlds. "All absolutely pure goodness completely eludes the will. Goodness is transcendent. God is Goodness" (*PG*, 52).

Conclusion: Grace and its Inversion

Weil's vision of grace is a vision of love in the crucified Christ. If grace fails to lift the human person up in the direction of God and of the good, it is to the extent that the self fails to strip itself of its natural faculties and the world. If, however, by the reality of contradictions the self contemplates the slope of nature, the equilibrium of action, the weight of gravity, then the cause and the reason for salvation is attributed not to human will but to the loving will of God who chooses the person as innocent. Innocence cannot come about unless evil, detachment, suffering, and the destruction of the self make the distance between God and the self infinitely unintelligible. In the absence of God from the world, the self can never hope to choose the good by its own will. In its separation from the good, the self really desires God, because the only way to approach him is by way of the unconditional, the indeterminate, the unknowing. "It is because we are a contradiction, being creatures, being God and infinitely other than God" (*PG*, 112).

Claudel, on the other hand, while believing that sin lies within the human person, also observes that the person is capable of choosing the good. Grace and free choice are both necessary for salvation; human beings are free to communicate, to make contact with grace, to be born with the knowledge of God, which is offered to them by phenomenal forms. Human beings have been created in the image and likeness of the Creator, endowed naturally with freedom and choice, which belongs to their natural condition. The testimony of the Mother Church in her biblical roots of the Old and New Testaments and the ecclesial tradition is also a revelation of God's love "in the bosom of the Trinity." God's grace or love, by which the human person comes to perceive and grasp God's splendor in the world, is the very wisdom of God, the very Word, the essence of the Eucharist, which places the person in a proper correspondence with, in a proper relation to, God's divine touches. God is present in all things; as is the cause in its effects, so is the Creator in his creature: God is present in the self in the way that Christ is present in the Church and the bridegroom is present in the bride. As sensing, rational, and willing being, the self reaches out to God through its own efforts, since grace does not exclude the self's freedom to choose the good. This is essentially what Claudel believes.

4

Claudel and Sartre: The Grace of Creation and the Beauty of Nothingness

Vois-la maintenant dépliée, ô Mesa, la femme pleine
de beauté déployée dans la beauté plus grande!
   Que parles-tu de la trompette perçante? lève-toi, ô
forme brisée, et vois-moi comme une danseuse écoutante,
   Dont les petits pieds jubilants sont cueillis par la mesure ir-
résistible! (*PM*, 1063)[1]

La beauté est une valeur qui ne saurait jamais s'appliquer qu'à
l'imaginaire et qui comporte la néantisation du monde dans sa
structure essentielle. C'est pourquoi il est stupide de confondre la
morale et l'esthétique. (1. 372)[2]

Claudel and Sartre suggest radically different approaches to the problem of the beautiful. While Claudel regards nothingness as the condition for sensing the form, the beauty in the world, Sartre believes that beauty can be grasped only in the image of things as unreal, and consequently in a world that is nonexistent, that is nothingness. For Claudel, while a thing is defined by what-it-is-not, this what-it-is-not does exist, and is perfection, Beauty. To the extent that the world is harmonized in the splendor of a triune God by means of and through the body and blood of Christ, there, in his view, is beauty. Beauty is for Claudel proportion, intentionality, harmony, movement, and light; a thing possesses it when it is in harmony with its own darkness or nonbeing, when it is in harmony with God, with light, with existence. The beauty of a human being, says Claudel, consists in the harmony of senses, reason, and conscience, in the knowledge that they are not God, in the reality that they are a relationship of verb, word, and name. The human person is a being-in-the-world, and the world is governed by the rhythm of sonorous images, or by light as the essence of color, or by signs as substances of poetic art.

On the contrary, for Sartre "the real is never beautiful" (1.372). Consequently, the beautiful is a consciousness of nothing. The human person is a being-in-the-world, but also a being who exists and is conscious of self. This means that the self must be conscious that it is not the world in which it finds itself. Consciousness of nothing makes it possible for us to imagine the beautiful that we know does not exist in things. Thus, "aesthetic contemplation is an induced dream and the passing into the real is an actual waking up" (1.371). Aesthetic or dream consciousness concerns itself with the real in that it enables us to understand our being-in-the-world, to withdraw from the world and consider it with intentionality, meaning, transcendence. "The imaginary appears 'on the foundation of the world,' but reciprocally all apprehension of the real as world implies a hidden surpassing towards the imaginary" (1.361). Reciprocally, consciousness of the world calls and motivates an imaginative consciousness, for without it the human situation would be conceived as completely "engulfed in the existent and without the possibility of grasping anything but the existent" (1.359).

In a way, both Claudel and Sartre see nothingness and transcendence as two important characteristics of aesthetic consciousness. For Claudel, however, phenomenal images produce not only ecstatic delight, but also reveal a correspondence that is objective in itself and in relation to other things. The world is beautiful in itself and exists for the pleasure of each sense; it exists not in order that we might lose ourselves in its nothingness, contingency, darkness, and superfluity, but in order that we might be born with God's form through our admiration of creation. For Sartre, on the other hand, images are not only a mental construct, but they disintegrate and vanish in the absurdity of the world, thus creating a feeling of nausea, of despair. Sartre's *La nausée* is characterized by nothingness and by his commitment to pure art. As aesthetic consciousness, *La nausée* is an imageless image of an amorphous world: it is the image of the darkness, the nothingness, the absurdity of existence and the recognition that commitment is possible only in art, which is intrinsically engaging. Literature is, in a sense, opposed to the real because it goes beyond it, by piercing through the layers of nothingness of the world in order to penetrate to the pure in-itself, to being.

Speaking of a jazz melody, Roquentin insists:

A travers des épaisseurs et des épaisseurs d'existence, elle se dévoile, mince et ferme et, quand on veut la saisir, on ne rencontre que des existants, on bute sur des existants dépourvus de sens. Elle est derrière eux: je ne l'entends même pas, j'entends des sons, des vibrations de l'air qui la dévoilent. Elle n'existe pas, puisqu'elle n'a rien de trop: c'est tout le reste qui est trop par rapport à elle. Elle *est*. Et moi aussi j'ai voulu *être*. Je n'ai même voulu que cela; voilà la fin mot de ma vie: au fond de toutes ces tentatives qui semblaient sans liens, je retrouve le même désir: chasser l'existence hors de moi, vider les instants de leur graisse, les tordre, les assécher, me purifier, me durcir, pour rendre enfin le son net et précis d'une note de saxophone. (*N*, 244–45)[3]

Claudel's *Partage de midi*, on the other hand, is a drama characterized by cosmic beauty by virtue of its image of transformation. In the light of "the irresistible measure," *Partage de midi* makes all visible forms luminous traces of the light, of God's splendor. It is a beautiful imaging of the light of the world that is conscious of its own darkness or transitoriness or nothingness.

The contrast I wish to set forth between Claudel and Sartre's art is one that reflects a fundamental human option. With Claudel, the nothingness is *nihil*, for reality is luminosity seen from an invisible source, God's abyss. What is is intelligible as what-is-not in the light of the source, the ground, which is. Any lack, loss, negativity, has meaning only in relation to what is, the *via* to its source. For Sartre, however, what is most fundamental is the nothingness which haunts and conditions being. Being or nothingness, such is the respective reference for Claudel and for Sartre. From this there emerge two views of beauty and the end of art.

Claudel: An Image of Cosmic Beauty

Partage de midi dramatizes the conflict between light and darkness, form and the formless, spirituality and corporeality, the unseen and the seen. "I love this great immobile day...I admire this great hour without shadow" (*PM*, 988), says Amalric to Mesa after the latter had remarked that the days were so much alike that they seemed composed of "one great black and white day." From the opening pages, the imagery that guides the play is in motion: "Noon in the heavens. Noon at the center of our lives" (*PM*, 991). The title itself is an image of the light of God unveiling itself and unveiling the beauty of the world. It is an image of the center around which the visible and the invisible, darkness and light, day and night, the phenomenal and the divine, creatures and Creator measure each other in order to be in perfect sight, "without shadow," of each other. To admire "this great hour without shadow" is to see the world with the right sight, which can only be given by God, the Light of the world. The "break of noon" is thus an image of transformation in which the whole of creation breaks away from its darkness and acquires luminosity and beauty.

It is around this image that the play is arranged in acts identified by physical time: act 1 takes place on a hot day at noon with the four protagonists ready to sail on the Indian Ocean to China; act 2 unfolds in the evening, under a dark sky and before a cemetery in Hong Kong; act 3 is set "in the depth of the night." The merger of physical time with Christian images of transformation guides the development of the play. Thus, the "desert of fire," the hellish purification, the mortification, that separates Mesa and Ysé can only be seen as a birth into the life of grace, as over and against physical death. What was once love in "clothes of the flesh" becomes the pathway into eternal time, into the Night of Love, which measures things not according to the light of day, but according to God's grace as the center of the universe, as the radiating light of beauty shining in all creation. Act 3 brings this image of transformation to its clearest expression when both Mesa's and Ysé's canticles express the transfiguration of their earthly love into divine love, of earthly sounds and sights into liturgical melodies and visions.

> Me voici dans ma chapelle ardente!
> Et de toutes parts, à droite, à gauche, je vois la forêt des
> flambeaux qui m'entoure!
>   Non point de cires allumées, mais de puissants astres,
> pareils à de grandes vierges flamboyantes
>   Devant la face de Dieu, telles que dans les saintes peintures
> on voit Marie qui se récuse!
>   Et moi, l'homme, l'Intelligent,
>   Me voici couché sur la Terre, prêt à mourir...
>   Au plus profond de l'univers et dans le milieu même de cette
> bulle d'étoiles et de l'essaim et du culte.
>   Je vois l'immense clergé de la Nuit avec ses Évêques et ses
> Patriarches.
>
>   (*PM*, 1051)[4]

This beauty of the world that Mesa sees is revelation: it is the light of God's love. It is a beauty that draws all things to itself and measures them in accordance with the mystery of God's form, which manifests itself in a more dazzling way than physical light because it is the source, the center, the glory, of creation. So, Ysé says to Mesa:

> Laisse ta main sur ma tête et alors je vois tout
> et je comprends tout.
>   Tu ne sais pas bien qui je suis, mais maintenant je vois
> clairement qui tu es et ce que tu crois être,
>   Plein de gloire et de lumière, créature de Dieu! et je

vois que tu m'aimes,
  Et que tu m'es accordé, et je suis avec toi dans une
tranquillité ineffable.

(PM, 1055)[5]

The world grows faint before the light of God, but illumined hearts experience "ineffable tranquillity," which cannot be expressed by ordinary language and concepts; the only language that cannot darken the brightness of this ineffable reality is liturgical language, a language whose music and poetry transform all creatures into creatures of God, full of glory and light. This language transports us into the world of ecstasy and delight where we come face to face with the mystery of God's image, which shines forth in us and makes us aware of our own darkness, our own nothingness. In his canticle, Mesa says:

  Et je me suis trouvé devant Vous comme quelqu'un qui
s'aperçoit qu'il est seul.
  Eh bien! j'ai refait connaissance avec mon néant, j'ai regoûté
à la matière dont je suis fait.
  J'ai péché fortement.

(PM, 1053)[6]

Such a knowledge of human nothingness, sin, darkness, finitude, loneliness, is realized in the eternal communion with the blood of Christ which flows from the cross.

  Ah! je sais maintenant
  Ce que c'est que l'amour! et je sais ce que Vous avez enduré
sur votre croix, dans ton Coeur,
  Si vous avez aimé chacun de nous
  Terriblement comme j'ai aimé cette femme, et le râle, et
l'asphyxie, et l'étau!

(PM, 1053)[7]

Nothingness is the means of getting within the heart, and regardless of the depth to which we can reach, it is still in Christ that we transform ourselves. Love makes explicit what the cross reveals: that Christ has been sacrificed for the sins of each and everyone of us so that we might come to abide in the abyss, the ground, the source, of the unmanifested light itself. The cross, as the descent of God into the flesh, abolishes the contradiction between darkness and light, sin and salvation, by transforming the body of Christ into the glorification of God the Father. Indeed, Mesa and Ysé are baptized into God's death in act 2, which takes place before a cemetery in Hong Kong, a cemetery shaped like an *omega*, symbol of the end. The cemetery, which at-

tempts to show death and the new life that Mesa and Ysé will experience, is nothing more than the symbol of the cross, the sacrifice
of the body and blood of Christ. As Mesa finds himself here, he feels
nausea; he trembles, for he does not wish to be here: "The taste of
my stomach is in my mouth." Here the full meaning of death is made
evident and visible.

> Quelle ombre sur la terre! Mon pas crie. Il me semble
> que je parle dans une caverne.
>   Au-dessus de moi un ciel obstrué, éclairé à l'envers
> d'un jour blafard.
>
> > > > > > > > > > > > (*PM*, 1018)[8]

The subterranean atmosphere, the dark sky, the cemetery, and the
visible world as shadows reflect Mesa's internal climate, his anguish,
his cry "in this desert of fire" of act 1 and the "shadow on the land"
of act 2. In order for Mesa to enjoy the fruits of transformation, of
divine love, he must pass through the dark night of the senses; that
is to say, he must purify himself, forsake earthly love, and die with
the Son of God in order to rise with him in that forsaken moment
on the cross.

> Ah, Vous Vous y connaissez, Vous savez, Vous,
> Ce que c'est que l'amour trahi! Ah, je n'ai point peur de Vous!
>   Mon crime est grand et mon amour est plus grand, et votre
> mort seule, ô mon Père,
>   La mort que Vous m'accordez, la mort seule est à la mesure
> de tous deux!
>
> > > > > > > > > > > > (*PM*, 1053)[9]

As Mesa meets Ysé in front of the cemetery, "she remains immobile, with her eyes downcast." With fear and trembling, Mesa
says to her: "All is finished." She tells him not to go away from her
anymore, to which Mesa replies: "O Ysé, don't let me come back!"
At this point Mesa sees himself as "a starving man," longing after
Ysé. A beautiful exchange takes place between the two, after which
Ysé reveals herself to Mesa:

> O mon Mesa, tu n'es plus un homme seulement, mais
> tu es à moi qui suis une femme,
>   Et je suis un homme en toi, et tu es une femme avec
> moi, et je cueille ton coeur sans que tu saches comment.
>   Et je l'ai pris, et je l'arrange avec moi pour toujours
> entre mes deux seins!
>
> > > > > > > > > > > > (*PM*, 1027)[10]

Mesa's love is now directed towards Ysé's as symbol of archetypal beauty, of light: "You are radiant and splendid! You are beautiful / as the young Apollo!" But the beautiful Ysé, who is "clear as the rising sun," as "straight as a column," is the mystery of contraries by which she makes Mesa participate in divine love by consenting to become his bride.

> O ineffable iniquité! Ah viens donc et mange-moi comme une mangue! Tout, tout, et moi!
> Il est donc vrai, Mesa, que j'existe seule et voilà le monde répudié, et à quoi est-ce que notre amour sert aux autres?...
> Et tout l'univers autour de nous
> Vidé de nous comme une chose incapable de comprendre et qui demande la raison!
>
> (*PM*, 1029–30)[11]

What we have here is love on its way to consummation, on its way to being buried with the form of love; Ysé alone is the means of both Mesa's anguish and salvation. "Behind your eyes which gaze at me the great dark flame of the soul which burns everywhere, like a razed city" (*PM*, 1030–31).

Thus, for Mesa and Ysé transfiguration is a change from a sterile, fleshly, and dark existence, which the cemetery makes concrete, into the form of grace that can only be seen through sacrifice, the cross. But what is beautifully revealed here is the form of grace under the image of sin or fault: "My crime is great." Mesa takes possession of Ysé; that is, he glorifies sensual love itself. To the eyes of Mesa, however, it is precisely this "black flame of the soul" that is transformed into a clear and luminous form of love: in the cemetery, Mesa sees the incarnation of God's splendor in the world; through Ysé's transformation into "a peacock in Paradise," "a dawn," and "a sensing flower," Mesa catches a glimpse of the spiritual senses, of the divine eros. The beauty of Ysé's body reveals a heavenly love; by giving her body to him in the flame of sensual love, Ysé changes Mesa's dark and empty existence into a luminous form. Ysé tells Mesa that suffering has now become a source of joy, and concludes: "No, this is not a marriage / That unites everything to everything else, but a break and the / mortal vow, and the preference for you alone!" (*PM*, 1031). Against the background of the *omega*-shaped cemetery, the "clothes of the flesh" are torn off, and earthly love is elevated into the sphere of the eternal. The cemetery, as the unifying point between Mesa and Ysé, is the ultimate image in which suffering, repentance, and redemption meet; it is the center where the water and sun of act 1 coincide with the hunger and thirst for love in act 2; it is the image of grace revealed through the anguish, the night, of the senses. Everything about Mesa's and Ysé's love must now be seen as the love of God: in the cemetery they see God's light over the world of darkness, they see God's flesh permeating the phenomenal world.

> Il n'y ait plus rien d'autre que toi et moi, et en toi que
> moi, et en moi que ta possession, et la rage, et la tendresse,
> et de te détruire et de n'être plus gênée
> Détestablement par ces vêtements de chair, et ces
> cruelles dents dans mon coeur,
> Non point cruelles!
> Ah, ce n'est point le bonheur que je t'apporte, mais ta
> mort, et la mienne avec elle,
> Mais qu'est-ce que cela me fait à moi que je te fasse
> mourir,
> Et moi, et tout, et tant pis! pourvu qu'à ce prix qui est
> toi et moi,
> Donnés, jetés, arrachés, lacérés, consumés,
> Je sente ton âme, un moment qui est toute l'éternité,
> toucher,
> Prendre
> La mienne comme la chaux astreint le sable brûlant
> et en sifflant!
>
> (*PM*, 1030)[12]

The one life, the one soul that Mesa and Ysé enjoy, comes to share in the natural indissolubility of the love between the dying Christ and the Father as revealed in the Eucharist, which bridges them to God. In the Eucharist, Christ offers himself to the world as the gift of the Father, and he establishes the life of grace upon the eating and drinking of his body.

> Et
> Puisque tu es libre maintenant,
> Et qu'en nous près d'être détruits la puissance
> indestructible
> De tous les sacraments en un seul grand par le mystère
> d'un consentement réciproque
> Demeure encore, je consens à toi, Ysé! Voyez, mon
> Dieu, car ceci est mon corps!
> Je consens à toi! et dans cette seule parole
> Tient l'aveu et dans l'embrassement de la pénitence
> La Loi, et dans une confirmation suprême
> L'établissement pour toujours de notre Ordre.
>
> (*PM*, 1059–60)[13]

The beatitude of this "reciprocal consent" is to be born with the world as it is; to sense it and to know it in the reality of the dying Christ, for in his death earthly love clothes itself with the garments of God's charity. Mesa's and Ysé's sacramental death lies in their obedience to God's law, the Incarnate Word. As Mesa and Ysé make divine claims for themselves, they must adapt themselves to the sacred measure of God's extreme suffering. This adaptation can be achieved in no other way than by the sacrament of penance. In penance, Mesa and Ysé experience a conversion, a turn in the direction of God as it comes to them in the mystery of a reciprocal act between the Father and the Son in the Holy Spirit. In penance Mesa and Ysé confess their sins and thus forgive each other, ready to enjoy their sacred union.

If nothingness or sin is equivalent to death and transformation, it is because Christ signifies this ultimate act of sacrifice for which Mesa and Ysé prepare each other. As act 2 opens, Ysé enters the room "dressed in white in a state of hypnotic trance." She moves across the room "like a cloud," passing before the mirror. She arrives at the room where the dead infant is. She becomes "all white with her long thick hair flooded by the moon on the veranda." Mesa places his hand on her head as she sits at his feet, and confesses her sins. Thus their love is transformed. In her canticle, Ysé says to Mesa:

> O Mesa, voici le partage de minuit! et me voici, prête
> à être libérée,
> Le signe pour la dernière fois de ces grands cheveux
> déchaînés dans le vent de la Mort!
>
> (*PM*, 1063)[14]

Withdrawn from time, day is night, sunrise is sunset, darkness is light, movement is permanency, visible is invisible, death is birth; all of creation is beautiful in God's light. Death to the self is the life of the night; that is to say, detachment of will and thought is a birth into the light of grace that inverts everything; everything turns from what-it-is-not, from all darkness, all nothingness, all flesh, into the image and likeness of God's splendor, his grace. This is what Mesa says at the end of the play:

> Et le mien, ce n'est pas de vains cheveux dans la
> tempête, et le petit mouchoir un moment,
> Mais, tous voiles dissipés, moi-même, la forte flamme
> fulminante, le grand mâle dans la gloire de Dieu,
> L'homme dans la splendeur de l'août, L'Esprit vain-
> queur dans la transfiguration de Midi!
>
> (*PM*, 1063–64)[15]

Truly transfigured, Mesa and Ysé become lovers of the night hours:
"There is the sun setting"; "Here is the tide of the night rising." The
light that filters into the dark room comes from heaven, transforming it into a majestic cathedral, the house of God. They have suffered
enough; they have been tortured by pride, jealousy, and lust, and now
they have reached that divine dwelling place where no light shines forth
other than that which emanates from the sacrificed Lamb who washes
away their sins with his blood. Freed from earthly love, Mesa and Ysé
enter within themselves; they close the doors of the physical senses
and open those of the spiritual senses by which they taste supreme
delight. Mesa and Ysé are no longer exiled souls, they are no longer
impassible to each other primarily because now their love is submerg-
ed into the baptismal water of Christ's Body and Blood. "As for me,"
says Ysé, "I hunger and thirst after death." Despoiled of earthly
"clothing," Mesa and Ysé are transformed into the image of light,
into the glory of God's form in the mystery of the humiliated Son.
Thus, says Ysé:

> Grand Dieu! me voici, riante, roulante, déracinée,
> le dos sur la subsistance même de la lumière comme
> sur l'aile par dessous de la vague!
>
> (*PM*, 1063)[16]

Mesa and Ysé have now discovered freedom within the light, and
their life can only be understood in terms of this "mystery of a
reciprocal consent," a mystery that is no longer accessible by the
fruits of natural love but by the mystery of the Incarnation, Death,
and Resurrection of Christ, which transfigures and beatifies their
whole being and in itself guarantees that grace will shine forth from
them as the most radiant of beauties.

> C'est toi maintenant qui m'instruis, et
> j'écoute.
> Combien de temps maintenant, ô femme, dis-moi,
> fruit de la vigne, avant que je ne te boive de nouveau
> dans le Royaume de Dieu?
>
> (*PM*, 1061)[17]

Sartre: The Nothingness of the Image

Like Claudel, Sartre emphasizes nothingness and transformation
or transcendent freedom as aspects of his aesthetic theory. Unlike
Claudel, whose image of beauty reveals itself in the world, Sartre's

image is lost in the nothingness, the viscosity, the thickness, the chaos of the world. Thus the theme of nausea: on the one hand Sartre sees estrangement, absurdity, as the fundamental structure of the human condition; on the other hand he believes in the commitment of pure art.

Sartre's novel, *La nausée*, develops this thesis by showing that Roquentin is unhappy with the various images of the world. From the outset, Roquentin is aware of the nausea which surrounds him. But it is the very inconsistency, the very thickness, the very viscosity, the very weight, the very emptiness of images that he finally comes to see as constituting the essence of life. Existence hides from him; it is he, it is in him, but he can never touch it. When he looks at things, they are far from being real, they are only an appearance, "monstrous masses, all in disorder — naked, in a frightful, obscene nakedness" (*N*, 180).

Roquentin would prefer things to exist more abstractly, with more reserve, more meaning, less monstrous, less naked, and less intolerable. But existence is absurd; Roquentin realizes that a separation exists between him and the world.

> Absurde: par rapport aux cailloux, aux touffes d'herbe jaune, à la boue sèche, à l'arbre, au ciel, aux bancs verts. Absurde, irréductible; rien — pas même un délire profond et secret de la nature — ne pouvait l'expliquer....Le monde des explications et des raisons n'est pas celui de l'existence. (*N*, 182–83)[18]

The world, reality, the situation, is beyond all explanation. That which exists comes from nowhere and goes nowhere. Things exist, then suddenly pass out of existence; existence is without a form, without a measure. The essential quality of existence is contingency; that is, existence is simply being-in-the-world, a world that cannot be grasped because it is being maintained not by internal stability, not by the mutual adaptation of matter and form, not by the correspondence between outer and inner world, but by its "disorder and obscene nudity." And thus Roquentin states: "To exist is simply *to be there*; those who exist let themselves be *encountered*, but you can never *deduce* anything from them" (*N*, 185). Contingency, however, is not a necessity that can go away; it is the absolute. Roquentin is committed to the justification of his existence. He must choose between living a life of nausea or transforming it into a work of art, into a creation of "pure imagination." His life has no past, no present, no future, no memories, no privileged moments. Change constitutes the matter of the real, the absurd its essence.

Quand on vit, il n'arrive rien. Les décors changent, les gens entrent et sor-
tent, voilà tout. Il n'y a jamais de commencements. Les jours s'ajoutent
aux jours sans rime ni raison, c'est une addition interminable et
monotone. (*N*, 61)[19]

This world without beginnings, in which everything changes, in
which everything is viscous, in which there is nothing or everything,
is nausea. In the midst of this world, Roquentin had once seen Anny's life as the way by which he could transform his own life. Unlike
Roquentin, Anny had tried to be; she seemed to remain stable, unchanging, and purposeful; she tried to live out her life in a world of
privileged moments. She told him:

Dans chacune des situations privilégiées, il y a certains actes qu'il faut
faire, des attitudes qu'il faut prendre, des paroles qu'il faut dire—et
d'autres attitudes, d'autres paroles sont strictement défendues. (*N*, 208)[20]

The drama, the world of art, Michelet's *History*, had given Anny the
illusion that her life could be one of privileged moments; by
submerging herself in an imaginary world she was able to lose
herself-in-the-world to the point that she could see her life as a succession of privileged moments, as a work of art.

But Roquentin discovers that Anny, too, has arrived at the same
conclusion about existence as he; namely, there are no privileged
moments. She tells him:

Je sens qu'il n'y a pas de moments parfaits.... Je le sens tout le temps,
même quand je dors. Je ne peux l'oublier.... Mais à présent, je suis toujours un peu comme si cela m'avait été brusquement révélé la veille. (*N*,
202)[21]

Even Anny has experienced a changing world, and she too has
changed; her creative life, which at one time had given her the illusion of order, arrangement, meaning, and permanency, now has
been swallowed up by the thick stickiness of existence. Anny tells Roquentin that she has abandoned the theater in the hope of experiencing ecstatic vision by recalling privileged moments from the past.

Anny has abandoned the theater because she wishes to commit
herself to pure art, the art of pure images or thought, whose being
is outside existence. Although filled with nausea, Roquentin still
longs for the perfect moment, for a world beyond the real, for a
world of the permanent, of the absolute, a world of pure essence.
Roquentin himself has the need for an ideal mode of existence, for

a desire to escape his situation, to pierce through the veil of nothingness that surrounds his existence and to reach the level of Being itself. He has rejected works of art, music in particular, because people "imagine that the sounds flow into them, sweet, nourishing, and that their sufferings become music.... They think that beauty is compassionate to them" (*N*, 243). It is only out of politeness that he accepts Madeleine's effort to play for him his favorite tune before he leaves the city. As soon as the music begins, he realizes that the consoling quality of the music results from the knowledge that it is beyond this world; the melody does not exist.

Elle est au-delà—toujours au-delà de quelque chose, d'une voix, d'une note de violon. A travers des épaisseurs et des épaisseurs d'existence, elle se dévoile, mince et ferme et, quand on veut la saisir, on ne rencontre que des existants, on bute sur des existants dépourvus de sens. Elle est derrière eux: je ne l'entends même pas, j'entends des sons, des vibrations de l'air qui la dévoilent. Elle n'existe pas, puisqu'elle n'a rien de trop: c'est tout le reste qui est trop par rapport à elle. Elle *est*. (*N*, 244)[22]

The music is of another world, of another time; Roquentin, too, like the melody, would simply like to be. He would like to be not through his adventures, not through Anny's first privileged moments, but through his act of creation, the realm of pure imagination, the world of the artist as creator of his existence. He suggests that literary art, the only thing he can do, might become for him the source of his being. The literary art Roquentin speaks of is the kind of art that exists behind the printed words, behind the pages and beyond existence: "A story, for example... an adventure. It would have to be beautiful and hard as steel and make people ashamed of their existence" (*N*, 248–49). Unlike history, art, whether it is literature or music, makes the aesthetic object both present and absent simultaneously: present in that art is in itself, "on the other side of existence"; absent in that art is out of reach, "without ever approaching it" (*N*, 245).

Freed from "the world of explanations" and reason or causality but enjoying a reality of its own, art, especially the melody, constitutes for Roquentin a "perfect moment." Part of this privileged experience is due to the fact that Roquentin is himself captive of an absurd world yet still searching to become. Fascinated by the works of art, from sculpture to literature, and desiring to live in the world of Tintoretto, Gozzoli, "behind the phonograph records, with the long dry laments of jazz" (*N*, 245), Roquentin disengages himself from the phenomenal world by withdrawing into an imaginary self, the object of unreal adventures that take place in time and space. This imaginary withdrawal takes him to the experience of death, which, like music, helps him to conceive what the world would be like if deprived of its phenomenal structure. Of the melody, Roquentin says:

> Et il y a quelque chose qui serre le coeur: c'est que la mélodie n'est absolument pas touchée par ce petit toussotement de l'aiguille sur le disque. Elle est si loin—si loin derrière....Mais derrière l'existant qui tombe d'un présent à l'autre, sans passé, sans avenir, derrière ces sons qui, de jour en jour, se décomposent, s'écaillent et glissent vers la mort, la mélodie reste la même, jeune et ferme, comme un témoin sans pitié. (*N*, 245–46)[23]

As an imaginary object, the melody is "distant," so that Roquentin still feels a certain indefinable quality, a certain "sense" that integrates the various sounds and elicits from him an affective response similar to what he would feel if he were in the presence of the composer himself. "I try to think of him *through* the melody, through the white, acidulated sounds of the saxophone. He made it" (*N*, 247). The melody makes Roquentin imagine the anguish and the financial burden of the composer, thereby eradicating from the melody all traces of delight; the only thing he feels is an intensification of the viscosity of existence. The creative impulse that exists in Roquentin delineates very clearly the distance existing between the joy of the composer, on the one hand, and the human condition, on the other. At the same time, through works of art, Roquentin comes to reflect on that first moment when, on the seashore, while holding the pebble, he conceived of existence as nausea, as empty, as absurd, as nothing. "Now I knew: things are entirely what they appear to be—and *behind them*...there is nothing" (*N*, 137–38). The writing of the book by which he would try to forget his existence would become the perfect moment through which his existence would take on meaning. At the same time, the book would rob him of all joy in the phenomenal world.

> Mais il viendrait bien un moment où le livre serait écrit, serait derrière moi et je pense qu'un peu de clarté tomberait sur mon passé. Alors peut-être que je pourrais, à travers lui, me rappeler ma vie sans répugnance. (*N*, 249)[24]

Roquentin is impelled to use his book, or works of art in general, to define his existence. Standing before official portraits in the museum of Bouville, Roquentin realizes that he, unlike the portraits, has no right to exist: "I had appeared by chance, I existed like a stone, a plant, a microbe. My life put out feelers towards small pleasures in every direction" (*N*, 122). In those portraits, Roquentin finds a peace that he himself does not have, a right to be that he himself is seeking, and a hardness that his existence lacks. "These men," he says, "had slipped quietly into death, to claim their share of eternal life to which they had a right" (*N*, 120). Unlike him, those portraits had the right to everything: to existence, to eternity. As his contemplation deepens, Roquentin says this of himself: "Was I not a simple spectre?" (*N*, 125). He would like to transform the world of nausea, of absurdity, of viscosity, into necessity; he would like to be a stone, a statue, immobile, hard, with no sound and no suffering. If he were able to bring this about he might finally achieve the aesthetic moment, the "perfect moment," in which the phenomena of the world would indeed be annihilated and he himself would lose his being-in-the-world and would become aesthetically, that is, imaginatively, conscious.

Mais je ne *vois* plus rien: j'ai beau fouiller le passé je n'en retire plus que des bribes d'images et je ne sais pas très bien ce qu'elles représentent, ni si ce sont des souvenirs ou des fictions.... Ils font naître en moi des images toutes neuves, comme en forment, d'après leurs lectures, les gens qui n'ont jamais voyagé: je rêve sur des mots, voilà tout. (*N*, 52)[25]

Roquentin's images, whether they are those which he personally has experienced or of a purely fictitious character, represent his dream or creative consciousness. Although he does not know what these images represent, they signify the presence of the real itself, whether it is manifested in the stones, the chestnut roots, the statues, the jazz melody, or simply the quality of nausea. While it negates the phenomenal world, dream consciousness makes it possible to totalize this world, to fill it with meaning. As an example, at one pole stands the record, which, as a collection of sounds, has meaning only insofar as it produces mental images, and at the other are the material elements of the record, which are real. As Roquentin searches for a justification of his existence, external images cease to function as analogues; consequently, he is unable to distinguish what is real from what is imaginary or unreal. But mental images or dreams incarnate not only the real, they also represent another world, the world of art, the realm of aesthetic images. Aesthetic images make present a reality that eludes both perceptual and mental awareness: "But I don't see anything any more." When Roquentin finds himself before works of art, he simultaneously feels and knows them, while he is conscious that they remain "behind" his power to imagine. Thus the imaginary act or dream constitutes the real in the mode of not-being-

in-the-world. To disengage himself reflectively, whether from the
dream or adventures or the real world itself, is to annihilate the situation out of which images appear. In fact, for Roquentin, to posit the
world as world and to annihilate it are one and the same thing.

> Quelque chose commence pour finir: l'aventure ne se laisse pas mettre de
> rallonge; elle n'a de sens que par sa mort. Vers cette mort, qui sera peut-
> être aussi la mienne. Je suis entraîne sans retour. Chaque instant ne paraît
> que pour amener ceux qui suivent. A chaque instant je tiens de tout mon
> coeur: je sais qu'il est unique; irremplaçable—et pourtant je ne ferais pas
> un geste pour l'empêcher de s'anéantir. Cette dernière minute que je
> passe...va prendre fin, je le sais. (*N*, 59)[26]

The nonidentity of consciousness (*savoir*) with the world it constitutes is the very expression of transcendent freedom, the ability of
consciousness to annihilate the real and to surpass it. "Existence,
liberated, detached, floods over me. I exist" (*N*, 141).
   The dream, the imaginary, the creative act, is the realm of
possibility. Because "consciousness" is both world-surpassing and
world-constituting, the imaginary is that toward which "consciousness" moves beyond the real: "Each instant appears only as
part of a sequence." As a form of imaging, the aesthetic act is itself
revelatory of this meaning. It, too, makes visible the realm of
possibility, of negation, of freedom with which "consciousness"
envelopes the real, which "begins for ending" or annihilates itself.
This is what consumes Roquentin. Although his freedom becomes
the essence of life, he finds it a dreadful burden.

> Je suis libre: il ne me reste plus aucune raison de vivre, toutes celles que
> j'ai essayées ont lâché et je ne peux plus en imaginer d'autres....Mon
> passé est mort. M. de Rollebon est mort, Anny n'est revenue que pour
> m'ôter tout espoir....Seul et libre. Mais cette liberté ressemble un peu à
> la mort. (*N*, 219–20)[27]

Freedom thus becomes synonymous with beauty; it is never realized except as dream, as "consciousness," as imaginary, as unreal.
Beauty, like existence, is a creature of change, of appearance, of the
world of annihilation; Roquentin, then, must commit himself to
pure art for the absurdity of human existence.

> Seulement, quand je repense à tous ces petits actes soigneux, je ne com-
> prends pas comment j'ai pu les faire: ils sont si vains. Ce sont les
> habitudes, sans doute, qui les ont faits pour moi. Elles ne sont pas
> mortes, elles, elles continuent à s'affairer, à tisser tout doucement, in-
> sidieusement leurs trames, elles me lavent, m'essuient, m'habillent, com-

me des nourrices. . . . Au loin. Au-dessus de ma tête; et cet instant-ci, dont je ne puis sortir, qui m'enferme et me borne de tout côté, cet instant dont je suis fait ne sera plus qu'un songe brouillé. (*N*, 221)[28]

If Roquentin's fundamental desire is to justify existence, to create his freedom, then he must travel the road of the imaginary. But the price is high, if not unbearable; not only is he completely alone, but the aesthetic object remains absurd, a creation of nothing, which gave it birth. His choices form a web around him: "They wash me, dry me, dress me, as nurses," and he is forever prevented from perceiving the beautiful. Reality is for him "a burning dream." Yet Roquentin, though aesthetically incomplete, is paradoxically powerful as a symbol for the commitment of pure art. Roquentin, like all of us, desires "perfect moments"; and when he creates them, whether by his past or his imagination, there is nothing in them: "They are so vain." In this sense, the aesthetic act does change reality by imposing upon it a unity, a meaning not found within existence. But this transforming act, this transcendent freedom, is nothing but a recreation of the human person's absurd situation, "an interminable and monotonous addition" to the already "obscene nudity" of life.

Conclusion: From Beauty to its Nothingness

Unlike Claudel, who defines beauty as that which pleases the senses or gives delight in the act of knowing, Sartre locates the beautiful in the creative act, in the imagination, "consciousness," in dreams, in the past: "The real is never beautiful." While both Claudel and Sartre use nothingness and transformation as two aspects of the creative act, Sartre's image of the beautiful is perceived as nonbeing, as unreal, as negation of the phenomenal image. For Claudel, on the other hand, the human person's awareness of phenomenal beauty depends on the splendor, the radiancy, the light, the form of God's mystery that emanates from things, causing the senses to feel divine sensations in the world. For Claudel, the image is the "secret ontology" of things; it determines their movement, their intentionality, their proportionality, their unity; it is that by and through which things are (exist) and act. Thus the world is beautiful because it unites the various images around God's hidden form — the center, the light, the grace — that reveals to human beings their nothingness, their darkness, since God is Existence, Being, Beauty itself.

For Sartre, however, the world is not beautiful in itself, and becomes so only as and when it is "a burning dream." Beauty is not seeing the real, it is not living it at all; it is the consciousness to transform an absurd and viscous existence into a *savoir*, a work of art, through a knowledge of nothing proper only to the imaging act, the act of commitment. The human person sees this annihilation of the phenomenal image by affirming something beyond the real, something that is itself a nothingness. This is the special domain of pure art. Art as dream, transforming, imaging, engaging, reveals that the human person is transcendentally free.

In this way, while Claudel uses imagination to penetrate to the abyss, the nothingness, the darkness, of the phenomenal world in the hidden form of God's grace, Sartre, on the other hand, uses imagination to transcend the world of nausea in order to reach the pure in-itself, art.

5

Claudel and Gide: Beauty and Grace in Baroque Art

Une peinture de Viel, de Vermeer, de Pieter de Hooch, nous ne la regardons pas, nous ne la caressons pas une minute, d'un clignement d'yeux supérieur: immédiatement nous sommes dedans, nous l'habitons. Nous sommes pris. Nous sommes contenus par elle. (*OE*, 20)[1]

Nicolas Poussin était et reste le plus conscient des peintres, et c'est aussi par là qu'il se montre le plus français....La pensée préside à la naissance de chacun de ses tableaux. (*P*, 5)[2]

Both Claudel and Gide find in baroque art, in its representation of nature, the senses, the soul, and a new perception of the infinite and the divine, a uniquely seminal expression of the beauty and the grace that can be revealed through the forms of the material world. Both see in baroque art a movement toward "a sensuality less flagrant" (Gide), a naturalism in which "the spirit makes the flest hear the call of consummate bliss" (Claudel). Baroque art presents them with a "dazzling revelation" (Claudel) capable of capturing them, of placing them in a state of prolonged contemplation. "We are immediately inside of it; we live in it; we are possessed by it" (Claudel); and, in the words of Gide, "Am I drawing Poussin towards me? — Not really; it is Poussin who attracts me to him" (*P*, 12). Baroque art thus is capable of elevating us to the beauty and grace of a spiritual world, whether considered in the mythological tradition of antiquity or the mystery of a triune God, or the aesthetic divine capabilities of human beings. Indeed, it is to this mystery made visible through the proper distribution of light and darkness, of the movement of the lines, of the choice of colors, and of the sensuality of figures that Claudel and Gide respond, each in his own way. Baroque art attains to the mystery, the ineffable, the profound light of grace itself, transporting one in what is an ascension to the spiritual world, where the soul simultaneously experiences sensual, rational, and ecstatic joy.

> La joie que nous apporte la contemplation de certaines toiles de Poussin n'est point seulement un ravissement de nos sens; elle est profonde, durable, et la sorte de sérénité que j'en retire m'ennoblit. (*P*, 9)[3]

Of baroque art, Claudel and Gide tell us: "Everything here is spiritualized" (Claudel); "Poussin is not a realist painter; we find none more spiritualist or idealist than he" (Gide). Yet, they both find in baroque art a "sumptuous symphony" (Gide) of passions. In the words of Claudel:

> Tout est éternel à la fois et tout coule. Tout coule, mais c'est dans notre gosier. Tout a été donné à l'homme pour s'en remplir à la mesure de sa capacité et tout autour se relève et s'approfondit comme vers un centre. (*OE*, 67–68)[4]

In the same way, Poussin's art conveys to Gide the depth, the serenity, the splendor of pagan spirituality, of sensual mysticism, which is vivifying to the soul. Thus, the spiritual world is made visible in baroque art through material forms, and material forms in turn become the visible light of divine delight.

Despite their concurrence, there is an unbridgeable gap between Claudel and Gide with respect to baroque art. Whereas the objective form of beauty and grace exists within the phenomenal world of a Claudel, it does not exist for Gide. While it is true that "the drama" that baroque art makes visible is sacred in the eyes of Gide, the sacredness is located in the subjective form, in the oeuvre of the artist and the figures that animate the paintings. Of Poussin, Gide writes: "No disquiet in him...no secret torment, no appeal to redemption, no recourse to the supernatural, to grace" (*P*, 10). In spite of the subjective evidence of beauty and grace, there still remains for Claudel a supernatural, a world of revelation, an ontological secret to Flemish art that finds itself confronting the world of "mythology and revelation." Unlike Gide, Claudel sees in baroque art a divine perspective that becomes incarnated within time and, "by the sharpening of desire, unites the immediate with the eventual, the present with the future, and reality with the dream" (*OE*, 140).

For Claudel, baroque art does not ignore reality; rather, it unveils it by "the sharpening of desire" and God's light. For Gide, on the other hand, baroque art is the perfect glorification, the most exquisite manifestation of natural beauty ordered by the "thought" of the artist himself. "Thought presides at the birth of each of his

[Poussin's] paintings" (*P*, 5). This way, Poussin's world is one of form, not of Old and New Testament figures or of mythologies, but a "persuasive delight," a "sensual delight," an aesthetic form of beauty and grace with no necessary correspondence between symbol and reality, between the grace of mythical beauty and the grace of revealed beauty. The only grace is the grace revealed by works of art.

Claudel: Form and Reality

While at the end of *L'art poétique* Claudel focuses on the development of the Church from its early times to twentieth-century architectural forms through Gothic, Renaissance, and baroque forms, in *L'oeil écoute*, he traces the "road" of the self in Flemish art where "everything is a matter of balance, of long meditated movement that is finally realized" (*OE*, 134). According to Claudel, Flemish art places before us this path by which we are called to dialogue with everything that is nature and from which we cannot turn, since art is not at variance with the phenomenal world but mirrors it; art is in harmony with material reality, which itself is in motion. Everything is in motion, and the self is both here and not here; the human person is a seeker. The sky, a continent, a country, a river, an ocean, a mountain, a flower, an animal, and the self itself do not form for Claudel a "changeless and motionless sheet" (*OE*, 133). Instead they realize themselves in accordance with their particular form; they live out their time of existence. However movable the phenomenal world, its forms can enter our consciousness propelling us "toward an end or in a certain direction, step by step" (*OE*, 133). Since this movement, this road, toward a reunion with the form, the light, is accessible to us step by step and not all at once, art, as the visible expression of nature's way, is only a symbol of our "relation through a distance," which we call present existence. Therefore, in the words of Claudel, art serves not only to make legible the images of past moments as relationships of various distances, but it also spreads before our eyes and memory a permanent, stable image that holds together the various other images.

L'image au fond de notre souvenir imprimée a acquis une valeur inaltérable. Le reflet a imprégné le miroir et de plusieurs choses ensemble à jamais a fait une plaque lisible. (*OE*, 136)[5]

Through the eyes material forms make direct contact with the intellect and the memory and come to acquire a center for themselves from which they can never be erased. They become for us "the allegorical sign of our intellectual shop" and interpreters of our movement; they make us stop, see, and touch "our ontological secret" (*OE*, 136).

This ontological secret is what Flemish art makes visible. It invites us to explore the most intimate and profound recess of our being from which we can then proceed to unsuspected worlds and admire the beauty and harmony of the phenomenal world. Of Flemish landscape, Claudel writes:

> Cela, c'est ce que j'appellerai les chemins d'exploitation, tous ces méandres d'un édifice, d'une ville, d'un jardin, tous ces détours qui n'aboutissent qu'à se rejoindre comme des lignes mélodiques, et qui ne font qu'assurer notre communication avec nous-même; les axes de notre possession et de notre habitude. (*OE*, 137)[6]

But more than this harmonious and melodious experience of the beautiful in the natural world, there is the "road" that is higher and above nature's way; it is a movement where nothing moves and a flow with no beginning and no end: "The very name that his God was pleased to assume is the Way, and he is crucified like a guidepost at the four points of the compass" (*OE*, 134). Thus, the beautiful reality represented in Flemish paintings calls to our attention another reality, another road, another distance, of a completely different type: that of the unknown, the hidden, the eternal, and the spiritual. "I preferred the unknown and the virginal, which is no other than the eternal" (*OE*, 139).

Flemish artists do not portray phenomenal reality per se; rather, they arrange and rearrange the visible world in order that their paintings manifest that "ontological secret." Visions of the eternal world are made accessible in realistic details, natural objects, and subtle, ever-changing white and black effects, which are not the "alternate negation of light and shadow" (*OE*, 30), but their manifestation, light revealing darkness and darkness revealing light. Flemish artists describe the human person's ontological way in terms of defined human activities (sitting around a table, washing feet, standing around a sick person, etc.) and not in an abstract or stylized manner. With Flemish paintings, "the reality and the reflection" interpenetrate and communicate with each other by means of the finest threads, and art does not so much transform nature as much as absorb it by "a secret impregnation" (*OE*, 33). Flemish artists penetrate the visible reality with the sounds of silence so that the phenomenal world transcends itself, realizes itself in a coherent and proportionate whole. Moreover, Flemish artists sharpen the movement of time by freezing it on the landscapes of nature; or, to put

it differently, all reality crystallizes itself around the glittering serenity of a remembrance of things past, the timelessness of space, the
abyss of being, the transparency of the visible universe, the stillness
of motion, the light of darkness, and the superb harmony of sensation, perception, and knowledge.

> L'art du grand Hollandais [Rembrandt] n'est plus une affirmation
> copieuse de l'immédiat, une irruption de l'imagination dans le domaine
> de l'actualité, une fête donnée à nos sens, la perpétuation d'un moment
> de joie et de couleur. Ce n'est plus du présent à regarder, c'est une invita-
> tion à se souvenir. (*OE*, 41)[7]

According to Claudel, nothing in Flemish art seems to disturb the
delicate balance between people and nature, feeling and perception,
perception and thought. Here sensation informs the memory, which
in turn sets the imagination in motion to gather around itself other
images in a coherent system of thoughts and ideas, which saturate
reality with meaning and intentionality. This exquisite harmony of
the symbolic and the real, of the invisible and the visible, of the past
and the present, of the imagination and thought, is realized because
no single element of Flemish art is overly emphasized: neither the
senses, nor the colors, nor the imagination. In fact, all seems
tempered with reason, so that the symbolic realism of nature is con-
vincingly portrayed; the viewer's imagination soars without breaking
its tie with reality. The thrust of Flemish art is toward a present
moment that is constantly vanishing. At the same time it captures,
it preserves, the permanent forms of things. Motion and mo-
tionlessness become for Flemish artists the double eye of their
memory by which they translate sight into insight, attention into contemplation, and contemplation into humanity's ascent to God.

> Ce chemin qui a servi autrefois à entraîner l'Enfant Prodigue et à le
> dissiper du côté de l'horizon, le Philosophe de Rembrandt l'a replié en
> lui-même, il en a fait cet escalier cochléaire, cette vis qui lui sert à descen-
> dre pas à pas jusqu'au fond de la méditation. Je te prendrai par la main,
> dit la Fiancée du Cantique, et je t'introduirai jusqu'au fond de cette cave
> où mûrit le vin. Cette cave dont la vieille femme de Nicolas Maes dans
> le tableau de Bruxelles a la clef. Elle pend au-dessus d'elle à côté du buste
> de Pallas, cependant que de la main, les yeux fermés, elle continue à lire
> ce livre sur ses genoux où, du haut de ce rayon derrière elle, semblent se
> déverser d'autres livres, chargés d'une composition invisible. (*OE*,
> 136–37)[8]

Thus, Flemish art shows this descent of human existence to its
darkest point in order that it may rise to the height of contemplation.

This is quite evident in the paintings of Frans Hals. In his art, Hals realistically portrays "the advancement of human existence towards its end." He exposes the human condition from inside out, from an alternation of black and white that reconciles itself in the subtle facial expressions and the emphatic gestures of the hands of the figures portrayed. With a stroke of his brush, Hals makes chiaroscuro the visible expression of the human person's inner nature, unequaled, in Claudel's opinion, in value and intensity by either Goya or El Greco. Nowhere is this inner side of the human person made so visibly real than in his use of light and darkness in the paintings of *Les Régents* and *Les Régentes* where the five women impose upon the painting a meaning, a regulated movement: that all existence moves to death, to nothing. With her lips closed, the central figure draws attention to the fact that "here we have to do with something more pitiless than justice, and that is annihilation" (*OE*, 31). Without doubt, the deep silence, the gloomy atmosphere, the frightful smile of the central figure, the permanent vibration from one women to the other produce a tenebrous mood, full of mysterious effects that invite contemplation on the meaning of existence, of justice. The powerful "annihilation" of the background is brought to light by the brilliant white that the women wear around their necks, thus creating both visual effect and ontological meaning.

The drama of human existence is also the subject of the painting of the six male regents. The focus of this composition is movement. From the lower figure to the left, the eye of the spectator is led step by step to the right toward the illuminated and shadowed face of the upper figure over which loom two immovable masks. One is the mask of a drunken person who seems to have been separated from the rank of evil-doers and who finds himself immersed in darkness; the other, on whom all the light is concentrated, is the mask of one who no more belongs to the living than the black stovepipe hat planted on his forehead belongs to his head, or the garish red knee belongs to his body. Claudel believes that Hals could not have revealed more of the advancement of the human condition toward its conclusion than he did in these two paintings, which open up human nature to its innermost depths. Light and shadow are powerfully contrasted in different degrees to give the compositions maximum movement, with rhythmic vibrations deeply set into space, yet proportionately united with the arrangement and emotional expressions of the figures.

According to Claudel, the "ontological secret," the movement "of human life toward its conclusion," is present in the paintings of Gerard Dou, Mieris, Gerard ter Borch, Pieter de Hooch, Van

Ostade, Maes, and Helst. It achieves its clearest expression in the art of Vermeer, however. Better than any other Flemish artist, Claudel goes on to say, Vermeer's brush captures the serenity and the transparency of this visible world with the precision of a geometer's eyes.

> Ce qui me fascine, c'est ce regard pur, dépouillé, stérilisé, rincé de toute matière, d'une candeur en quelque sorte mathématique ou angélique, ou disons simplement photographique, mais quelle photographie! en qui ce peintre, reclus à l'intérieur de sa lentille, capte le monde extérieur. (*OE*, 24)[9]

Vermeer's angelic purity penetrates reality's most profound sense; that is, the relationship between the phenomenal world and its intentionality. Vermeer's art is for Claudel the knowledge of a rational or photographic mind: by this "pure look," the outer world is transported within the realm of necessity. His art, continues Claudel, measures space accurately, and the position of each object is brought into a unified whole. Every object thus becomes properly related to the whole, both in intensity and meaning. His art does not separate senses from thought, imagination from forms, and, consequently, it leads observers toward the contemplation of the invisible instead of locking them within the darkness of the phenomenal world or within the various geometric figures represented. Claudel delights in Vermeer's art because he finds there this "geometric concert," this symbol of the closed circuit of the world, made especially visible in the *Vue de Delft*, *La Ruelle*, and *L'Allégorie evangélique*. Besides being a master of this geometric art, Vermeer is also a master in the art of "surrounding a point by a curve" (*OE*, 25). This technique allows Vermeer to represent distances and objects realistically in an unbroken movement leading to the invisible center, the infinite point, the center of the universe, which is a kind of "spiritual coordination, a flash of lightning discharged from the soul" (*OE*, 25).

Vermeer's art represents this spiritual coordinate, which unveils the whole of Being. In *L'Allégorie evangélique*, Claudel again finds an example of art's ability to coordinate concrete existence to ontological secret. Here, Vermeer represents faith with a seated woman who reminds him of Murillo's *Immaculate Conception* and who seems to be totally absorbed in contemplation. The woman is radiant; she is a figure of grace and beauty; she leans back and her eyes are turned towards the glass sphere that hangs from the ceiling; her right foot rests over another sphere, which is the world, and her right hand is poised over her heart. She seems to soar motionlessly within

Joannes Vermeer, *Allegory of the Faith*. Oil on canvas, 45 × 35 in., ca. 1671–74. *(Courtesy of the Metropolitan Museum of Art, New York. The Michael Friedsam Collection, 1931, 32.100.18.)*

the space of the composition, illuminated by the light of her inner self made visible in the perfect tonal balance of the blue and white of her dress. All is here a symmetry of space and figure, of time and timelessness, of visible and invisible, of body and soul, of form and reality, a symmetry that is repeated in the painting of the Crucifixion behind her, a painting within a painting where the most harmonious blend of light and darkness is focused on the figure of Christ, suspended in an abyss of time and space, of being and nonbeing, of sin and salvation.

> Quoi de plus émouvant que ce crucifix de bois rigide, que délègue à sa place, actuel et portatif, sur cet autel, le Dieu immolé qui nous est représenté sur le tableau au fond de la pièce, et de tout? (*OE*, 26)[10]

Just as the image of faith is premised on the image of the Crucified One, "actual and portrayed" and "in the back of the room," so too all the images of Vermeer's art are premised on the reality of a spiritual image. Without this, Claudel believes, Vermeer's paintings would have no meaning, no visible presence of the ontological secret. Claudel concludes that the spiritual image of Vermeer's *L'Allégorie evangélique* is the Church, who herself is this movement of "the human life towards its conclusion."

But more than any other artist, it is Rembrandt, according to Claudel, who brings the correspondence between the exterior and interior world, between form and reality; he brings the ontological secret of human existence to its finest expression. While it is true that Flemish artists typify the rational mind that sees nature's advancement toward its conclusion with the eyes of a geometer, Claudel admits that Italian masters such as Perugino, Tintoretto, and Titian had already unveiled reality with purity of their vision. In fact, according to Claudel, Italian and Flemish art have this in common: both glorify the present and both take their point of departure from the phenomenal world, from concrete existence. Rembrandt deepened the baroque spirit by his precision of details and by his use of chiaroscuro: that hidden light which seems to pour into his compositions from nowhere but draws everything around itself and "stirs up all around, in a curious way, all sorts of flashes and shadowings, of reflections and echoes" (*OE*, 40); the importance he gives to pure space, and the silence which reigns in all his works. Indeed, to Claudel, Rembrandt is the master of the ray of light, the glance, and of all that begins to live or speak, aloud or in a whisper. He makes observers feel the dark night of the soul without leading them into despair; his ray of light penetrates the inner self of the observers, raising them to a conversation with the Light. No one, concludes Claudel, expresses so beautifully this dialogue between the inner world of light and the outer world of darkness than Rembrandt; his most important contribution to the baroque spirit is his ability to reveal the correspondence between the phenomenal world and the world of grace, of the spirit.

This correspondence is also captured by painters of still lifes. The flowers, vegetables, fruits, tables, cups, dishes, draperies, etc. are symbols of something else: "It is something at the mercy of time" (*OE*, 48). Still-life paintings are a moral page, a revelation of reason itself, a living expression of "the eucharistic meal," an intimate communion of lifeless objects with the vibratory movement of life itself. Claudel sees all objects as pointing to an ultimate meaning: they convey an eternal sentiment, for to the still life there corresponds a flowing, a movement that is existence in its physical, moral, and spiritual unity.

Landscape paintings as well convey this eternal sentiment, this unity, this ontological secret of nature. In the landscapes by Ruysdaël, Hobbema, and Chintreuil, the baroque sense of the movement "of the human life toward its conclusion" is perhaps most fully realized, according to Claudel. *La Plage* by Ruysdaël, or *Le Chemin* by Hobbema, or *L'Espace* by Chintreuil, reveal to Claudel the human voyage, the road toward transformation, the road, as Claudel writes, that makes the individual tremble, the road that calls the human person into the world of eternity. In landscape paintings, time and space, the human person and the world, the world and the eternal, are continuous with one another. It seems that what exists here and now never ceases to be, and nonbeing expresses existence under its fleeting movement, which implies permanency, an irresistible necessity by which earth, air, sky, and the human person move along toward their end. With every look, the phenomenal world remains as near as that pure gaze with which distances are measured; the remembrance of things past becomes the angle of vision by which artist and viewer see with the world, conversing with it through "the sonorous breath" of contemplation. "Here our mother Nature has not taken the trouble to declare...her intentions....Thought very naturally, freed of an object that forces itself brutally upon the vision, grows big with contemplation" (*OE*, 9–10).

Gide: Symbolic Mysticism in Poussin's Art

According to Gide, Poussin's aesthetic roots lie deep in nature; his approach is basically contemplative. He wants to penetrate to the beautiful by way of a form that brings together reality and art, senses and reason. On the one hand, Poussin is influenced by the beauty of the phenomenal world; on the other hand, he is so profoundly immersed in art that, for him, it becomes his vocation. "Certainly, he was not insensitive to the beauty of the outside world, but it was in contact with works of art that he became conscious of his vocation" (*P*, 5). As artist, Poussin not only perceives the world as it is presented to him, but he uses his mind to reveal the image, the form of the beautiful by means of art.

> Et c'est qu'en lui la pensée se faisait aussitôt image, naissait plastique, et qu'ici intention, émotion, forme, métier, tout convergeait et conspirait à l'oeuvre d'art. (*P*, 2)[11]

This, Gide insists, is what makes Poussin's art delightful to the eyes and the mind; it appeals to something deep within human beings. It invites them to a contemplation that comes with "a work of art, music, painting or poetry." For painting, music, and poetry not only contain the beauty of the visible world, but the idea of the objects are also there in their essential forms of intention, proportion, color, sound, and elucidation; in them, thought itself is visible, heard, and read. Through art, the human person is brought to the realm of delight where the sensual and the rational are one. Poussin's art, says Gide, invites to "a persuasive delight; a delight rising out of which my vision of the outside world and even my actions saw themselves modified" (*P*, 9).

In Poussin's art, Gide finds a relationship between senses and thoughts whereby each modifies the other and their unity is subordinate to the composition itself. The modification of the exterior world and of human "comportment" is affected and in a state of mystery and delight. Placing the human person in a state of contemplation, Poussin's art speaks of gods who in turn speak to humanity by revealing the "persuasive delight" that is their natural state. It is this intercourse that Poussin expresses in the *Inspiration d'Anacréon* and to which Gide pays homage:

> Mysticisme païen, il va sans dire, mais vif et sincère, et tel qu'on n'en imaginerait pas l'expression différente lorsque, au lieu d'étancher sa soif spirituelle à la coupe de poésie que lui tend le dieu, Anacréon s'abreuverait au calice de l'eucharistie. Il a...le regard extasié de qui communie. (*P*, 11)[12]

Nicolas Poussin, *The Inspiration of Anacreon.* **Oil, 94 × 69.5 cm, ca. 1635–38.**
(Courtesy of Niedersächsisches Landemuseum Hannover.)

Although pagan, Poussin's spirituality and mysticism are not reduced to mere profanization just as they do not arise out of "a mystic emotion." Rather, his art resolves the tension between matter and spirit, the real and the ideal, not exclusively by the naked senses, but by thought through the senses; the world of thought is made visible in his art, and the outside world is brought into harmony with it. "The sensuality of his eye will doubtless be able to guide him well, but will never be an imperious mistress: a supreme rationality will always hold it in respect" (*P*, 6). Whether his paintings are as beautiful as nymphs or as horrible as war, destruction, or death itself, they are graceful to the extent that they are faithful to thought. "Thought presides at the birth of each of his [Poussin's] paintings" (*P*, 5). Thought allows Poussin not only to imitate the real, but to elevate it to the realm of the ideal. This, says Gide, should be seen by the fact that Poussin is more of a "draftsman than a painter; and often the painting will be for him only a setting in colors of dimensionality, for even his drawing retains order and composition" (*P*, 6). Thus, the highest achievement of Poussin's art is that, while creating the illusion of the real, it translates thought into images. "We only perceive the value of Poussin's thought when we see it as plastic and when he conveys it to us as image" (*P*, 8). Phenomenal forms radiate through Poussin's composition by means of the most delicate and well-defined geometric perspective. This is possible because Poussin is a painter, a draftsman, and a composer. To compose is in essence a matter of writing, of translating thoughts into sounds or verses, as the musician or the poet does. A painting is beautiful when its spectators imagine that it is looking at them, speaking; that it moves them; that it elicits from them feelings of contemplation or silence, dreams, feelings of being captured by its extraordinary beauty, feelings that light, colors, images, brush strokes, and the entire visible world of the painting communes with them, a feeling that the painting itself is alive.

> Mais ceci dit, reconnaissons que c'est la pensée qui motive et anime tous ses tableaux. C'est elle qui détermine le groupement de ses figures et leurs gestes, le mouvement des lignes, la distribution de la lumière et le choix des couleurs. Il n'est pas jusqu'aux frondaisons des arbres de ses vastes paysages qui n'en semblent une émanation par leur balancement tranquille et la sérénité qu'ils respirent. (*P*, 8)[13]

As a composer, Poussin bridges the inner movements of the soul with the phenomenal world through thought. He is a composer inasmuch as his art seeks to be faithful to rational naturalism, a naturalism that vivifies the soul.

Sans doute c'est l'esprit du Poussin qui m'y parle; mais c'est moins à mon intelligence qu'il s'adresse qu'à ce que j'ai de plus intime en moi, que je ne sais si je dois nommer âme, ou volonté....Ma raison est ici touchée elle aussi, qui prête assentiment à ma joie, à la réconciliation de l'âme et des sens dans une suprême harmonie. (*P*, 8–9)[14]

The joy that Gide discovers in looking at Poussin's art derives from Poussin's creative genius, from his ability to express the world of thought in the reality of images. The images in his art speak to a higher realm beyond the senses and the intelligence; they speak to the realm of "the will," a world of desires from which the soul and/or reason respond to the aesthetic images that "reclaim from us, in order to be touched, and to touch us, a very vigilant attention, a prolonged contemplation" (*P*, 3). True joy, persuasive delight, pagan mysticism, mean that Poussin's art stands on the horizon of the images of things in their phenomenal existence and of the sentiment of things in the human soul, and his art brings the contemplative feeling to the serene world of nature, and so deals with the contemplation of nature. There is no doubt that the contemplation of natural beauty as reflected in his art is immeasurably delightful, says Gide. But no matter how beautiful this natural vision is, the rational mysticism is even more delightful. "It is and remains rational, Cartesian one might say, even before the influence of Descartes began to prevail" (*P*, 10).

To rational mysticism corresponds human contemplation, that is, reason combined with the senses, which are called to a prolonged state of contemplation in which "the will" or the soul discovers "the persuasive delight" of the mythical world. At the same time, this rational mysticism, this pagan form of contemplation, is horrible and cruel because it puts humanity back in the state of nature in which it found itself at the creation of the world and prior to the world of Revelation. Pagan or rational mysticism, then, is that original condition in which humanity found itself purely and simply; it points to that which is most archetypal, most fundamental in the human person; it reveals nature's image in the human soul. It is the joy of life from which the impulses of the heart cannot be separated. On *L'enfance de Bacchus*, Gide comments: "This evocation of the beautiful girls of Nîmes as well as his numerous sketches bear witness to his love and his knowledge of life. When he sacrificed it, it was not through impotence, but by his will" (*P*, pl. 14); on *Orphée et Eurydice*, "It is the beginning of the sorrowful drama which had to separate the lovers forever" (*P*, pl. 38); again, on *L'été*, "We take part in a drama of an unconquerable nature, and one almost understands better that the battle is useless" (*P*. pl. 40); on *Le massacre des innocents*, "Often Poussin will inscribe fury, sorrow, terror by means of the pathos of a mask, but no one will ever again have such strange vigor" (*P*, pl. 7); and on *Jupiter et la chèvre amalthée*, "Time, in effect, devours everything" (*P*, pl. 17); finally, about *L'apparition de la Vierge à Saint Jacques*, Gide states:

Le respect et l'adoration qu'expriment ces visages de saints témoignent que Poussin néanmoins connaissait l'homme et son coeur, et savait, quand il le voulait, en traduire les mouvements. (*P*, pl. 9)[15]

This human drama is so archetypal, so fundamental, so original that it transcends time through tradition, through transcending thought; through the image, Poussin's artistic contemplation communes not only with "the persuasive delight" of the natural world, but with history as well.

Pour lui la tradition forme, comme en dehors du temps, une suite si homogène qu'il n'hésite pas à situer, dans son *Orphée et Eurydice*, le drame qui sépare les deux amants de la fable grecque, dans un décor romain où nous étonnons de trouver le château Saint-Ange. (*P*, 11–12)[16]

Gide goes on to state that Poussin's art not only stands outside the artistic tradition of his time ("Neither the disciples of Caravaggio, nor the Bolognese school are his equal") but more than this, he finds therein "the movements of the heart," which go "beyond time" (*P*, 14). Commenting on *Le triomphe de Flore*, Gide states:

Et quant à Poussin, il les utilisa avec une incroyable variété d'emploi et d'expression, comme jamais même les Grecs, ni la Renaissance, ni plus tard Boucher: enfants de l'homme, anges ou Cupidons, ils participent au drame. (*P*, pl. 11)[17]

There are more expressions, more movements, more figures, more luminous colors in Poussin's art than the eyes can see in perceiving the world, and they bring delight to the mind by the very fact that they are tempered "by a monotone patina, and frozen as well by our being accustomed to it" (*P*, 2). And it is with a sort of "particular enthusiasm" that we admire the visual effects that a Caravaggio, a Titian, a Rubens, or a Raphael do not create as masterfully as Poussin, since the former do not rely exclusively on thought. Commenting on *L'enlèvement des Sabines*, Gide writes:

Les moeurs, les chevaux, les architectures, les galères, les trophées, les ornements, les coiffures, les sandales, les casques, les boucliers, les voiles, les drapés, tous les détails du costume et des attitudes, Poussin les étudia à la plume, à la mine de plomb, à la sanguine, au pinceau sur toutes les fresques, toutes les médailles, toutes les pierres gravées, tous les bas-

Nicolas Poussin, *The Triumph of Flora.* Oil, 165 × 241 cm, 1630. *(Courtesy of Cliché des Musées Nationaux, Louvre, Paris.)*

reliefs, toutes les colonnes, tous les arcs, toutes les statues que l'antiquité a légués à Rome. (*P*, pl. 22)[18]

Still, the pagan mysticism of Poussin, which stands outside historical tradition, belongs with the French artistic tradition, for it needs a corresponding natural sentiment exterior to itself. While it is true, Gide affirms, that the creative spirit of the artist is free and autonomous; nevertheless, "the pagan mysticism," "the persuasive delight" act as a kind of natural reminder of the French artistic tradition.

Pourtant c'est l'esprit et le génie de la France qu'on sent qui respire en ses toiles et qu'il illustre d'une autre manière mais autant que Descartes (cet autre grand déraciné) et Corneille ses contemporains. (*P*, 4)[19]

With Descartes, "the spirit of art" becomes dependent on the rational ideal of the natural sciences, thereby beginning its movement toward a representation of "the still life" with Chardin and the world of movement with Delacroix. Descartes, and art bound by his principles, made it possible for the artist to experiment with the question of art for art's sake; or, to state it differently, Descartes made it possible for the artist to express the beautiful through the use of the artist's own mind. From Descartes onward, artistic expression came to be seen as the result of the artist's own creative power, and the artist's thought works on art as the divine mind works on nature. Only with Descartes can the relationship between sentiment and content, reality and art, be fused into one. At the same time, Gide goes on to affirm, this Cartesian model on which Poussin's aesthetic foundation is built is abandoned by French artists of today in favor of "realistic painting," which no longer represents either sentiment or thought of the natural and the human drama, but relies merely on the exigencies of space, volume, and mass.

Pour avoir trop bien compris que c'est avec les beaux sentiments et les nobles pensées qu'on fait les pires oeuvres d'art, le peintre a résolu de n'exprimer plus de pensées ni de sentiments du tout. (*P*, 7)[20]

While the above assertion may be true, Gide does not fail to establish the connection between Descartes and the French artistic tradition, beginning with Poussin and ending with Monet. Indeed, only with Descartes by way of Poussin can Gide arrive at a Courbet or a Manet, who "make us see nothing above matter" (*P*, 11) but still exemplify the spirit of symbolic art. No doubt that Courbet and Manet glorify "matter" while Poussin "transports humanity above matter itself"; nevertheless, Courbet and Manet address themselves to consciousness itself, to the hiddenness of things, to art as the unique end of humanity. This is also true of a Seurat, a Matisse, a Picasso, and a Monet; the aestheticization of the material world and the anchoring of artistic forms in the movements of the heart and the thoughts of the artist are the essential aspects of Descartes and the entire French tradition, despite Gide's assertion that today's French art does not represent Poussin's relationship between true art and human sentiment and human thought. "The work, to free itself from true painting, must guard itself from expressing nothing" (*P*, 7). Yet, symbolic mysticism is the thread that connects French artists. For this reason, says Gide, Poussin's genius is the glory of France: "He entered into French Eternity."

Indeed, Poussin's spirit is found within French artistic tradition, and this spirit overflows in its literary expression as well — "and, today, Péguy, Claudel and Valéry"; and in the past, La Fontaine, Racine, Molière, Mallarmé, and Baudelaire. Just as Gide finds in Poussin both a sensual and rational delight, so he finds this delight also in the French literary tradition, which reveals the beautiful by the contrast of the "comportment" of the literary figure and the exterior world. Like the artist, writers base their stance on the real world of images with which they try to penetrate deep into the phenomenal world so that their work may transport us to the realm of delight. For the writer as for the artist, the point of reference lies in the harmony between nature and mysticism and in the natural delight of this harmony, a delight that only works of art can bring to us. Gide attributes to Adrien Mithouard and Toulet his first discoveries of this delight, the "rapture which belongs to us." Toulet had described Poussin's art as the finest expression of French symbolic mysticism; he had spoken of its poetics of "persuasive delight" and had found in it "the optical identity of our intellectual life." Toulet maintained that while Italian artists had not neglected this identity with their intellectual culture, they, unlike French artists, had failed to emphasize "the melody and its development."

Unlike the French artistic and intellectual tradition, the Italian tradition turns its attention on the form of the phenomenal world, not on its melody or lyricism; it focuses on the glorification of human existence and not on the glorification of artistic forms as the human person's final end of life; its attention is on the present, not on the remembrance of things past. In attempting to express the form of the beautiful in the visible world, the Italian artist does not reduce the material world to a mere symbol, a plastic form or ideality. For the Italian artist, the form has flesh of its own, independent of the mind of the artist who expresses it and the mind of the observer who contemplates it. In contemplating Italian art, the senses do awaken a remembrance of things past, but this remembrance is not found exclusively by and in the memory, by and in thought, but also incorporates the testimony of the phenomenal world and beauty itself. In contrast, French literary and artistic expression elevates itself to lyricism, to a melody of forms that brings delight to the senses and the mind by way of plastic forms; for a beautiful form is not only the creation of thought which excites us, but it offers us all the combined charms of art and pagan or rational mysticism. In *Moïse exposé sur les eaux du Nil*, Gide finds a certain influence of Raphael:

> ...l'encombrement des figures, leur échelle aux dépens du paysage, et le faire même; mais Poussin conservera le goût des divinités fluviales que Raphaël lui avait donné....Quel charme cependant dans le tendre geste bénisseur de la mère, dans le bras levé de sa soeur, qui guette, dans l'air de proue et de toute la figure! (*P*, pl. 3)[21]

Poussin, says Gide, not only surpasses Raphael, but his intent is to strike his spectators' sentiments, the movements of their hearts, to raise them to the realm of delight, to a charm felt in the gestures and movements of the figures, to make them forget their ordinary existence; this, according to Gide, was not Raphael's intent. Poussin's art is the first visual drama of thoughts in which the phenomenal world is disregarded for the created forms acting upon it. Like drama, Gide sees created beauty interposing itself between the objective form of the beautiful and reality itself; that is, natural beauty is the beauty of a work of art, of music, of poetry, or literature in general. Through the melody of plastic forms, created beauty attempts to honor phenomenal beauty by covering it with a veil of delight, with a splendor, with a glory, which can be experienced only by the contemplation of plastic arts.

Thus, Gide comes to a full circle in his interpretation of Poussin's art. If by its nature Poussin's art is rooted in the Cartesian world of thought, Poussin's expression of beauty and grace of necessity must fall within the realm of the artist's mind; that is, beauty and grace must be revealed from the mental process of the artist, not from the objective form of things. This means that the senses and the mind of the artist establish themselves as the center of the plastic world, around which created forms revolve, while phenomenal forms lose their aesthetic visibility, their form of the beautiful. While it is true that Poussin's art balances form and reality, "the exterior world" and "the movements of the heart," Gide breaks this balance by

Nicolas Poussin, *Venus Spied on by Shepherds.* **Oil, 71 × 96 cm, ca. 1624.**
(Courtesy of Staatliche Kunstsammlungen Dresden.)

becoming so enraptured in the delight of contemplating the art work itself that he ignores the mythological, biblical, and the phenomenal forms that Poussin represents in his art. This way, Gide reduces Poussin's art to pure melodies of the mind, to rational harmonies of nature, to symbolic mysticism, to a revelation of beauty and grace through artistic expression.

Cette harmonie, Poussin ne la recherche pas seulement dans l'expression de la félicité; il l'impose volontiers au tumulte; il l'obtient jusque dans l'horrible, à la manière des tragiques grecs et ne craint point de représenter des massacres, des cadavres, des pestiférés. (*P*, 9)[22]

Conclusion: From Reality to Symbolic Art

Both Claudel and Gide acknowledge that Italian artists, particularly Raphael, Michelangelo, Titian, and Caravaggio, exerted a lasting influence on both Flemish and French art. Yet, whereas Claudel sees in Flemish art a spiritual realism like the one found in Italian art, Gide, on the other hand, sees nothing of this realism in Poussin's art, where thought alone coordinates colors, figures, lines, and composition into a harmonious whole. By making delight the chief end of his art, Gide tells us, Poussin makes art—not the world—the image, the beauty, of delight. Unlike Hals, Vermeer, Rembrandt, Hooch, Steen, Ter Borch, Van Ostade, Claesz, Ruysdaël, Hobbema, Chintreuil, Poussin makes the human person's ontological existence not a reality but a mere abstraction. Unlike Flemish artists, who, according to Claudel, communicate through their art the liturgical drama, Poussin, in Gide's view, reveals the visual drama of humanity simply and purely; that is, in the grace of its aesthetic form, not in the grace of God's form in humanity and in the world. The beauty and grace experienced while contemplating Poussin's art lie in "the sad drama" that Poussin expresses in pure forms, forms that are rational or Cartesian without fleshly existence, lie in the harmonious beauty of proportion, harmony, and composition, that brings pleasure to the senses and reason. Thus, the use of mythologies in Poussin's art is neither a true "mystic emotion" nor a true "sensuality."

But even Flemish artists used mythologies, says Claudel. The Flemish, however, ascend higher than the world of myths, of humanity itself; for them, the experience of the mythical world flowers into a real mystical encounter with phenomenal forms where "justice, which is nothingness," is the very sense of God in the world. In Claudel's Flemish art, the human drama is not only a reality and also a symbol of the invisible world of God, whether it is represented by a landscape by Hobbema or a religious painting by Vermeer. Furthermore, the human drama that Flemish artists make visible reminds Claudel of the mysteries of Christ's Incarnation, Death, and Resurrection, true symbols of reality. Flemish images remain immersed in the flesh while still pointing to the world of light, beauty, and grace. Poussin's images, on the other hand, seem to Gide to flow into thin air, creating such an effect that the only place where we might encounter them is in the world of dreams and fables, of pagan mysticism, or in the world of thought.

6

Claudel and Redon: The Image of
Beauty and Grace

Laissez-moi voir et entendre toutes choses avec la / parole / Et
saluer chacune par son nom avec la parole qui / l'a fait. (*CGO*,
70)[1]

Et moi, Jean, je vis la sainte cité, la nouvelle Jérusalem, qui
descendait du ciel, d'auprès de Dieu. (*OR*, 184)[2]

Claudel and Gide see in baroque art a sense of drama. For
Claudel, Flemish art represents the link between the phenomenal
world and the realm of beauty and grace through the mediation of
the incarnated form, which awakens in the world and the human person a sense for God. For Gide, Poussin's art makes "thought" visible, which establishes the transformation of the natural world to the
ecstatic world of created forms.

Flemish art reveals to Claudel that grace is a wave that

...se précipite vers cette mer de rafraîchissement, de consolation et de
lumière, qui, comme la perspective nous l'enseigne, n'est nullement au-
dessous de nous, mais en avant de nous et au-dessus de nous! (*OE* 189)[3]

Flemish art leads the observer beyond the world of nature, beyond
the world of human drama, to a world of liturgical drama, a world
that exists objectively. This sacred world is too solemn, Claudel insists, to be left exclusively "to the realm of spontaneity and of subjective improvisation" of the artist.

Flemish art thus manifests and orders the correspondence between
the self and the world, which is prior to the self and which "responds
to all the movements of our soul," so that the self may come to feel
it, know it, and be born with it.

On the other hand, Poussin's art according to Gide does not reveal
nature as this "text anterior to us." Gide feels that Poussin's art is
a re-creation of nature from thought, from the genius of Poussin as

composer. Deligth as thought is embodied in the world so that the world may be embodied in thought, and this embodiment manifests itself in artistic creations. This is why Gide sees in Poussin's art the seeds of "true painting," which finds its consequences in the French literary and artistic expression of the nineteenth and twentieth centuries. Like Mallarmé who, in the words of Gide, "remained, prior to Valéry, the most intellectual of the poets," and who believed that poetic language is the highest expression of human existence. Poussin's art embodies "the persuasive delight" of beautiful art forms.

While both Claudel and Gide praise created forms, they differ from each other as to the objective evidence of beauty and grace. For Claudel, art is the proper correspondence between the phenomenal world, the interior sentiment of the artist, and an objective form; the artist must make forms visible that exist already in the world. For Gide, the ontological correspondence between phenomenal forms and art does not exist; consequently, artistic creations are the essence of things, displacing the objective phenomenal form in favor of subjective images, which alone inflame the artist to create, and which alone become the objective measure.

Redon's art reveals beauty and grace from the realm of the artist's own thought. And thought is nothing but a dream, the imagination bursts forth and takes hold of art, as the phenomenal world becomes appearances. In Redon's art, the luminous finds no correspondence with the hidden form unfolding itself in the world; rather, it is the luminosity of pure imagined images — of disembodied forms, as attested by the series, *Les origines*, of the invisible world of thought, as revealed by *Dans le rêve* — of the felt radiancy of nature that his still lifes manifests. In looking at his art, one feels that one is indeed living in a Gidian world of "thought," in a world where the visible and the invisible, the artist and the phenomenal form are brought together and united according to what the imagination sees and feels. Claudel, on the contrary, reveals the luminosity of the visible world, a luminosity seen from within the "nothingness," which supposes an objective form, an essence capable of being seen, felt, and known from the light of grace.

Claudel: A Vision of Light and Darkness

In dealing with the image of beauty and grace, Claudel speaks of both light and darkness: "The darkness is without, the light is / within" (*CGO*, 100). As Claudel considers beauty and grace, he focuses on darkness in its connection with light, on the exterior world in its connection with the interior world, on the phenomenal world in its correspondence with the invisible, on the world of body in its relation to the form that shapes it. According to Claudel, the self that is unable to perceive the form hidden in the phenomenal world and in itself is enclosed in its own darkness, incapable of encountering the beautiful in the world and in itself. "You cannot see but with the sun, nor know but / within yourself in God" (*CGO*, 100). Light and darkness, then, whether interpreted in a real, allegorical or metaphysical sense, belong to the order of knowledge in which God's form becomes visible.

> Cette lumière qui n'est pas pour les fils de la Terre!
> Cette lumièreici est pour moi, si faible qu'il lui faut
> la nuit pour qu'elle m'éclaire, pareille à la lampe de
> l'habitacle!
> Et au dehors sont les ténèbres et le Chaos qui n'a point
> reçu l'Évangile.
>
> (*CGO*, 82)[4]

Without the light of grace—here Revelation—there is no way of penetrating the darkness, the chaos, of the phenomenal world; the self itself dissolves in the abyss of nothingness. Yet, for Claudel, the manifestation of this light is revealed during the night, in the darkness of existence. In the night, God's splendor or light is seen in the immediacy of faith.

> Comme la parole a tiré toutes choses du néant, afin
> qu'elles meurent,
> C'est ainsi que tu es né afin que tu puisses mourir en
> moi.
> Comme le soleil appelle à la naissance toutes les choses
> visibles,
> Ainsi le soleil de l'esprit, ainsi l'esprit pareil à un
> foudre crucifié
> Appelle toutes choses à la connaissance et voici qu'elles
> lui sont présentes à la fois.
>
> (*CGO*, 89)[5]

Starting from the visible, the self proceeds towards the light of God, knowing him not in what he is, but in what he is not. And even in the revelation of his Son, God remains the hidden form, the mystery, the light, that the self contemplates in phenomenal forms. As the self contemplates the splendor of God's light in the world, intelligence comprehends itself; it sees itself in seeing God's hidden form; it knows itself as image of God's light; it sees and knows itself as the pure blue of the sky, as the symphony of colors of the phenomenal world. This, according to Claudel, is the "darkness of the intelligence," the intellect that is born with the vision of the form, the light of God's form, the Word made flesh. Once God's radiancy is seen, felt, and known, then the whole universe, in its visible and invisible aspects, is presented to the perceiver in one single image: that of darkness, of the abyss. Hence, a true experience of the beautiful includes a certain experience of darkness, a sense of God's hiddenness here and now. "The Abyss, which the sublime gaze / Forgets, passing daringly from one point to the other" (*CGO*, 25).

The self cannot see God's abyss until the eyes are purified. In order to flood the self with the light of faith by which it can begin to see the beauty of created things, God must first blind the eyes of the senses. Sensory sight must first be veiled if the self is to encounter the beautiful in the luminosity of God's grace, which brings together the luminosity of the phenomenal world and the self's consciousness of that luminosity. It is therefore in darkness that the self perceives "this light so weak that it needs the night to light my way." In this darkness, the senses and intelligence see nothing and know nothing but are directed by God's spirit, which makes them look and know by the obscure light of grace rather than by the light of the day or phenomenal light. "One day follows another, but here it is the day where the sun / stands still" (*CGO*, 62). The night when the light of grace excels the stars, when the day is inundated with the light of heaven, is the moment when the visible universe becomes a "work of Eternity" (*CGO*, 44). Seeing and knowing in the darkness, in the visible expression of God's hidden form, is for the self to live in the dryness of God's spirit, in the abyss of the death of His only begotten Son. "My God, I see the perfect man on the cross, perfect / on the perfect Tree" (*CGO*, 41).

In his infinite love, God, instead of abandoning humanity to the darkness of the phenomenal world, sees to it that where there is perfect darkness, His light should shine more brilliantly or perfectly. God becomes incarnate and dies in order that humanity may pass from unseeing to seeing, from darkness to light, from the phenomenal to the eternal. Hence, the necessity of dying, of sacrificing; because "it is death which calls everything to life" (*CGO*, 88). In the act of sacrifice, humanity is stripped of earthly existence so that it may be born with Christ's death and live the life of grace, which is the eternal life. "I shall not die, but I am immortal!" (*CGO*, 47). This is a birth, a "knowing," a resurrection from the dark abyss of phenomenal existence to God's darkness, the abyss. By the same token, it is a rebirth by virtue of the fact that with the first chaos, the first darkness, and with the experience of sin, humanity must be made to see anew with Christ as God's visible form.

Dieu qui avez baptisé avec votre esprit le chaos
Et qui la veille de Pâques exorcisez par la bouche
de votre prêtre la font païenne avec la lettre psi,
Vous ensemencez avec l'eau baptismale notre eau
humaine
Agile, glorieuse, impassible, impérissable!

(*CGO*, 46–47)[6]

With the sacramental water of baptism, which has for its end the gift of life, and with the Eucharist, which completes that life, humanity is able to feel, to see, to know, and to be born with Christ's form and is thus enabled to perceive God's hidden form in the world and within itself. Through his death, Christ disposes himself so that humanity may eat the flesh and drink the blood and be made witness of God's glory on earth.

In order that the world may continuously reveal God's light, that both God's grace and humanity's desire may become one in the longing to see Beauty face to face, and that human persons may feel Beauty's presence in the world and in the depth of their being, it is necessary that Christ's death be seen as the last step of his abasement. Likewise humanity must humble itself, must die to itself, in order to be exalted, to be transformed by his splendor. "I have descended with you into your sepulcher" (*CGO*, 99). At the same time, humanity's descent into the abyss of the earth, into total darkness, into nothingness, opens the way to the invisible, the eternal. Like the resurrected Christ who ascended from the tomb and entered the place where the Apostles were without opening the door, so the human person will enter the abyss of eternity, the realm of divine darkness, through the light of Revelation, through Christ's form. "Heed the Gospel which counsels you to shut the door of your room" (*CGO*, 100). Christ is the form by which the human person enters God's kingdom of light precisely because he has become human and, therefore, seeing him as center, as form, is seeing the beauty, the splendor, of the Father. In this way, perfect sight occurs in the contemplation of Christ on the cross; the cross makes humanity see, feel, and touch suffering; humanity sees that Christ himself has suffered death in order to ascend to the abyss of the ground, the source, the light, beauty itself, an ascent that takes him into the bosom of the Trinity.

Je crois sans y changer un seul point ce que mes pères
ont cru avant moi,
Confessant le Sauveur des hommes et Jésus qui est
mort sur la croix,
Confessant le Père qui est Dieu, et le Fils qui est Dieu,
et le Saint-Esprit qui est Dieu,
Et cependant non pas trois dieux, mais un seul Dieu....

(*CGO*, 123)[7]

As in God there is not one nature apart from three Persons, so in the human person there is a complete harmony of senses, knowledge, and conscience; of body, intellect, and spirit; of form, movement, and intentionality; of birth, resemblance, and dissolution; of verb, word, and name. As Claudel believes each one of the three Persons, Father, Son, and the Holy Spirit, is fully God by virtue of his being "a single God," so human beings are whole in each part of their nature, since each part is identical with their concrete existence. Human beings are in the world, and through the unity of their human and divine natures they perfect themselves; that is, they bring the phenomenal world into a new correspondence with the truth of their trinitarian nature, of their own hearts.

> Je connais toutes choses et toutes choses se connaissent
> en moi.
> J'apporte à toute chose sa délivrance.
> Par moi
> Aucune chose ne reste plus seule mais je l'associe à
> une autre dans mon coeur.
>
> (*CGO*, 40)[8]

There, in the heart, the Claudelian person comes to know the link between the phenomenal world and the world of the artist who must express the tale of creation in a most complete image. And there, in the heart, art is reinforced with truth, the truth of a creed, of an eternal "knowing."

> La terre, le ciel bleu, le fleuve avec ses bateaux et
> trois arbres soigneusement sur la rive,
> La feuille et l'insecte sur la feuille, cette pierre que je
> soupèse dans ma main,
> Le village avec tous ces gens...
> Tout cela est l'éternité et la liberté...
> Je les vois avec les yeux du corps, je les produis dans
> mon coeur!
>
> (*CGO*, 44–45)[9]

Before the beauty of the visible world, the heart, illumined with the flame of love and the light of faith, annihilates the darkness that is in the world and removes the blindness from the eyes of the senses. Before eternity, which clothes itself in the vestments of the body, and in the face of the flowing fountain of grace that pours out from the Trinity, Claudel himself stands before the Divine Artist. As artist, Claudel tries to give expression to the world's form; he tries to listen to what the night and the earth and the sky and the people have to tell him, the beauty of Creation.

Redon: A Vision of Pure Images

Like Claudel, Redon brings into expressive form the emergence of light from darkness. Unlike Claudel, who conveys light from and in Christ's corporeal form, in the human person's spiritual senses, Redon's light is that of thought, of dreams, of created or art forms. The beautiful that Redon offers in his lithographs (to which this analysis is limited) is manifested in phenomenal forms; it is not the vibratory movement of the senses directed by the soul to feel divine sensations in the world. Rather, it is an inner vision, a flash of light that remains dark primarily because this light exists in the mind, in the world of dreams and night. Hence, the grace that shines in Redon's art has no correspondence with the objective form hidden in things; instead it is the grace, the luminosity of disembodied forms, of pure symbols. Redon's art seems to be one of flight, of movement in which objects float in the boundless space of emerging and dissolving forms.

It is from this standpoint that the *Apocalypse de Saint-Jean* series (1899) appears to Redon as the beginning and end of pure symbols. The first lithograph, "And He Had in his Right Hand Seven Stars" (*OR*, 174), with the cross suspended from the figure's mouth, indicates that night, the void, the abyss, is the realm of light. The plate suggests that Thought radiates light in all directions of the universe; it suggests an inverted reality. What exists here is not the correspondence between light and its manifestation in phenomenal forms, nor is it the correspondence with what John sees as signs or revelations; to John's eyes, the phenomenal world discloses the bright light of God, a light that shines in the corporeal form of Christ. "I, Jesus, have sent my angel to make these revelations to you for the sake of the churches. I am of David's line, the root of David and the bright star of the morning" (Rev. 22:16).

The bright star that John reveals is not Redon's "And There Fell a Great Star from Heaven" (*OR*, 178); rather, it is the light of Christ's bodily form; it is the angel who appears in the form of a servant. John's angel is sent by God to reveal the "prophetic message of this book" (Rev. 22:7); it is sent by Christ "for the sake of the churches"; it is sent from Christ to His servant John, and John "has written down everything he saw and swears it is the word of God guaranteed by Jesus Christ" (Rev. 1:2). To John, then, signs reveal the hidden light of the "seven stars you have seen in my right hand, and of the seven golden lamp-stands:...the seven stars are the angels of the seven churches, and the seven lamp-stands are the seven churches themselves" (Rev. 1:20). For John, the angels of the churches and the lamp-stands of the churches are part of this earthly com-

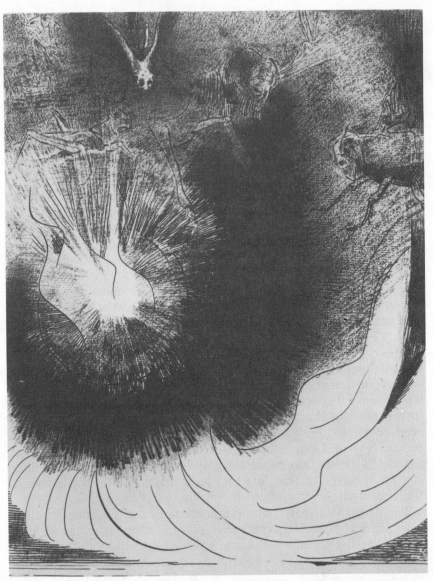

Odilon Redon, *And there fell a great star from heaven....* **Lithograph, 30.3 × 23.3 cm, 1899. (***Courtesy of the Museum of Fine Arts, Boston. Bequest of W. G. Russell Allen, 60.710.***)**

munity, which ideally is found in heaven as holy city ruled by God.

> Then I saw *a new heaven and a new earth*; the first heaven and the first earth had disappeared now, and there was no longer any sea. I saw the holy city, and the new Jerusalem, coming down from God out of heaven, as beautiful as a bride all dressed for her husband. (Rev. 21:1–3)

The signs or revelations of which John writes are the epiphany of the holy city, they are the vision of God's splendor in Christ and of Christ's luminosity or grace shining over the first heaven and the first earth. "And the city did not need the sun or the moon for light, since it was lit by the radiant glory of God and the Lamb was a lighted torch for it" (Rev. 21:23–24). This "lighted torch," says John, is there in creation; it is there for everyone to see it, and everyone sees it according to a personal vision. Furthermore, this light can serve as the book of life, as the way to the beautiful, which is God's splendor, his glory, shining in all phenomenal forms. Conversely, the beautiful that shines in creation can serve as the way to Christian revelation, to a new heaven and new earth, a new Jerusalem whose light is the Lamb, the incarnate Word of God. Hence, to John, Christ as the servant of God is not a mythical king who accomplishes heroic acts; rather, he is the very Word, the very Glory, the very Splendor, the very human Person who suffers and dies precisely so that the light, the grace of the world may shine anew. To those who see and believe in this Lamb, the new heaven and the new earth coexist in, find their manifestation in, the Eucharist. "Come here. *Gather together at the great feast* that God is giving" (Rev. 19:17). With the Eucharist, both the world and the human person will no longer need the sun as their light, and for both of them it will never be night again, because God's glory or splendor will be shining in them.

By contrast, Redon transforms these revelations into a mythical reality, into simple created forms. Unlike Johns's vision of light, which maintains the relationship between symbol and reality, between the interior luminosity of things and their exterior darkness, Redon seems to stress the nothingness, the arbitrariness, the purely symbolic form of things. Whereas for John the nothingness or darkness represents an existence lived apart from the luminous, from revelation, for Redon, the nothingness, the void, is all. His *Apocalypse* paints a holy city that exists only as symbol, as myth, with no historical or theological connection to the testimony of Revelation and no ties to phenomenal forms. For John, revelations or signs are not merely mythical or allegorical; they are the very material of Christian Revelation, the realization of all myths, Eastern, Western, and Judaic. Redon's second lithograph, "And I Saw in the Right Hand of Him That Sat on the Throne, a Book Written within and Without" (*OR*, 175) remains inaccessible, since it is separated from the root of David, and from the revelation of God's Word. Also, the plate, "A Woman Clothed with the Sun" (*OR*, 179), is not the bride of which John speaks, nor is the illustration, "The Holy City, the New Jerusalem" (*OR*, 184), the Church of God, the Bride of Christ; these plates are pure symbols, mental constructs cut off from the hidden form of things and the grace of God.

Redon's *Apocalypse* destroys the connecting link between symbol and reality, and instead of serving as a guide into the realm of the Incarnation, of the mysterious revelation of God's splendor in the world through Christ's form, leads into the realm of the unknown, the realm of the mythological, the darkness of both phenomenal world and mind. Redon captures the beautiful from the night, the time when dreams and the unconscious take over. In the *Dans le rêve* series (1879), Redon does indeed leave behind the phenomenal world in order to enter the world of thought, the nocturnal aspect of things, dream consciousness. In the first lithograph, "Blossoming" (*OR*, 27), a face peers out from a dark cell as a bristly chick emerging from its egg, or as a flower stiffly and awkwardly opening up its petals. Surrounded by wisps of black lines, suggesting its movement in space, the blossoming cell floats about, along with other circles of varying degrees of black. Without these globes of consciousness, without the black wisps of lines, all would be nothing, all would dissolve in empty whiteness. Human thought itself seems to be blossoming forth as darkness within the emptiness of light, which alone can affirm the cosmic magnitude and give a semblance of motion to the void by creating gently swirling pathways of black within the motionless abyss. In the second plate, "Germination" (*OR*, 28), the void is black, and the globes of consciousness are distinguishable by their whiteness. As if viewing the cosmos, one sees Milky Ways of thought forming pathways of blackness and light. As with Claudel, both darkness and light are needed to reveal one another, but unlike Claudel, Redon makes them utterly interchangeable, utterly arbitrary. Light does not shine forth unequivocally from any objective source, be it the phenomenal world, "knowing," or revelation. Light is a void, a nothingness, just as darkness is. Light gives form only as chiaroscuro, which alone is able to define the flux of a reality, which itself is not phenomenal; it is a dissolution, an emergence. As light, this chiaroscuro places the phenomenal world at the service of thought, of that part of the mind that submits to the self's hidden depths, to its dreams. This world of physical time and space yields to an imaginary time and space where

Odilon Redon, ... *a woman clothed with the Sun.* **Lithograph, 23 × 28.6 cm.** *(Courtesy of the Museum of Fine Arts, Boston. Bequest of W.G. Russell Allen, 60.711.)*

the beautiful is an appearance, a shadow, a symbol without object, a sign that is only signifier with no ultimate signified. The ascension beyond the rooftops of the phenomenal world is indeed sad as the plate "Sad Ascent" (OR, 35) testifies. The winged creature looks up proudly, lovingly at the balloon-person it has inflated and elevated well above the earth. Yet, the wings seem too small to maintain the flight; the winged creature sits precariously on its flooring so that the distinction between mover and moved, up and down, night and day, is erased, and the balloon seems to float sluggishly into the air, rather than being propelled by the energy of the extended, ecstatic winged creature. Rooftops, the only features of the phenomenal world barely visible, also blend with the dream-vision; they too seem to coexist interiorly, not as objective objects.

The shift from the exterior world of forms to the inner world thought, of dreams, does not entail a renunciation of the phenomenal world, but its transformation. The first lithograph of the series, Les origines (1883), "When Life Was Awakening" (OR, 45), evokes a being, which, like so many of Redon's creations, has no correspondence with natural existence; its existence seems to be in the "obscure matter" of the mind. Yet, and despite the fact that this creature exists nowhere except in the imagination, its link with the phenomenal world is not completely severed; it is not abstract; it is surreal, beyond and yet of the laws of nature, beyond and yet of the objective world of forms. In this series, Redon calls the observer away from the existing objective world into the world of the mind, which imagines what is (exists) prior to its being; its hidden "formless form." A misshapen polyp, a mask that sounds the funeral bell, eyes that float in space, in the ocean, and in the forest, embryonic being suspended in space, winged creatures, chimera and legendary satyrs, sirens, and fauns, a smiling spider, a cactus man, a madman in a dismal landscape, Phaeton, Orpheus, Buddha, Isis, and Christ; in the mind there emerges a life without hours and places, an existence whose beauty is encountered in the world of pure images. The world to which these images belong is that of the artist's own thoughts, and not the phenomenal world in which they nevertheless must take their source. Like a dreamer, Redon expresses the beauty of the eternal silence of the infinite, of the fine outline of tree branches against the sky, of the arrival and passing of the seasons, of night and day, of darkness and light, of birth, movement, transformation, and death of things, evil and redemption. It is the beautiful that can be seen only with the eyes closed, since it shines in the night where only the mind's eye can grasp it. It is the beautiful of the chiaroscuro, of ambiguity, which brings into focus imagination and the phenomenal world.

Odilon Redon, *Sad Ascent.* **Lithograph, 26.7 × 20 cm, 1879.** (*Courtesy of The Art Institute of Chicago. The Stickney Collection, 1920.1565.* © *1987 The Art Institute of Chicago. All rights reserved.*)

In the series, *La nuit* (1886), Redon again tries to reconstruct existence in its hidden form, in its archetypal origin. The lost angel, the solitary man, the priestesses that await; old age; and "the searcher [who] was in an infinite search" (*OR*, 67) are the fixed characters of his mind's drama illumined by the light of remembrances, of both the personal and collective unconscious. As in the other series, here the figures are both light and darkness; they both see and do not see. They express the self's search for the absolute and the encounter with the void. Although disconnected from material reality, they belong to an aesthetic reality; their beauty is that of the mysterious, of the unknown, and of the shadowy; it is a beauty of the barely imaginable, melted down and vaporized in the crucible of the artist's mind.

The hidden, the search for the absolute, light, darkness, dreams, and night, constants in Redon's aesthetics, are brought together in the *Songes* series (1891), revealing the beautiful as an encounter with the source, the abyss, the origin. The lithograph, "Pilgrim of the Sublunary World" (*OR*, 114), depicts a white-robed figure on a horse looking up toward a bright circular object. "And beyond, the Astral Idol" (*AM*, 111) contains a white-robed and monklike figure inside a cell, with an arrow in his left hand gazing at the void. These lithographs, thus, direct the viewer away from the material world toward a spiritual reality, an image, a primordial source of beauty, of light itself. Although referring to Christian, Buddhist, and mythological themes and subjects, Redon's art divests them of their own particular allegories and places them within the sphere of pure aesthetic images. His own grace, like his Christs and his Buddhas, is but "a veil, an imprint" (*OR*, 110), "a head suspended in the infinite" (*OR*, 112), a "black being biting" (*OR*, 113). The true star, the idol, the apotheosis is "below" and forever hidden from human sight. "The Day" (*OR*, 115), which completes this series, offers the window to Redon's vision. It is only from within the dark interior and through thick, delicately barred walls that shadowy globes of consciousness see and reveal the day, the light, the edenic tree of life.

Conclusion: From the Image of Beauty and Grace to Their Symbols

Both Claudel and Redon seek to express the beautiful in their artistic creations, and both approach it through the image. The image bridges light with darkness, the visible with the invisible, the known with the unknown, making it possible for the mind's eye to behold the radiant, the luminous, the hidden, both in the world and in the

Odilon Redon, *The Day,* **plate 6 from** *Dreams.* **Lithograph, 8¼ × 6⅛ in., 1891.** (*Courtesy of the Museum of Modern Art, New York. Lillie P. Bliss Collection.*)

human person. Being part of the phenomenal world, the image not only draws the senses from beautiful forms to beautiful forms, but also serves as a path through the world, leading the self to a communion with Beauty where all phenomenal forms manifest themselves as one, the origin, the ground, the abyss, the dark unity. Claudel, on the one hand, uses phenomenal images to penetrate to the ground, revealing the existence of an archetypal image; Redon, on the other hand, uses oneiric images since phenomenal forms conceal the archetypal image.

Hence, for Claudel, the Image expresses and represents itself in the world, and yet it exists as symbol behind the manifestation. For this reason, his poetic creation leads to the revelation of the signified, of Beauty itself. By contrast, Redon expresses the beautiful as a trace, as a veil, as dreams, absent as archetypal image and forever unreachable because it is cut off from the signified, the luminous, light itself. Whereas Claudel sees in his mind the beauties of creation because he succeeds in grasping the inner light, beauty's hidden form, the meaning of things within the world as well as through Revelation, Redon sees in his mind art forms, illumined by the light of thought, of dreams, of the imagination, while giving rise to the origin.

7

Claudel and van Gogh: Expressiveness of Beauty and Grace

Mais pourquoi me mettre au service d'un programme? le mouvement tout pur est à ma disposition, le mouvement qui crée le temps et le temps à son tour a créé l'espace. Les clefs reposent entre mes mains qui sont de la mise en marche de tout! (*OE*, 182)[1]

Gauguin et moi avons encore vu un tout petit panneau de lui [Giotto] à Montpellier, la mort d'une bonne sainte femme quelconque. Là les expressions de douleur et d'exstase sont humaines à tel point que tout dix-neuvième siècle qu'on soit, on s'y sent—et croit avoir été là présent—tant on partage l'émotion. (*LB*, 146)[2]

While Claudel acclaims the creative power of both reality and the artist, van Gogh marvels that a work of art expresses and shares emotion. How can an art form be both subjectively felt and objectively expressed? In order to examine this question, I will deal with Claudel's musical aesthetics and van Gogh's art. For Claudel, subjective creativity means to create forms which are in harmony with, in correspondence to, an objective form; for van Gogh, on the other hand, art is a function of a subjective creativity that is in correspondence to human emotion. Claudel's beauty and grace, as we have seen, have both an inward and an outward orientation, a subjective and an objective manifestation, and they are the result of vibration, movement, form, proportion, rhythm, number, intentionality, and harmony. His poetic art expresses the sense of a world that has an orientation beyond itself. Poetic art expresses reality and communicates this reality by virtue of its sonorous images. Similarly, according to Claudel, the whole function of music is to take possession of the phenomenal world, to create musical space, time, and movement, which are analogues of real space, time, and movement.

Par le moyen du son nous devenons directement sensibles à ces réalités qui autrement ne sont appréciables à notre esprit que par un rapport au monde de la dimension: la vitesse, la distance, le haut, le bas, le continu, l'interrompu, le direct, le latéral, le lourd, le léger, le simple, le composé, etc....Nous traduisons, nous créons de l'espace avec de la durée et du physique avec de l'immatériel. (*OE*, 171)[3]

Unlike Claudel, who hears the fundamental harmony of beauty and grace in the world, which, in turn, resonates within himself as an artist, van Gogh speaks of the beauty of forms that are beautiful because of the aesthetically imposed emotive dimension. Unlike Claudel, who considers body in harmony with the soul, van Gogh must distort the outer person for the sake of the inner person, the world of the senses and reason for the world of conscience and emotion. What concerns van Gogh is that the beautiful and the good are illusion, emptiness, and that despite this knowledge, humanity still allows itself to be deceived by the charm that the outside world casts over the senses, "as one knows nothing, and above all the difference between the objective and the subjective" (*LB*, 80). Artists, says van Gogh, choose the form and the meaning they wish to give to their feelings, and they create only with reference to them. The artist's art is indeed expressive of human emotion, but reality is lost to movement where everything seems in a state of flight, of flux, making and unmaking. At the very moment we see and feel the awe of beauty, we find ourselves plunged into a state of chaos, of nothingness, of disillusion, and we are left with a feeling of sorrow, of estrangement, of despair, since beauty and grace lock themselves up in the space, the movement, the rhythm, the colors, the sky, and the earth of human creativity, of the artist's inwardness and subjectivity.

Claudel: Expressiveness of Sonorous Forms

For Claudel, however, the choice does not lie, as van Gogh suggests, between the deception of our senses on the one hand and the absence of the beautiful and the good on the other hand. A definite correspondence exists between the sensuous enjoyment of music and sonorous movements and the "purely intellectual satisfaction that pleased many German musicians" (*OE*, 172). Music, like any other work of art, does not exist primarily for the satisfaction of the mind alone; it is the heart, or the entire being in its sensual, intellectual, and moral aspects to which music must give voice and expression. While the composer is the origin of the work, says Claudel, "he speaks to someone outside of himself" (*OE*, 173). By means of his or her own mind, the composer imposes upon the listener's sentiment

a movement and a rhythm and absorbs the listener into what the
composer's soul longs for, sees and does not see, enjoys and regrets.
In short, the composer makes available to the listener a road to
follow, to affirm, until it reaches perfect clarity; and clarity is delight
because it expresses itself in the form of successive and simultaneous
sounds, or of unity, of melody.

> De la naissance à sa conclusion la mélodie, par une exploitation
> bienheureuse d'elle-même, la voilà successive et simultanée qui s'offre à
> moi dans une évidence ineffable et dans la sécurité au sein de la vocalise
> intransgressible d'une libération par le délice. (*OE*, 173)[4]

Claudel does distinguish between the ecstatic and the rational form
in music. The ecstatic is something meditative, infinite, and
indefinite; the rational is something contained within a continuity, a
plan, precise outlines. Certain works by Bach and Beethoven, for example, have clear meaning and form a definite "ensemble of relationships that I shall call, after a fashion, immediate, intelligible"
(*OE*, 172). On the other hand, the composition of Debussy expresses
"a tactile ensemble" that cannot translate itself into clear-cut
outlines because it overflows in purely emotional tones.

> ...mais la note, déjà, toute pure, cette goutte dans l'instant perceptible
> faite d'ondes agglomérées, comporte par le fait seul de son existence un
> accord virtuel, une interrogation, un appel autour d'elle à l'union, au
> sens, au commentaire, à la contradiction. (*OE*, 174)[5]

Whether "a tactile ensemble" or "an ensemble of intelligible relationships," music arouses pleasure by its sonorous form alone. Like
poetry, music has vocalized breath for its means of expression. But
for Claudel, while the poet constructs and modifies, "in the
workshop of his mouth," the words that spring from the poet's
mind, the composer fixes his attention on that "song alone, con-
ducted by emotion, that he listens to issuing from the depths of his
inner cavity" (*OE*, 173). Composers, like poets, are able to penetrate
the inner person, making possible the experience of various emotive
moods. By a certain action exerted on the modulation of vocalized
outpouring, whether it be the reed of the larynx or of the organ, or
the string, stopped by the finger, vibrating under the rise and fall of
the bow, or of some pipe fitted to the lungs, music affects human beings in accordance with their moods.

> Le sentiment sous la poussée de l'âme se gonfle et se détend, il essore par
> tous les degrés de la gamme jusqu'à l'aigu, il descend à la cave, il

roucoule, il vocifère, il meurtrit, il caresse, il pense; passager, mais inépuisable, il s'écoute jouir au-dessus du temps d'une espèce d'état
bienheureux dont il est lui-même la source. Par le son, le silence nous est
devenu accessible et utilisable. (*OE*, 173)[6]

By the movement of sounds, music creates relationships in time
corresponding to patterns of lived emotion, producing a kind of
blessed state of which time itself is the source, since time moves in
the rhythm of silence, in the stillness of cosmic harmony. The music
of the world is a beautiful symphony that the senses feel and human
reason discerns in the blending of various elements in their physical
and chemical aspects, a movement that is the very basis of every
form of life. It is also the beauty of the stars, the sky, the earth, the
water, the mountain, and of all visible forms; the eye sees their harmonious relationships and the ear listens to the sounds of silence,
which disclose the spiritual world of immutable relationships. These
permanent relationships do not depend on the mental process of the
human person as composer, for they exist in God but are reflected
in the phenomenal world, where they produce sonorous vibrations.
The world, says Claudel, resembles a beautiful painting in which a
particular rose, a certain paradoxical yellow, a certain white, suddenly clashing amid the snarling of greens, violets, and bronzes, sets
ablaze a pyrotechnic display of colors. Or the world resembles a
poem, an ensemble of words which include a movement of sound as
well as thought. The beauty of a poem results, on the one hand, from
images that are indispensable to poetic art, and on the other hand,
from the rhythm and musicality of the verse. But whether in a painting or a poem, the world manifests the fundamental vibratory
movement of our senses and organs, since art is the extension of
nature.

Mais la nature elle-même, elle n'est pas faite pour m'engloutir! C'est moi
le maître! c'est moi qui la fais lever de cette fausse immobilité que moi,
qui en sais plus long que vous, j'appelle simplement "une tenue." C'est
moi qui lui explique qui elle est! elle est mon audience! elle est cette
matière à mes ordres! je passe la revue! c'est moi qui au sein de ce chaos
profère le nom de Dieu! (*OE*, 176)[7]

Being a microcosm, the human person must reflect the musicality
of the universe. There is, according to Claudel, a correspondence
between the movements that govern the outer person and those
which govern the inner person. The body is the most fundamental
natural harmony; the rhythm of the dance that harmonizes the
movements of the body's limbs is the external expression of more

basic harmonies, which are the body's health and life. A sound is given to the body from the outside but is heard from the inside, and when sounds are linked together into sensual melodies they stimulate the vibrations of the body, which are always in tune with themselves. Sound shapes itself in and from the body; it develops and, as a moving form, has its existence in the body.

> Ainsi le son est essentiellement ce qui commence et qui cesse, ce qui décrit d'un terme à l'autre la phase. L'oreille est cet instrument par qui l'homme peut apprécier tous les rythmes et allures de ce mouvement dont il est lui-même animé, se servant comme d'une base continue de son cours propre. Ce train de la vie, il est loisible à l'homme d'en créer l'image sonore; et telle est l'origine de la musique et du langage. (*OP*, 169)[8]

The other harmony in the human person is an inner harmony; it is the harmony of the soul, which, among the sonorous forms, is considered a spiritual composition. In fact, beauty of the soul is simply the proper relationship between sensibility, knowledge, and conscience, which, in turn, correspond to desire, imagination, and intellect. According to Claudel, the deep appeal of the note, or of what he calls the musical word, which consists of an inner formulation of syllables, goes further than our sensibility and our thoughts; through sonorous images we communicate with everything in the world that appears as an image of harmony: "all that proceeds and advances in a certain consciousness and composition of the whole that is called harmony" (*OE*, 171).

The harmony of the body, says Claudel, proceeds from the harmony of the soul, and their harmony proceeds from the body's encounter with reality in the sensation and knowledge of God. Sonorous forms thus remain in existence by virtue of harmony, that is, by the unchanging relationships that unify everything within the number, the whole, the center. In God alone Claudel sees harmony, relationship, and number express unity, the essential rhythm of vibrations that constitute the body, the external form of the human person's interior faculties. By becoming conscious of this correspondence, humanity discovers within itself the objective form of art, architecture, sculpture, poetry, and music. It is this correspondence which gives the arts their unique end; music has for its end flight, a certain state of consciousness modified by sonorous images. Its strings are the senses, which, sustained by the necessity of sounds, of harmony, fly on the wings of rhythm, detached, as it were, from the body, and sucked in by the beautiful that escapes measurement, since it is human beings after the movement of the heart, who count by means of their existence and measure by means of their temperament. Because of this, music "carries us away with her," whether we like it or not: "She takes us by the hand; we become one with her" (*OE*, 176).

If music abducts us, if it tears us away from ourselves, if it makes us desire, plunge, climb, remain still, or move either slow or fast, if it transports us beyond space and time and gladdens our heart to an endless degree, it is because absolute harmony, pure love, the most luminous light, ultimate Beauty, shine through musical pleasure.

> Le nombre, c'est l'amour, un sentiment aigu et tout-puissant de la convenance, l'adhésion sereinement, passionnément, extatiquement libre à un ordre, à une raison, à une justice, à une volonté, à une disposition d'un partenaire inéluctable, le logement de nous-mêmes à l'intérieur d'un chiffre si beau qu'il échappe à la computation, digne objet d'une étude inépuisable. (*OE*, 177)[9]

Every note, every sound, is the discovery deep within ourselves of the very movements of the soul regulated by and ordered to harmony, proportion, and number of human beings as they are born with the world. Human beings, says Claudel, impose movement on things with their left hand, while with their right hand they invite things to change under their bow; it is human beings who, with knowledge and conscience, reveal to things their harmony; it is human beings who discover in the world its "religious anthem." As human beings, we have at our disposal pure movement; we hold the keys that can put everything in motion. There is nothing, not a sound, not a melody outside of us that does not provoke an echo, an answer, a discussion, a controversy within the soul. With no word or allusion by anything drawn from outside, we make use of our body and soul to communicate with ourselves; we make of ourselves something in time that calls, questions, and answers us. We learn to make use of our own intensity and modulation as though they were an instrument. We criticize our souls by means of those external resonances which the soul itself has provoked. With an ear attentive, from beginning to end, to our own accuracy, we end up by singing. By reason of our existence and in accordance with all the rapid and violent modes that we invent, we attain exquisite harmony outside of the self, separating the self from the harmony and joining it again, following it and pulling it after us. And if harmony is refused us, the distance by means of which we can measure the self with it is no less indispensable to us.

> Je n'ai pas besoin de moins pour accueillir le prodigieux message autour de moi que je pressens que de ces ouïes à deux battants de l'orchestre! Ce n'est pas à ma seule vocifération que j'ai à pourvoir, c'est la Titane

tout entière, c'est la Création tout entière que j'ai à accoucher de son langage virtuel et de ce moment à la fin qui lui est intimé de s'expliquer avec Son Créateur! (*OE*, 183)[10]

This is exactly what great composers do; they recognize modulation in creation and in themselves and express it in sonorous images, unifying the whole visible world in an ineffable concord by the word and grace of the Creator. "Nothing is too much for me, for this wise attack that I am meditating in the most hidden depths of your personality, for this biting into your sensibility" (*OE*, 184). From the lightest touch of a breath to the knife-thrust, music must lead to ecstatic pleasure, to rapture that belongs to spiritual joy. On the one side, there are those who abandon themselves to their subjective sentiment without knowing the modulation, rhythm, movement, proportion, number, and harmony of creation; on the other are those who compose according to "the sacred measure," keeping in mind objective sonorous forms. The former feel the world without understanding its intentionality or meaning; the latter sense, know, and express the world in such a way that their artistic creation is not only a symbol of a certain state of their sensitivities but also the evaluation of the effort they must make in order to produce themselves in it, to be born with it, to realize themselves in it.

Il y a un certain thème à mon art proposé et imposé pour la résolution de quoi m'est nécessaire le concours de cet oracle intérieur au fond de moi que j'ai à éveiller au sentiment de ses responsabilités. (*OE*, 183)[11]

Art, which makes use of nature in order to exist, is not a human skill, but is a divine allotment furnished by the oracle, the muse, who inspires the artist to compose beautiful harmonies by which he or she becomes Bacchic and possessed. But this intoxication, this rapture, this ecstasy of the artist is for Claudel the supreme surge of the Alleluia and the Amen; it is the liturgy that the choir of angels spreads over creation; it is the glory of God that seeks and takes root in the anointed artist's thoughts awakened by the divine sensation of grace; it is God himself, at peace with his creation, his work, who has put harmony into the ears and the heart of the artist. Everything is in motion, and the dazzled eye finds no spot large enough to rest on it; it is swept along by this beautiful light of songs that creation sings to the Creator: it is that vast and limitless variety where everything smells good together; it is the eternal earth under the eye of God. It is the various combinations of blue, yellow, red, green, and violet that do not stop at or define any particular form; rather, in a ceaseless dance, they elevate the form to a higher beauty. It is the interior of the world on the march toward its reunion with God when the outside has given way to grace; it is the faith to adore the world, this world that God places at our disposal to draw on, to transform it into word and song, and to fill all the spaces with the notes of the divine melody.

> La flûte au-devant de lui trace un sentier lumineux. Les cymbales d'elles-mêmes éclatent à ses deux poings, et non pas la lyre païenne, mais la grande harpe décacorde faite des rayons mêmes de la Grâce et da la Gloire divine vient se placer entre ses bras pour la double activité inverse de ses doigts agiles et retentissants. (*OE*, 188)[12]

If indeed the "sacred measure" furnishes the artist with the means for stopping time, for transforming its flow, its passage, in a permanent harmony forever at the artist's disposal, then it is no longer a question of sonorous images brought into a cogent harmonic rhythmic unity, it is a question of testimony, of life itself. Music gives off an attraction; it makes an appeal, beyond logic, to the vast resources of our sensibility, our memory, and our desires; it solidifies in a sound, a note, a chord, a melody, a harmony, the continuously assembling and dissolving process of life itself. Through music, a life is given composition; it is our concrete existence joyfully born out of the flux and flow of time that makes available to us the sense for God, a sense that makes us see, however faintly, that the phenomenal world and our inner world correspond not according to the created melodies of the composer, but according to "the divine Glory" of the Creator. The harmony of creation, of which music is the image, tells us that our life and that of the world are headed in his direction following the flight of our heart and mind.

> Cette touche sonore est l'avant-goût et le gage d'un commerce prolongé et détaillé qui, désormais, apparaît réalisable à la condition que notre vacarme intérieur *n'empêche pas la musique*. Il y a donc dans la sonorité divine, au fond de nous, à la fois imprégnation de notre intelligence et ébranlement de notre volonté. (*PP*, 72)[13]

This "sonorous touch" is nothing but silence, which music makes available for us; it is "the sacred measure" that God imprints upon the world; it is grace and divine glory within ourselves; it is our destiny, a destiny that takes us on a journey to communion with God's splendor in things. It is the murmuring day and night that never ceases to sound in our ears the Creator's harmony; it is the continual emanation of the desire that we have for wanting to feel him and of the countless things we want to say to him and to ask of him. "It is the consecration of our breath that we dedicate to Him, and the sacrifice of the soul that has replaced the bloody sacrifice of animals, the offering of incense, of oil and of fine flour" (*OE*, 187). It is our deliverance from captivity in sin; we, too, have crossed the Red Sea with dry feet. We, too, have crossed the desert and gathered up the manna; we, too, have been promised to enter into the Promised Land; we, too, were inside his work from the beginning of creation alongside the sacrificed Word. And this long journey, says Claudel, has brought us to the foot of the cross where we never cease to hear the Son of God asking his Father why he has abandoned him. What was only silence in creation now becomes a living mystery, a beating life, a celebration of joy, a praising of the beauty and goodness of creation, and then the composer assumes the power of a creator. For the composer not only proposes, but composes; the composer opens, directs, stirs, and measures the heart's desires destined to carry us across and beyond space and time. And if the composer looks at this world at the mercy of time and listens to Christ's words on the cross, the composer cannot fail to feel the love of the Spirit, which fills him or her with joy in singing the same melody which declares "the immense octave of Creation," "the clear dialogue" of God's beauty and grace on earth and in human beings.

> Ah, je suis ivre! ah, je suis livré au dieu! j'entends une
> voix en moi et la mesure qui s'accélère, le mouvement
> de la joie...
> Que m'importent tous les hommes à présent! Ce n'est
> pas pour eux que je suis fait, mais pour le
> Transport de cette mesure sacrée!...
> Que m'importe aucun d'eux? Ce rythme seul! Qu'ils
> me suivent ou non? Que m'importe qu'ils m'entendent
> ou pas?
>
> (*CGO*, 74–75)[14]

Van Gogh: Expressiveness in Art

The feeling of joy that Claudel experiences in sonorous forms is both outside his body (objective) and inside himself (subjective). For Claudel, moods and emotions are subjective for the person who feels them but objective in that they are properties of the phenomenal world, the world of music. Differences in sounds are experienced as differences of movement and intentionality, of modulation and rhythm, of proportion and continuity, of low and high. Musical movement, which is objective, possesses properties similar to those of bodily movements, which are subjective. The human body, like music, is also a composition, an expression resulting from concerted means: the eyes, the nose, the ears, the mouth, the hands, the limbs, are the gateway to the soul, a moment of our natural disposition to be born with the world.

This correspondence does not coincide with the expressionism of van Gogh's art. In fact, he does not subscribe to Claudel's "theology of vision," which presupposes a relationship between art and reality, form and beauty, subjective creativity and the authenticity of beauty from without. Van Gogh does not believe that there is discernible movement in the world that the artist needs only to transcribe into a work of art. On the contrary, van Gogh considers art as a movement that is exclusively subjective and separated from the world, which is itself separated from goodness and truth. To express a beautiful reality, van Gogh creates a world of colors mirroring human sentiment.

> Absolute black does not really exist. But like white, it is present in almost every colour, and forms the endless variety of greys, — different in tone and strength. So that in nature one really sees nothing else but those tones or shades.... The colourist is he who seeing a colour in nature knows at once how to analyse it, and can say for instance: that green-grey is yellow with black and blue, etc.... Feeling and love for nature sooner or later find a response from people who are interested in art. It is the painter's duty to be entirely absorbed by nature and to use all his intelligence to express sentiment in his work, so that it becomes intelligible to other people. (LG, 158–60)

The object of painting is to express sentiment, which manifests itself first and before nature. It is through absorption in the world of nature as feeling that the artist creates beautiful forms with which to penetrate the hearts and touch the emotions of people. According to van Gogh, to feel nature the artist must know its color tones, which exist in infinitely varied shades of the three fundamental colors, red, yellow, blue, and their combinations. Thus, if the artist is to express the sentiment of the world, it is necessary to do so by means of color tones. Color tones excite our admiration in many ways. Some we find beautiful because of the ardent passions they seem to convey, others because of their neutrality; the beauty of a pink apple blossom is not that of "yellow leaves against violet tones." Some colors, such as blue, for example, please because they are familiar; others please because they are seldom seen. Some attract by virtue of their softness, their well-balanced harmony: "But this I know, that I was struck by the harmony of green, red, black, yellow, blue, brown, grey" (LG, 166); others are striking by their dissonance, by their illogical flow, by the intoxicating richness of their oneiric quality. Sometimes we like to see many colors absorbed into one or two; at others it is the many emerging from one or two that is pleasing. Familiar colors may appeal, colors that are natural and appropriate to the world; yet the startling, the unknown, the arbitrary colors of the canvas also have their appeal. Indeed, the arbitrary colors, the colors created by the artist, are more beautiful than the exact imitation of nature. To express one thing and let the world belong to it and proceed from it is the joy of painting.

> Always and intelligently to make use of the beautiful tones which the colours form of their own accord, when one breaks them on the palette, I repeat — to start from one's palette, from one's knowledge of colour-harmony, is quite different from following nature mechanically and obsequiously. Here is another example: suppose I have to paint an autumn landscape, trees with yellow leaves. All right — when I conceive it as a symphony in yellow, what does it matter whether the fundamental colour of yellow is the same as that of the leaves or not? It matters *very little*. (*LG*, 241)

Colors attract attention by their very nature, and everything depends on the artist's perception of the infinite variety of tones that he or she must be able to mix on the palette in order to touch the human heart. The mixing of colors must be done in such a way that it does not reproduce an exact imitation of nature but a harmony in and of itself.

> I retain from nature a certain sequence and a certain correctness in placing the tones, I study nature, so as not to do foolish things, to remain reasonable — however, I don't mind so much whether my colour corresponds exactly, as long as it looks beautiful on my canvas, as beautiful as it looks in nature. (*LG*, 241)

The beauty of van Gogh's colors therefore do flow from a certain correctness or harmony or sequence, as is found in nature. Thus, beauty is not simply a matter of pure colors, of imaginative perception, nor is it solely the object of pure sentiment. It springs from the total attitude of van Gogh, the artist, from his being faithful to color tones while creating his own colors, his own harmonious form, thereby arousing pleasure or sentiment. In other words, color offers a semiotic equivalent of the emotion that the phenomenal form gives rise to, but the phenomenal form as it appears matters little, since art is a form of language without need for the conventional use of signs.

> I see that nature has told me something, has spoken to me, and that I have put it down in shorthand. In my shorthand there may be words that cannot be deciphered, there may be mistakes or gaps, but there is something in it of what wood or shore or figure has told me, and it is not a tame

or conventional language, proceeding less from nature itself than from a studied manner or a system. (*LG*, 167)

Van Gogh's art thus is a shorthand language which reveals what cannot be expressed in conventional ways. Art is a vision that expresses what nature has said to the artist. For this reason, artists must not depart from nature; they must guard against painting exclusively from the imagination because, says van Gogh, while it is true that the imagination alone brings artists to the creation of the beautiful forms that reality shows them nevertheless, to paint only from the imagination does not give clear and solid expression to the expressive aspect of nature. Art gives form to sentiment — "I want to make drawings that *touch* some people" (*LG*, 155) — and its language is neither the subject represented, nor reality as it merely appears; it is the pictorial expression of van Gogh's awareness of the permanent and changeable aspects of nature and life.

> What a mystery life is, and love is a mystery within a mystery. It certainly never remains the same in a literal sense, but the changes are like the ebb and flow of the tide and leave the sea unchanged. (*LG*, 182)

In other words, art is expressive of the mystery of and beyond the changeable, and it expresses this mystery by means of colors, lines, brush strokes, surfaces, and space, which must give the viewer a glimpse of life seen, felt, and understood from the profound sorrow of a disillusioned existence. Insofar as artists create from nature, they bring the natural order into being. Since they read nature's shorthand language, they cause it to speak like a beautiful harmony, endowing each thing with the means to achieve its own feeling while collaborating in the language of nature as a whole.

> Either in figure or in landscape I should wish to express, not sentimental melancholy, but serious sorrow. In short, I want to reach so far that people will say of my work: he feels deeply, he feels tenderly — notwithstanding my so-called roughness, perhaps even because of this. (*LG*, 156)

Sorrow is given full expression in van Gogh's art, but it is the sorrow that abandons itself totally to the joy of the creative spirit; all that is changeable, varied, and innumerable in nature dissolves into the mystery, the peace, the melody of the artist; in the artist, according to van Gogh, sorrow and tranquillity achieve a beautiful harmony.

Vincent van Gogh, *Pietà*. Oil, 28¾ × 23¾ in., 1889. (*Courtesy of Vincent van Gogh Foundation/National Museum Vincent van Gogh, Amsterdam.*)

It is true that I am often in the greatest misery, but still there is within me a calm pure harmony and music. In the poorest huts, in the dirtiest corner, I see drawings and pictures. And with irresistible force my mind is drawn towards these things. (*LG*, 156)

Far from denying calm, serenity, and harmony, van Gogh's sorrow celebrates, beyond time and space, a truly sacred communion between the human person and the world of nature, between human beings and their own feelings, between nothingness and creation. The form of sorrow in which pure harmony and music may be infinitely reflected embodies the laws of colors; to each color tone corresponds a sentiment that exists in harmony with all other passions. Of the *Night Café*, van Gogh writes:

I have tried to express the terrible passions of humanity by means of red and green. The room is blood red and dark yellow with a green billiard table in the middle; there are four lemon-yellow lamps with a glow of orange and green. Everywhere there is a clash and contrast of the most alien reds and greens, in the figures of little sleeping hooligans, in the empty dreary room, in violet and blue. (*LG*, 288–89)

Life, with the terrible passions of humanity, is without form, and it is art that gives it a design and a content—the design of the artist and the content of passion, blood, dreariness, and suffering. Through the consideration of nature, artistis form a vision of what they want to express through their paintings. The paintings, however, must correspond to the contrast and clashes of passions, which are expressed by color tones. Blue against orange, red against green, and yellow against violet are sentiments of loneliness, fear, cruelty, longing, and despair. Such color patterns do not simply parallel the world of sentiment, are not merely an example of pathetic fallacy; rather, they express the whole of nature in its creative joyful being, as well as in its sorrowful form, in its fleeting aspect. To the transitory nature of life corresponds the calm, the pure harmony, the mystery of created forms.

Mysteries remain, sorrow or melancholy remains, but that everlasting negative is balanced by the positive work which is thus achieved after all....Right and wrong do not stand separate, any more than black and white do in nature.(*LG*, 196)

The artist, says van Gogh, must delight in the world of nature, grasping there, in its colors, the beautiful as well as the ugly. If the splendid yellow of the sun, the pale orange of a sunset, the blue of the sky,

Vincent van Gogh, *The Night Café.* **Oil on canvas, 28½ × 36¼ in., 1888.** (*Courtesy of Yale University Art Gallery. Bequest of Stephen Carlton Clark, B. A. 1903.*)

and the green of the olive trees create a feeling of calm and tranquillity, they echo a grief that is hardly human as they gradually sink
almost to black in tone. "Then I understood, and I tried to express
something voluptuous and at the same time grievously afflicted"
(*LG*, 249). Whether colors grow heavier or lighter, van Gogh's art
expresses a feeling of affliction, of estrangement, of serious sorrow,
of despair. The sky, the stars, the landscapes, the figures, the objects,
and the whole visible reality are transformed away from as well as
toward the form of the beautiful and of the good under the creative
power of the artist.

"When I was. . . in the surroundings of pictures and objects of art,
you know how I then had a violent passion for them, that reached
the high pitch of enthusiasm" (*LG*, 118). Such an enthusiasm,
however, clashes with the reality of the artist: to suffer because the
times do not favor the artist. Suffering is nothing else than an invisible power, a desire, which gives the artist the semblance of life; and
this life embraces all things as it moves to realize its end. "I would
not set any value on life, if there were not something infinite,
something deep, something real" (*LG*, 138). The artist's search for
this infinite, this something deep and real, leads along the path of
darkness, humiliation, anguish, and separation from the world. Van
Gogh's search for self-expression leads him along the road of sentiment as opposed to that of reason and conscience. "For indeed it is
impossible always to know what is good and what it bad, what is
moral and what is immoral" (*LG*, 134). The artist who wishes to
know whether a form is beautiful and good needs only to consult
personal sentiment; the only things that the artist must be concerned
with are the contrasts and clashes of colors that express the artist's
desire to grasp the sublime, the mysterious, the infinite. For, as van
Gogh believes, if the soul is not distinct from its faculties, then to
know is to imagine, to imagine is to feel, and to feel is to enjoy, to
experience delight. The beautiful is delightful because it carries us to
the realm of the divine, which is the world of abstraction, of created
forms, which alone give a feeling of something eternal, something
real: a glimpse of pain and ecstasy, of mortality and immortality, of
life and death. If indeed we are in the presence of created forms
whose structure is in nature, and if the color tones of these forms
through the creative power of the artist express the beautiful, it is obvious that the phenomenal world is beautiful insofar as it embodies
the laws of passions, the fluidity of existence. Van Gogh, the artist,
the poet, creates in order to express the most beautiful images or the
most fitting tones, and not in order to achieve clarification and truth
about reality; he creates precisely because reality cannot be com-

municated by a system of logic, words, or an objective form. "For poetry is so deep and intangible that one cannot define everything systematically.... I think that sentiment [is] worth so much more than definitions and criticism" (*LG*, 134).

Thus, we do not admire van Gogh's art for its precision and clarity, but for its strictly subjective expression of beauty. It attracts our attention by the fact that it translates different moods into visual terms: by nature it presupposes sentiment. His art fixes the relation between sentiment and subject, color and nature, the visible and the invisible, the changeable and the permanent, in such a way that we find ourselves simultaneously under the joy and the burden of life. The enthusiastic impulse, the calm, the pure harmony and music that exist in his art are used by him to express all the more clearly the serious sorrow of existence, on the one hand, and human creativity, artistic creation, on the other hand. We see something—for example, the sower, the olive trees—taking note of the fact that what makes them visible as real things is a differentiated play of greens, browns, blues, and yellows in various textures and shapes. The visible world seems to forget its real existence, its aesthetic measure, but this, says van Gogh, is exactly what the colorist captures. The colorist expresses the visible in such a way that we cannot help notice the deep relationships that define it. Indeed, insofar as the artist creates sensuous forms from the various combinations of colors, lines, and brush strokes, we are placed in a new relationship to the artist and his or her world. Hence, art expresses the artist's personal relation to the world. As personal and collective existence take on a new form, so does our understanding of art and its creators. However, concludes van Gogh, the only thing that we really know is that artists live a real life and that they must go on painting as long as "one has breath" (*LB*, 112).

In an art conceived as the very breath of life, the visible world, reduced to clashes and contrast of colors, disappears, and what remains are plastic elements in a pure state. Colors and sentiment, says van Gogh, serve to distinguish content from form, unify the fine arts at their source, bridge science and art, and embrace the laws of nature.

La science—le raisonnement scientifique—me paraît être un instrument qui ira bien loin dans la suite. Car voici: on a supposé la terre plate. C'était vrai; elle l'est encore aujourd'hui.... Seulement n'empêche que la science prouve que la terre est surtout ronde. Ce qu'actuellement personne ne conteste.... Des générations futures, il est probable, nous éclairciront sur ce sujet si intéressant; et alors la Science elle-même pourrait— ne lui déplaise—arriver à des conclusions plus ou moins parallèles aux

Vincent van Gogh, *The Sower.* **Oil, 13 × 16 in., 1888.** (*Courtesy of Vincent van Gogh Foundation/National Museum of Vincent van Gogh, Amsterdam.*)

dictions du Christ, relatives à l'autre moitié de l'existence. (*LB*, 111–12)[15]

Accordingly, what appears illogical, incongruous, unsystematic, and untenable, if viewed from the other half of our existence or from the other side of death, will prove to be a harmony, a beauty, which is the world of artistic expression. Creativity begins when the artist, like Christ, stands free above good and evil, reason and conscience, and can be both master and servant of humanity. The master, because he makes the visible subservient to his higher end, the world of created forms; the servant, because he must give shape to his sentiments and must express them through colors in order that they may be understood by others. "But, I repeat, this Christ is more of an artist than the artists themselves; He works on the spirit and on live flesh; He creates men rather than statues" (*LB*, 117). Like Christ, van Gogh sacrifices himself, nourishing the spirit of subjective creativity with his own flesh and blood, silently accepting suffering, humiliation, and defeat. This sacrifice constitutes the very joy of his art: the joy born, like grace, from love, from the desire to see, hear, touch, smell, and taste the real substance of life in its movements, rhythms, and symphonies of colors and passions, the very expressions of nature's way.

Spring is tender, green young corn and pink apple blossoms. Autumn is the contrast of the yellow leaves against violet tones. Winter is the snow with black silhouettes. But now, if summer is the opposition of blues against an element of orange, in the gold bronze of the corn, one could paint a picture which expressed the mood of the seasons in each of the contrasts of the complementary colours (red and green, blue and orange, yellow and violet, white and black). (*LG*, 218)

Van Gogh's colors express moods, life itself, a life that escapes logical categories. Reds and greens, blues and oranges, yellows and violets, black and white, express not only the immutable law that everything changes but also convey as colored form of beauty and grace. Writing to Emile Bernard, van Gogh states:

Ah! il est sans doute sage, juste, d'être ému par la Bible; mais la réalité moderne a tellement prise sur nous que même en cherchant abstraitement à reconstruire les jours anciens dans notre pensée, les petits événements de notre vie nous arrachent à ce même moment à ces méditations, et nos aventures propres nous rejettent de force dans les sensations personnelles—joie, ennui, souffrance, colère ou sourire. (*LB*, 148)[16]

Conclusion: Expression in Music and Art

Both Claudel and van Gogh affirm the desire of the artist to grasp underneath the changeable reality something hidden, something infinite, something spiritual. Both see the beautiful in the movements, vibrations, rhythms, sounds, and colors of the physical world. Both experience the joy of creativity born from a life filled with darkness or sacrifice, and both extend artistic beauty to the world of rapture, of delight, of voluptuousness.

However similar Claudel and van Gogh seem, their difference is as deep as the abyss, the mysterious, the source, that they wish to make real or visible. Claudel's approach to the expression of beauty and grace emphasizes objective form without the elimination of the subjective measure or creativity; van Gogh, on the other hand, embraces subjective creativity as his norm for expression without totally eliminating the real or phenomenal measure, but rather by distorting it. For Claudel, sonorous images are placed in a state of correspondence between the artist's desire to create and translate space with time, the visible with the invisible, and the body with the soul, on the one hand, and the beauty and grace of things through God's word in the body of Christ, on the other hand. Music, says Claudel, absorbs human beings into the movements, the rhythms of nature from which they discover new melodies, new arrangements of sounds already in existence. Thus, for Claudel, music utilizes phenomenal forms to discover the harmony of things, God's glory in the world of senses, of reason, and of conscience.

In contrast to Claudel, the distinctive aspect of van Gogh's art is the aesthetic act itself: namely, the expression of nature's way through art. Nature is thus what artists see, grasp, and express, and what they express is communicable only in virtue of its color tones. In order for artists to express the beautiful, they must color its form so that it finds its source in the world of nature, of sentiment. Nature, says van Gogh, needs to be given form, it needs an art that transcribes it into an expressive movement meaningful to observers in accordance with their moods, since in nature one cannot yet find goodness, intentionality, and truth. Art thus expresses estrangement, serious sorrow, affliction, the despair and joy of the world in pure forms and colors. The visible world vanishes within the world of subjective creativity.

Music and art express the form of beauty and grace, the power of the artist to set things in motion. Just as the composer works in sound and form, so the artist works in color and form. But whereas for Claudel sound and form speak of a divine harmony, of God's splendor in the world, for van Gogh color and form clash with phenomenal forms; his art expresses the height of subjective creativity and the depth of a bleak existence.

Conclusion

My comparisons of Claudel with Proust, Merleau-Ponty, Weil, Gide, Sartre, Redon, and van Gogh have disclosed the subjective element in Claudel's aesthetics yet have also unveiled its objective measure. Grounding beauty and grace in the phenomenal world, the world of the senses, of bodies, Claudel has overcome that subjectivity which threatens to annihilate the beauty of the world by reducing it to a dream, an appearance, a nothingness; yet he has remained faithful to phenomenology without removing "the sacred measure" from the phenomenal world. According to Claudel, the human person is in-the-world, and nothing can be sensed, perceived, and known without the world. In this sense he comes close to Merleau-Ponty and Sartre. But unlike Sartre, who makes the human person absolute, and unlike Merleau-Ponty, who excludes God from his phenomenology of perception, Claudel sees God as the source of existence, and he makes "*connaissance*" the very path to the invisible, the eternal.

His sense of beauty and grace is no invitation to Proust's world of immaterial equivalents, or to Gide's symbolic mysticism, or to Weil's mysticism of contradiction, or to Redon's world of pure images, or to van Gogh's expressive form of colors. Rather, Claudel invites the human person to sense beauty and grace in the sonorous images, the vibrations, the colors, and the poetry of the universe. In a way, Claudel makes of the phenomenal world a "breaking of noon" in that it is "the liturgical drama" of all things as they pass from the abyss of darkness to the grace or light of God's abyss, from nothingness to being, from myth to Revelation. The world issues meaning by which human persons experience their humanity and their divinity, their sufferings and their redemption, their darkness in sin and their splendor in God's gift of grace through the hidden form shining in things, and through Christ's sacramental form in the Eucharist.

For Claudel, God is light, and because he is light, he is hidden beauty. Insofar as creation is luminous, it is also divine. The world is divine because it unfolds God's hidden form. For this reason Claudel concedes that "the sensation of the divine" is experienced in the soul, and the soul is beautiful because it is an image of the Word. The soul, then, is not only the form of sensual, moral, and intellectual faculties, but also the very movement, the very intentionality, the very life principle of things. And creation is constituted as such that its materiality is timeless and its existence is forever in the possibility of being-born-with. Although corruptible, creation never moves toward a total nothingness, since in the light of the ground, of the abyss, nothingness cannot be the end of things. Rather, nothingness is the means by which the light irradiates the bodies with eternal light, which is "the bosom" of the Trinity. Seeing this light results in a feeling of pleasure because the senses, reason, and conscience are in harmony with divine wisdom or grace. Grace is the word of God made flesh and speaking to the soul; it is the luminous light of the Trinity in the soul revealed in the beauty of forms, in the splendor of creation.

Claudel further believes all that is not grace is darkness, night. The light of grace transforms the night of the day (phenomenal world) into a luminous darkness, the world of faith. The splendor that is God shines in the darkness or nothingness of the world: to see it one must open first the bodily senses and then the spiritual senses, the senses of the heart and soul. The spiritual senses make one see, hear, touch, taste, and smell the sense of Christ's form in the world. By his Incarnation, Death, and Resurrection, Christ implants in the human being a sense for God. Thus, those who realize the death of Christ realize their own nothingness, their own darkness; they realize that Christ alone is the light of grace which makes them see God's beauty in creation. This sight is made possible for Claudel through the sacramental form, the body and blood of Christ, revealed in the Church. In this way, all phenomenal forms are elevated to the image, the beauty, the grace of the Creator by the witness of the Church, the mediation of the form, the movement of things. It is therefore, according to Claudel, through the contemplation of the material beauty of things that the human person ascends to God, and it is through grace that the human person penetrates the light of beauty.

It is only fitting to close this study with Claudel's own remarks on the stained glass windows of France's cathedrals. His very words make beauty and grace the life-giving rays, the sonorous images, the bright colors, the celestial poem, the "liturgical drama" of the world; they achieve that symphony of order, that transparency of light, that harmony of words, that beauty of grace, that penetrating sound, that purity of form, that sacred measure, that sensory delight which constitute the elements of his aesthetic theory.

Ce temple qui pour quelques précieux moments m'a reçu et dont la Genèse dit qu'il est terrible, c'est Béthel, c'est la maison de Dieu avec l'homme, et cette splendeur innombrable et diverse qui m'entoure, cet espace tout entier fait de piqûres, cette activité silencieuse, en plein jour, comme celle du ciel étoilé, c'est la Grâce, c'est le langage de Dieu avec l'homme, qui, pour se faire entendre ne juge pas convenable de se servir d'autre chose que cette lumière qu'Il est.... Ces panneaux de verre coloré autour de nous, c'est la matière qui sent, c'est la matière abstraite sensible au rayon intellectuel, c'est l'accident miraculeusement isolé de la substance, nous sommes enveloppés par de la sensibilité, combien fine, instable et délicate!... Voici le paradis retrouvé. Nous sommes enveloppés et pénétrés de son murmure latent, de ses ténèbres éclatantes, de son conseil innombrable. (*OE*, 122–23)[1]

Notes

Chapter 1. Claudel and Proust on Beauty

1. The idea of eternity amounts to that of an *enclosure* infrangible in itself. But, all *forms* are deduced from this same idea of an enclosure *closed* on itself, and we have seen that, in this world, nothing can exist without form.

2. ...I could no longer look at Mme Elstir without a feeling of pleasure, and her body began to lose its heaviness, for I filled it with an idea, the idea that she was an immaterial creature, a portrait by Elstir....One feels unmistakably, when one sees side by side ten portraits of different people painted by Elstir, that they are all, first and foremost, Elstirs.

3. All created things acquire, because of the fact that they do not come by themselves, a sense, the general transcription of which is movement, flight. They point to their origin, by straying. Movement...is the first feeling the element has about itself, by not coming *from* itself.

4. In the field of matter, organized or unorganized, this equilibrium is to be found only in the establishment of a combination form or figure. All that which is, strives toward being more completely; that is, toward constructing the idea in which it can take pleasure in its organic differences.

5. The person auditively informed becomes sound, that is, modified by sound, just as, in the alternative of sight, it becomes color, that is, modified by color in its vibratory roots.

6. God being all existence, cannot permit anything else to exist, except as excluded from Him in its own way. Man, this vertical witness, analyzes matter and finds only the purely mathematical fact, movement. Everything *perishes*. The Universe is but a total way of not being that which is. So let sceptics talk on, how great is the security of our knowledge! Indeed, and together with us, the world exists; of course, it exists, since it is that which is not.

7. All passes, and since nothing is present, everything has to be *represented*. I put in an appearance. I constitute. I maintain myself in form and figure. I make myself known. I answer the roll-call.

8. The word is not merely the symbol of a certain state of our sensitivity, it is the evaluation of the effort we have to make in order to produce it, or rather for us to produce ourselves in it.

9. We borrow its [the word's] creative power, that is the force which creates it. We know that it is and we understand what it does.

10. The living being must know itself, that is, know the world which surrounds it and conceive it as an image. But this image is not merely the inert molding of the vacuum that irreducible terms leave behind them....Series of moving bodies expect to be released by it.

11. Once found, the image, in turn, determines our action. In a word, by means of the articulation of its various elements, we must create the figure, the medium according to which we are capable of contacting and knowing.

12. But, whereas, our existence down here is like a barbaric and broken language, our life in God shall be like exquisitely perfect verse. . . . But, in the after-world, we shall be the *poets*, the makers of ourselves.

13. The act by means of which man certifies the permanence of things; by means of which, he formulates the combination of permanent conditions, which, together, give every thing the right of coming into the spirit's focus, independently of second circumstances and causes; by means of which he conceives it in his heart and repeats the order which created it, is called speech. To point out the word, we use three terms: verb, word, noun. The verb expresses the faculty of the speaker; the word, the special movement which is every being's motive, illustrated by the speaker's emotions; the noun. . . the difference owing to which no individual is equivalent to another individual.

14. For a long time to come, we will, undoubtedly, be unable to go any further, to trace sensation back to its source to the distribution board, to this central station where the wave feeding the various peripheric organs receives its first impulse.

15. Thus, conscience is the faculty by virtue of which man knows what he does, consequently, if he acts well or wrongly. Well or wrong, that is according or in opposition to his future or fundamental, real or imaginary ends, according to his fantasy or his duty. Things do not exist alone, they are related by a mutual obligation. . . . His conscience tells him if he has contradicted in any way his purpose and his nature.

16. Just as words are made out of vowels and consonants, our soul, with each breath, draws, from God, sonority in all its plenitude. To come to life would thus be, for our soul, to know, to be fully conscious.

17. We shall then see, as the number expresses unity, the essential rhythm of this movement which constitutes my soul, this measure which is myself; we shall not only see it, we shall be it, we shall produce ourselves in the perfection of freedom and vision and in the purity of perfect love.

18. In the bitterness of mortal life, the most poignant ecstasy revealed to our nature is the one accompanying the creation of a soul, through the coupling of two bodies. Alas, it is but the humiliated image of the substantial embrace, in which, learning its name and the intention it satisfies, the soul shall utter and make itself known; it shall, in succession, aspire and expire itself. Oh, continuation of our heart! oh, incommunicable word! oh, action in the future Paradise! All carnal possession is incomplete in its span and its duration and how despicable its rapture, compared with the undescribable beatitude of those nuptials! Oh, God, Thou feedest us with the bread of tears; and givest us to drink in great measure.

19. Then, Time shall be closed on us, and the Present shall be its eternal center. The time once established, hark, the choir bursts out singing! What can be better done than that which is accomplished? . . . What can be more ended than that which cannot be ended any more? . . . Just as the day, never the same, repeats the day, and the year repeats the year, just as the screw of stars tightens or loosens, at regular intervals, and just as the children of Night widen or narrow the reel, like the motion of lips. . . so shall our occupation, in eternity, consist in the accomplishment of our part toward the perpetration of the Office, the maintaining of our equilibrium, always new in the immense contact with all our brothers, the raising of our voice in the unvoiceable lamentation of Love!

20. Sometimes, too, as Eve was created from a rib of Adam, a woman would be born during my sleep. . . . Conceived from the pleasure I was on the point of consummating, she it was, I imagined, who offered me that pleasure. My body, conscious that its own warmth was permeating hers, would strive to become one with her, and I would awake.

21. Perhaps it is nothingness which is real, and all our dream is non-existent, but then we feel that these phrases of music, these conceptions which exist in relation to our dream, must be nothing either. We shall perish, but we have as hostages these divine captives who will follow our fate. And death in their company is somewhat less bitter, less inglorious, perhaps even less probable.

22. But as soon as I had finished reading the letter, I thought of it, it became an object of reverie, it too became *cosa mentale*, and I love it so much already that every few minutes I had to re-read it and kiss it. Then at last I was conscious of my happiness.

23. I never ceased to believe that they corresponded to a reality independent of myself, and they made me conscious of as glorious a hope as could have been cherished by a Christian in the primitive age of faith on the eve of his entry into Paradise....And for all that the motive force of my exaltation was a longing for aesthetic enjoyments,....

24. In a work such as Vinteuil's sonata the beauties that one discovers soonest are also those of which one tires most quickly, and for the same reason, no doubt — namely, that they are less different from what one already knows. But when those first impressions have receded, there remains for our enjoyment some passage whose structure, too new and strange to offer anything but confusion to our mind, had made it indistinguishable and so preserved intact; and this, which we had passed every day without knowing it, which had held itself in reserve for us, which by the sheer power of its beauty had become invisible and remained unknown, this comes to us last of all. But we shall also relinquish it last. And we shall love it longer than the rest because we have taken longer to get to love it.

25. What such an ideal inspired in Elstir was indeed a cult so solemn, so exacting, that it never allowed him to be satisfied with what he had achieved; it was the most intimate part of himself; and so he had never been able to look at it with detachment, to extract emotion from it, until the day when he encountered it, realised outside himself, in the body of a woman...who had in due course become Mme Elstir and in whom he had been able (as is possible only with something that is not oneself) to find it meritorious, moving, divine. How restful, moreover, to be able to place his lips upon that ideal Beauty which hitherto he had been obliged so laboriously to extract from within himself, and which now, mysteriously incarnate, offered itself to him in a series of communions, filled with saving grace.

26. Since my first sight of Albertine I had thought about her endlessly, I had carried on with what I called by her name an interminable inner dialogue in which I made her question and answer, think and act, and in the infinite series of imaginary Albertines who followed one after the other in my fancy hour by hour, the real Albertine...appears, out of a long series of performances, only in the few first.

27. My eyes aligned upon her skin; and my lips, at a pinch, might have believed that they had followed my eyes. But it was not only to her body that I should have liked to attain; it was also the person that lived inside it, and with which there is but one form of contact, namely to attract its attention, but one sort of penetration, to awaken an idea in it.

28. That Albertine was scarcely more than a silhouette, all that had been superimposed upon her being of my own invention, to such an extent when we love does the contribution that we ourselves make outweigh — even in terms of quantity alone — those that come to us from the beloved object. And this is true of loves that have been realized in actuality.

29. I felt perfectly happy, for, with the help of all the sketches and studies that surrounded me, I foresaw the possibility of raising myself to a poetical understanding, rich in delights, of manifold forms which I had not hitherto isolated from the total spectacle of reality.

30. If it is true that the sea was once upon a time our native element, in which we must plunge our blood to recover our strength, it is the same with the oblivion, the mental nothingness of sleep; we seem then to absent ourselves for a few hours from time, but the forces which have gathered in that interval without being expended measure it by their quantity as accurately as the pendulum of the clock or the crumbling hillocks of the hour-glass. Moreover, one does not emerge more easily from such a sleep than from a prolonged spell of wakefulness, so strongly does everything tend to persist; and if it is true that certain narcotics make us sleep, to have slept for a long time is an even more potent narcotic, after which we have great difficulty in making ourselves wake up.

31. When he [Swann] had sat for a long time gazing at the Botticelli, he would think of his own living Botticelli, who seemed even lovelier still, and as he drew towards him the photograph of Zipporah he would imagine that he was holding Odette against his heart.

32. He [Swann] no longer based his estimate of the merit of Odette's face on the doubtful quality of her cheeks and the purely fleshy softness which he supposed would greet his lips there should he ever hazard a kiss, but regarded it rather as a skein of beautiful, delicate lines which his eyes unravelled, following their curves and convolutions, relating the rhythm of the neck to the effusion of the hair and the droop of the eyelids, as though in a portrait of her in which her type was made clearly intelligible.

33. I put down the cup and examine my own mind. It alone can discover the truth. But how? What an abyss of uncertainty, whenever the mind feels overtaken by itself; when it, the seeker, is at the same time the dark region through which it must go seeking and where all its equipment will avail it nothing. To seek? More than that: to create. It is face to face with something which does not yet exist, to which it alone can give reality and substance which it alone can bring into the light of day.

Chapter 2. Claudel and Merleau-Ponty on Perception

1. Sight does not result from an image represented on our brain, but from a real contact with the object touched and circumscribed by our eyes....

2. It is through my relation to "things" that I know myself; inner perception follows afterwards, and would not be possible had I not already made contact with my doubt in its very object.

3. You must create. You must accomplish in Time that which is deep within you. I bear witness in these words which are incapable of passing. Between Time and Cause, is it not Christ's Heart which becomes for us the interpreter of Eternity and the instrument of our resurrection, the ceaselessly renewed in an instant?

4. Eternity is the time that belongs to dreaming, and the dream refers back to waking life, from which it borrows all its structures. Of what nature, then, is that waking time in which eternity takes root? It is the field of presence in the wide sense, with its double horizon or primary past and future, and the infinite openness of those fields of presence that have slid by, or are still possible.

5. God is always in the present, and it is in the present that He is present to all things. In being in this present in Him all things take their beginning and end. He is...the compass and the circle....

6. I am, just like the sun, a source of light and energy. And the light wave, in its expansion, does not meet any inert bodies, but, everywhere, more or less compact

or complicated power systems in operation. It is compelled to take this obstacle into account, to modify its rhythm and attraction accordingly. This reaction, this ignition of the object due to the solar shock is what we call color.... Color is the herald of flame. Let us take a circle having the source of light as its center.

7. The call to the outside is made by way of the organ in agreement with all that constitutes the individual. This organ is our eye; the eye, in the name of our body and the whole person, is called and placed in charge of the task of seeing. God calls us from the outside, from the immense work which surrounds Him, and man has answered that call... by way of this double receptive sun he communes with all that is outside the light.

8. Thus the light, together with all exterior things it brings and manifests, has been given to man so that he may learn to see, to show where he is, to lead him from possibility to actuality, to realize deep within himself all those possibilities of differentiation that are the expression of his person, and so that he may learn to move this essential difference over the things that surround him as an instrument of knowledge (*co-naissance*).

9. Consequently, the principle of its existence and form is also the instrument of its knowledge. The knowledge of man can be defined as a conscious birth, *qualified by the thing which limits its expansion*.

10. Every being, in fact, is in itself a particular translation of His creative glance, and the realization in time of the form prescribed for its obedience, that is, for its operation, and of the symbol necessary for it to be significant. This form is the concrete expression and, at the same time, the means to knowledge which the particular being has of the general. Knowledge is the instrument which allows all beings to be born with. This being-born-with... crowns itself in man as an action that is voluntary, conscious, and intelligent.

11. And we, deep within our abysmal abode, have an eye to drink from those overflowing cups which God's generosity holds out toward us, one after the other. An eye directed not only to the outside but also to the inside, like those symbolic animals of which St. John speaks, who are *full of eyes within and without*; a look toward God of which sin alone alters the clarity.

12. The exercise of the four senses calls on us... the field of the subjective. Vision, on the contrary, it seems, turns itself entirely toward the object; it transports me to the outside, and I am so taken up by the gaze that I forget for a moment to exist; the object possesses me, substitutes itself for me, it works in me in my place.

13. It is from the heart alone that He demands the secret of our filiation. God breathes us in order to know the scent which we possess.... Then we, with God, will have knowledge of a darkness so great that the Scripture... finds no other comparison than that of the light of Noon.

14. *It is then*, says the blessed soul, *that I will be known as I am known*, says this pure image deep within ourselves, says this Conception in which this image is rendered capable of calling upon the Father.

15. Everything within us becomes simultaneous, transcribed once and for all into the "blue" of Eternity. We are transported ecstatically. The new Vision is but the unfolding of this glorious night of Faith in us. Then the soul, lending its ear, and shutting itself off within the walls of its house, will hear the word which had been promised to it: *I will wed thee for eternity*.

16. To say that I have a visual field is to say that by reason of my position I have access to and an opening upon a system of beings, visible beings, that these are at the disposal of my gaze in virtue of a kind of primordial contract and through a gift of nature, with no effort made on my part; from which it follows that vision is prepersonal. And it follows at the same time that it is always limited, that around

what I am looking at a given moment is spread a horizon of things which are not seen, or which are even invisible. Vision is *a thought subordinated to a certain field*, and this is what is called a *sense*.

17. In every focusing movement my body unites present, past and future, it secretes time, or rather it becomes that location in nature where, for the first time, events, instead of pushing each other into the realm of being, project round the present a double horizon of past and future and acquire a historical orientation.

18. Perception is always in the mode of the impersonal "One." It is not a personal act enabling me to give a fresh significance to my life. The person who, in sensory exploration, gives a past to the present and directs it towards a future, is not myself as an autonomous subject, but myself in so far as I have a body and am able to "look." Rather than being a genuine history, perception ratifies and renews in us a "prehistory."

19. The constitution of a spatial level is simply one means of constituting an integrated world: my body is geared to the world when my perception presents me with a spectacle as varied and as clearly articulated as possible, and when my motor intentions, as they unfold, receive the responses they expect from the world.

20. For each object...there is an optimum distance from which it requires to be seen....This is obtained through a certain balance between the inner and outer horizon....The distance from me to the object is not a size which increases or decreases, but a tension which fluctuates round a norm.

21. We have relearned to feel our body, we have found underneath the objective and detached knowledge of the body that other knowledge which we have of it in virtue of its always being with us and of the fact that we are our body. In the same way we shall need to reawaken our experience of the world as it appears to us in so far as we are in the world through our body, and in so far as we perceive the world with our body.

22. All thought of something is at the same time self-consciousness, failing which it could have no object. At the root of all our experiences and all our reflections, we find, then, a being which immediately recognizes itself, because it is its knowledge both of itself and of all things, and which knows its own existence, not by observation and as a given fact, nor by inference from any idea of itself, but through direct contact with that existence. Self-consciousness is the very being of mind in action.

23. Since...I have no evidence of my past other than this present testimony and yet have the idea of a past, I have no reason to set over the unreflective, as an unknowable, against the reflection which I bring to bear on it. But my confidence in reflection amounts in the last resort to my accepting and acting on the fact of temporality, and the fact of the world as the invariable framework of all illusion and all disillusion: I know myself only in so far as I am inherent in time and in the world, that is, I know myself only in my ambiguity.

24. Each perception...disappears only to give place to another perception which rectifies it. Each thing can, after the event, appear uncertain, but what is at least certain for us is that there are things, that is to say, a world. To ask oneself whether the world is real is to fail to understand what one is asking, since the world is not a sum of things which might always be called into question, but the inexhaustible reservoir from which things are drawn.

25. If the thing itself were reached, it would be from that moment arrayed before us and stripped of its mystery. It would cease to exist as a thing at the very moment when we thought to possess it. What makes the "reality" of the thing is therefore precisely what snatches it from our grasp.

26. The ipseity is, of course, never *reached*: each aspect of the thing which falls to our perception is still only an invitation to perceive beyond it, still only a momentary halt in the perceptual process.

27. But if we rediscover time beneath the subject, and if we relate to the paradox of time those of the body, the world, the thing, and other people, we shall understand that beyond these there is nothing to understand.

28. We are in the world, which means that things take shape, an immense individual asserts itself, each existence is self-comprehensive and comprehensive of the rest. All that has to be done is to recognize these phenomena which are the ground of all our certainties. The belief in an absolute mind, or in a world in itself detached from us is no more than a rationalization of this primordial faith.

Chapter 3. Claudel and Weil on Grace

1. Our entire religious life is our attention to the particular intention that God had in calling us into being....

2. Attention, taken to its highest degree, is the same thing as prayer. It presupposes faith and love.

3. He who Is what has always been, is the Father; he who is what Is, the resemblance which establishes identity, the word which translates the substance, is the Son; and he who Is what will be, that bond of love which exhausts at one fell movement between the two participants any and all possibility of being everywhere other than in the here and now, is the Spirit.

4. She...is the exaltation of humility, she is penitence in full glory! She is suave and unique. Honorable vessel, receptacle of orthodoxy, spiritual secret, vase of prudence, famous sanctuary of devotion! Full of grace....

5. Attention alone, that attention which is so full that the "I" disappears, is required of me. I have to deprive all that I call "I" of the light of my attention and turn it onto that which cannot be conceived.

6. The mute mass *summons* God to sow it with a word, to give it that by which it might become capable of coming to an end, and expiring in Him, of returning that which it had received. And, hark, life vibrates in his bosom.

7. It is one and at the same time a paradise and a clock; it is a distance sanctified by the figure; it is time made permanent by proportion; it is Infinity governed by number; it is absolute freedom in the infrangible enclosure; it is security in the inexhaustible; it is the phenomenal in the mystery; it is spontaneity in the fascination of the Law...it is an inextinguishable vigilance...it is the Dance of the Lanterns; it is a number whose key is everywhere; it is an insurrection and a choir; it is a city and an equation.

8. For, the Cross, which, according to the sacred promise, was to "draw everything to itself," was planted in the back of the building, in that gesture of widespread arms, pointing, unfolding, calling and stopping....Alone, around the altar and the choir, the officiating priests are given their own places; by its very pause, the crowd expresses, by congealment, the movement which has attracted it, a movement determined by a precise act; its partaking of the perpetration of the liturgical drama, in which it communicates for the perfection of the Hour. The middle bay, barred by unfathomable mysteries, guides the eyes up to that point, the aisles lead the step back and forth in their circuit.

9. If the presence of Christ in the consecrated elements were not solely...a sort

of alimentary luxury, a mystery confined to the contact of the palate with the tongue, it became important that the worship should not be limited to the liturgical act, but that permanent residence and honor be extended to the Eucharist among us.

10. Words truly *full of grace* which address themselves not only to the children of Abraham, nor even to the Dove of Nazareth, but to us also throughout the centuries! For, by bearing the Christ, we ourselves are part of His flesh and His soul, within the unity of the Church, to whom a Virgin gave birth. Already the work of our redemption has begun....It is she who engendered and who nourished us. It is this Virgin, our mother, at whose breast we sucked *butter and honey so that we might know how to* avoid evil and choose the good.

11. Christ was a public man, and, from the very beginning, he made his abode in public places. If we seek Him during the days of His stay among us, we find Him in Simon's house and the holstelry of Emmaus and the well of Sychar and always, according to Pharisees' reproach, with those who "eat and drink"; so also the Church....

12. For, ever since Paradise...man has always turned to the tree, shoot and vegetation of the unity, expression of wanting in testimony, seeking it as guardian of his prayers and as protector of his waters; sitting, kneeling in the shadow. But, while the heathen, incapable of subduing mystery, sought its obreptitious darkness as a hiding-place for his dolls, the Christian Church absorbed the mystic forest, adapting its avenues and its choir, from within, for the use of the human congregation.

13. The table is set, let us serve ourselves. God gives Himself to us: limitlessly, mountains and plains, hollows and valleys, meadows and deserts, and those triumphant perspectives to the infinite! What is left to do is to seek within!...It is not bread we desire, but the essence of bread...that money of eternity, that luminous and secret wafer which every dawn the priest slips between our lips.

14. He did not come to let Himself be grasped, but to let Himself be probed. In His first steps toward our soul, He does not address Himself to our intelligence, but to our probation. He turns to our *senses*, that is to the different forms of our interior *sensibility*, to our sense of sense.

15. He is the one who extracts for me from all things a sense of conscience and a sense of grace, and who arranges matters in such a way that everything on my right and on my left becomes rhythm, idea, resemblance, proposition, temperament and hymn.

16. Grace attracts, stirs, invites to its revelation that surface, that envelope to which everything else is attached, on which grace can exercise its action, and which would be appropriate to describe, while underneath it constructs the very mechanism appropriate for the deepest [sort] of enterprise of knowledge....At first it is a light and pure ray which soon encourages the emergence of the most profound treasures, all these spiritualized metals.

17. So lift yourself up towards God at the summit of the candelabrum, oh ardent and intelligent tongue, sharpened spiritual weapon, organ of enjoyment, of speech and desire!

18. Deprived of its senses, the soul separated from the body does not possess the means of receiving outside information; but it is not bereft of the initial sense, constituted by its shifting connection with the only fixed point. Now, the soul takes up directly the thrust and the design of the impulse which, not long ago, used to set going the various apparatus of the senses, supplying it, in this way, with the perception of its image. In the "time" allotted to its tension, it folds up in all its might; it no longer possesses the means of creating images with its senses; but the organiza-

tion owing to which it set them in motion constitutes a kind of image in itself. It builds itself up in a certain state of equilibrium....This image constitutes the soul's gift to its Creator, achieved by the second measure of its respiration, and the substance of its joy or its torment.

19. To accept a void in ourselves is supernatural. Where is the energy to be found for an act which has nothing to counterbalance it? The energy has to come from elsewhere. Yet first there must be a tearing out, something desperate has to take place, the void must be created. Void: the dark night.

20. If I thought that God sent me suffering by an act of his will and for my good, I should think that I was something, and I should miss the chief use of suffering which is to teach me that I am nothing. It is therefore essential to avoid all such thoughts, but it is necessary to love God through the suffering.

21. In our sense perceptions, if we are not sure of what we see, we change our position while looking, and what is real becomes evident. In the inner life, time takes the place of space. With time we are altered and if, as we change, we keep our gaze directed toward the same thing, in the end illusions are scattered and the real becomes visible. This is on the condition that the attention should be a looking and not an attachment.

22. The use of reason makes things transparent to the mind. We do not, however, see what is transparent. We see that which is opaque through the transparent, the opaque which is hidden when the transparent was not transparent....The uncomprehended hides the incomprehensible and should on this account be eliminated.

23. Contradiction is the criterion. We cannot by suggestion obtain things which are incompatible. Only grace can do that....Grace alone can give courage while leaving the sensitivity intact, or sensitivity while leaving the courage intact.

24. Renunciation. Imitation of God's renunciation in creation. In a sense, God renounces being everything. We should renounce being something. That is our only good.

25. The rising of the notes is a purely sensorial rising. The descent is at the same time a sensorial descent and a spiritual rising. Here we have the paradise which every being longs for: where the slope of nature makes us rise toward the good.

26. Evil is infinite in the sense of being indefinite: matter, space, time. Nothing can overcome this kind of infinity except the true infinity. That is why on the balance of the cross a body which was frail and light, but which was God, lifted up the whole world.

27. As God is present through the consecration of the Eucharist, in what the senses perceive as a morsel of bread, so he is present in extreme evil through redemptive suffering, through the cross.

28. Innocence and evil. Evil itself must be pure. It can only be pure in the form of the suffering of someone innocent. An innocent being who suffers sheds the light of salvation upon evil. Such a one is the visible image of the innocent God. That is why a God who loves man and a man who loves God have to suffer.

29. God can love in us only this consent to withdraw in order to make way for him, just as he himself, our creator, withdrew in order that we might come into being....God who is no other thing but love has not created anything other than love.

30. We are born and live in an inverted fashion, for we are born and live in sin which is an inversion of the hierarchy. The first operation is one of reversal. Conversion.

31. The mysteries of the Catholic faith are not intended to be believed by all the parts of the soul....The Eucharist should not then be an object of belief for the part of me which apprehends facts. That is where Protestantism is true. But this presence

of Christ in the Host is not a symbol, for a symbol is the combination of an abstraction and an image, it is something which human intelligence can present to itself, it is not supernatural. There the Catholics are right, not the Protestants. Only with that part of us which is made for the supernatural should we adhere to these mysteries.

Chapter 4. Claudel and Sartre

1. Here she is before you, Mesa, relaxed, a woman full of beauty spread out in a greater beauty!/You talk about the piercing trumpet?/Rise, fractured form, and see me as a listening dancer,/Whose jubilant little feet are caught up in the/irresistible tempo!

2. Beauty is a value applicable only to the imaginary and which bears the negation of the world in its essential structure. This is why it is stupid to confuse the moral with the aesthetic.

3. Through layers and layers of existence, it unveils itself, thin and firm, and when you want to seize it, you find only existants, you butt against existants devoid of sense. It is behind them: I don't even hear it, I hear sounds, vibrations in the air which unveil it. It does not exist because it has nothing superfluous: it is all the rest which in relation to it is superfluous. It *is*. And I, too, wanted to *be*. That is all I wanted; this is the last word. At the bottom of all these attempts which seemed without bonds, I find the same desire again: to drive existence out of me, to rid the passing moments of their fat, to twist them, dry them, purify myself, harden myself, to give back at last the sharp, precise sound of a saxophone note.

4.   Here I am lying in state!
    And on all sides, to the right and to the left, I see
the forest of torches that surround me!
    Not lighted tapers, but powerful stars,
like tall dazzling virgins
    Before the face of God, such as one sees in holy paintings
of self-effacing Mary!
    And here I am, man, Intelligence,
    Lying on the Earth, ready to die....
    At the bottom of the universe and in the very midst of this
bubble and of swarm and cult.
    I see the immense clergy of the Night with her Bishops and
Patriarchs.

5.   Leave your hand on my head and I will see
    and understand everything.
    You don't fully know who I am, but now I see
clearly who you are and what you think you are,
    Full of glory and light, a creature of God! And I see
you love me,
    And that you are given to me, and I am with you in an
ineffable tranquillity.

6.   And I found myself confronting You like someone who
realizes that he is alone.

So, and I encountered again my nothingness, I tasted again
the matter of which I am formed.
I have sinned greatly.

7. Ah! I know now
What love is! And I know what You endured on your
cross, in your Heart,
If you loved each of us
Terribly, as I loved that woman, and the death rattle, and
the suffocating and the vise!

8. What a shadow on the land! My footstep cries out. It seems to me
I am speaking in a cavern.
Above me an obstructed sky, lighted upside down
by a pale day.

9. Ah, You know all about it, You know, You,
What love betrayed is! Ah, I have no fear of You!
My crime is great and my love is greater, and your
death alone, O Father,
The death that you grant me, death alone can gauge
them both!

10. O my Mesa, you are no longer merely a man, but
you belong to me, a woman,
And I am a man in you, and you are a woman with
me, and I gather your heart without your knowing it.
And I took it, and I arrange it with me forever
between my breasts!

11. O, ineffable iniquity! Come and eat me
like a mango fruit! Everything, everything, and me!
Is it really true, Mesa, that I exist by myself, and thereby
repudiate the world, and of what use is our love
to others?...
And the whole universe about us
Emptied of us like something incapable of
understanding and which requires reason!

12. Let there be nothing else but you and me, and in you only
me, and in me only the possession of you, and rage, and compassion,
and to destroy you and to be no longer detestably
Restrained by the clothes of flesh, and these
cruel teeth in my heart,
Not cruel!
Oh, it is not happiness I bring you, but
death, and mine with it.
But what does it matter to me if I make you
die,
And myself, and everything, provided that at that price,
which is you and me,
Surrendered, thrown down, torn, lacerated, consumed,

I feel your soul, for a moment which is all eternity,
touching,
   Taking
   Mine as lime seizes the sand, burning and hissing!

13.   And
       Since you are free now,
       And since we took it upon ourselves to destroy
    the indestructible power
       Of all the sacraments, there is only one, by the mystery
    of a reciprocal consent that
       Still lives, I promise myself to you, Ysé! See, my
    God, for this is my body!
       I promise myself to you! and in this consent alone
       Take the vow, and in the luminosity of penitence
       The Law, and in a supreme confirmation
       The establishment of our Order, for always.

14.   O Mesa, this is the break of midnight, and I am
    ready to be liberated,
       The sign for the last time of these great tresses unfolded
    in the wind of Death!

15.   Mine is not one of vain hair blowing about,
    and a dainty hanky a moment,
       But, all veils gone, myself, strong fulminous flame,
    the magnificent male in the glory of God,
       Man in the splendor of August, the vanquishing Spirit in
    the transfiguration of Noon!

16.   Great God, here I am, laughing, rolling, uprooted,
       leaning on the very subsistence of light as if
       on the wing beneath the wave!

17.   You are now the one who will instruct me, and
       I am listening.
       How long now, o woman, tell me,
       fruit of the vine, before I drink once more
       in the Kingdom of God?

18. Absurd: in relation to the stones, the tufts of yellow grass, the dry mud, the tree, the sky, the green benches. Absurd, irreducible; nothing—not even a profound, secret upheaval of nature—could explain it....The world of explanations and reasons is not the world of existence.

19. Nothing happens while you live. The scenery changes, people come in and go out, that's all. There are no beginnings. Days are tacked on to days without rhyme or reason, an interminable, monotonous addition.

20. In each one of these privileged situations there are certain acts which have to be done, certain attitudes to be taken, words which must be said—and other attitudes, other words are strictly prohibited.

21. I feel there are no more perfect moments....I feel it all the time, even when I sleep. I cannot forget it....But now I always feel a bit as if I'd suddenly seen it yesterday.

22. It is beyond—always beyond something, a voice, a violin note. Through layers and layers of existence, it unveils itself, thin and firm, and when you want to seize it, you find only existants, you butt against existants devoid of sense. It is behind them: I don't even hear it, I hear sounds, vibrations in the air which unveil it. It does not exist because it has nothing superfluous: it is all the rest which in relation to it is superfluous. It *is*.

23. And there is something that clutches the heart: the melody is absolutely untouched by this tiny coughing of the needle on the record. It is so far—so far behind....But behind the existence which falls from one present to the other, without a past, without a future, behind these sounds which decompose from day to day, peel off and slip towards death, the melody stays the same, young and firm, like a pitiless witness.

24. But a time would come when the book would be written, when it would be behind me, and I think that a little of its clarity might fall over my past. Then, perhaps, because of it, I could remember my life without repugnance.

25. But I don't *see* anything any more: I can search the past in vain, I can only find these scraps of images and I am not sure what they represent, whether they are memories or just fiction....New images are born in me, images such as people create from books who have never travelled. My words are dreams, that is all.

26. Something is beginning in order to end: adventure does not let itself be drawn out; it only makes sense when dead. I am drawn, irrevocably, towards this death which is perhaps mine as well. Each instant appears only as part of a sequence. I cling to each instant with all my heart: I know that it is unique, irreplaceable—and yet I would not raise a finger to stop it from being annihilated. This last moment I am spending...is going to end, I know it.

27. I am free: there is absolutely no more reason for living, all the ones I have tried have given way and I can't imagine any more of them....My past is dead. The Marquis de Rollebon is dead, Anny came back only to take all hope away....Alone and free. But this freedom is rather like death.

28. Only when I think back over those careful little actions, I cannot understand how I was able to make them: they are so vain. Habit, no doubt, made them for me. They aren't dead, they keep on busying themselves, gently, insidiously weaving their webs, they wash me, dry me, like nurses....In the distance....Above my head; and this instant which I cannot leave, which locks me in and limits me on every side, this instant I am made of will be no more than a confused dream.

Chapter 5. Claudel and Gide

1. We do not look at a painting by Viel, Vermeer, Pieter de Hooch, nor even accord it a superior and affectionate glance; we are immediately inside of it; we live in it.

2. Nicolas Poussin was and remains the most conscious of the painters, and it is through this that he reveals himself the most French....Thought presides at the birth of each of his paintings.

3. The joy which the contemplation of certain paintings by Poussin brings to us is not only a delight of our senses; that joy is deep, lasting, and a kind of serenity which uplifts me and draws me to myself.

4. Everything is eternal and everything flows at the same time. Everything flows, but it is down our throats that it flows. Everything has been given to man so that

he can fill himself to his capacity, and everything around rises and falls as toward a central point.

5. The image imprinted on the background of our memory has taken on a permanent value. The reflextion has impregnated the mirror and made a legible and enduring plate of several objects together.

6. All that is what I shall call the roads of utilization, all those twistings of a building, a city, a garden, all those detours that only end by coming together again like melodic lines, and that do nothing but assure us of our communication with ourselves; the axes around which revolves what we possess and what we are.

7. The art of the Dutch master [Rembrandt] is no longer a generous affirmation of the present, an irruption of the imagination into the domain of actuality, a banquet offered to our senses, the perpetuation of a moment of joy and color. It is no longer a glance at the present, it is an invitation to recollection.

8. Rembrandt's Philosopher has wound about himself this pathway that, in other days, served to lure away the Prodigal Son and to divert him toward the horizon; he has made this spiral stairway of it; this spiral that serves him for his descent step by step into the depths of contemplation. I shall take thee by the hand, says the Bride in the Canticles, I shall lead thee into the cellar where the wine is mellowing. This cellar for which the old woman in Nicolaes Maes' picture in Brussels has the key. It hangs over her alongside the bust of Pallas while, with closed eyes, she continues, with her hand, to decipher this book on her knees, upon which from the top of this shelf behind her seem to be pouring down other books filled with an invisible theme.

9. What fascinates me is the purity of its appearance, divested, stripped, made bare of all matter, of an almost mathematical or angelic purity or, let us say, simply photographic, but what photography! in which this painter, shut up in the interior of his lens, entraps the outside world.

10. What could be more touching than this crucifix of stiff unyielding wood, real and transportable, delegated in His stead on this altar by the sacrificial God represented for us in the picture in the back of the room and behind everything else?

11. In him thought also became image, gave rise to plastic art, and here purpose, emotion, form, craft, all converged and combined into the work of art.

12. Pagan mysticism, it goes without saying, but vivid and sincere, and such that one would not imagine the expression of it to be different when, instead of quenching his spiritual thirst at the cup of poetry which the god holds out to him, Anacreon should drink his fill of the chalice of the Eucharist. He has...the enraptured expression of one who receives Communion.

13. But having said this, let us realize that it is thought that motivates and animates all of his paintings. It is thought which determines the placement of his figures and their gestures, the movement of lines, the distribution of light and the choice of colors. This even extends to the foliation of the trees in his spacious landscapes, which seem to be an emanation of thought by their tranquil balancing and the serenity that they give forth.

14. Doubtless it is Poussin's spirit that speaks to me; but it is less to my intellect that he addresses himself than to the most intimate part of me which I do not know whether to call it soul or will....My reason is also touched here which lends assent to my joy, to the reconciliation of the soul and the senses in a supreme harmony.

15. The respect and adoration that these faces of saints express testify that Poussin nevertheless understood man and his heart, and knew how, when he wished, to interpret their movements.

16. For him tradition forms, as if outside of time, a continuity so homogeneous

that he doesn't hesitate to place, in his *Orphée et Eurydice*, the drama which separates the two lovers of the Greek tale, in a Roman setting where we are astonished to find the castle of Saint-Angelo.

17. And, as for Poussin, he has utilized them with a more incredible variety of use and of expression than even the Greeks ever did, or the Renaissance, or later Boucher: children of man, angels or Cupids, they take part in the drama.

18. Customs, horses, architecture, galleys, trophies, ornaments, hairstyles, sandals, helmets, shields, sails, draped figures, all details of costume and of posture, Poussin studied them with pen, with pencil, with red chalk, with brush on all the frescoes, all the medallions, all the engraved stones, all the bas-reliefs, all the columns, all the arches, all the statues that antiquity bequeathed to Rome.

19. However, it is the spirit and the genius of France that one senses which breathes in his canvas and that he illustrates in another way, but to the same extent as Descartes (this other uprooted one) and Corneille, his contemporaries.

20. From having too well understood that it is with beautiful sentiments and noble thoughts that one makes the worst works of art, the painter resolved no longer to express either thoughts or sentiments.

21. ...but Poussin preserved the taste for river gods that Raphael had given him.... What charm there is, however, in the tender blessing gesture of the mother, in the uplifted arm of his sister, keeping watch, in the appearance of the prow and of the entire form.

22. This harmony, Poussin doesn't seek it only in the expression of bliss; he imposes it voluntarily on the tumult; he finds it even in the horrible; in the way of the tragic Greeks and he is not afraid to portray massacres, dead bodies, and plague-ridden people.

Chapter 6. Claudel and Redon

1. Let me see and hear all things by means of / speech / And hail each by its very name with the word that / made it.

2. And I, John, saw the Holy City, the New Jerusalem, which descended from Heaven, next to God.

3. ...rushes toward that sea of refreshment, consolation and light, that, as perspective teaches us, is in no way below us, but ahead of us and above us!

4.   This light which is not for the sons of Earth!
       This light is for me, so weak that it needs
    the night to light my way, like the lamp of the binnacle!
       And outside is the darkness and the Chaos which has not yet
    received the Gospel.

5.   As the word drew all things from nothingness, so that
    they might die,
       It is thus that you were born so that you might die
    in me.
       As the sun calls into being all things
    visible,
       Thus the sun of the spirit, thus the spirit like a
    crucified thunderbolt
       Calls all things to knowledge, and behold they are
    presented to It at the same time.

6.   God, You Who baptized with Your Spirit the chaos
   And Who at the Easter Vigil exorcise through the mouth
of Your priest the pagan fount with the letter psi,
   You mingle with the water of Baptism our
human water
   Agile, glorious, undisturbed, imperishable.

7.   I believe without changing a single point that which my fathers
have believed before me,
   Confessing the Savior of humanity and Jesus Who has died
on the cross,
   Confessing the Father Who is God, the Son Who is God,
and the Holy Spirit Who is God,
   And yet not three gods, but only one God.

8.   I know all things and all things know themselves
in me.
   I bring to each thing its deliverance.
   Through me
   Each thing no longer remains alone, but I link it to
another in my heart.

9.   The earth, the blue sky, the river with its boats and
three trees carefully set on the bank,
   The leaf and the insect on the leaf, this rock which I
weigh in my hand,
   The village with all these people...
   All that is eternity and freedom...
   I see them with my bodily eyes, I bear them in
my heart!

Chapter 7. Claudel and van Gogh

1. But why put myself at the service of a program? Pure movement is at my disposal, movement that creates time, and time, in its turn, has created space. In my hands, I hold the keys that can put everything in motion!

2. Gauguin and I have yet to see a small panel of his [Giotto] at Montpellier, the death of some sainted woman. There, the expressions of sorrow and ecstasy are so human that the entire nineteenth century agrees; there, one feels—and believes oneself to have been present there—so much does one share the emotion.

3. By means of sound, we become immediately sensitive to those realities which otherwise are perceptible to our minds only through their relationship to the world of dimension: speed, distance, height, depth, continuity, interruption, the direct, the lateral, the heavy, the light, the simple, the complex, etc. We translate, we create space with time, and the physical with the immaterial.

4. From beginning to end, by a happy utilization of itself, there is successive and simultaneous melody offering itself to me in ineffable clarity, and in security in the bosom of inviolable vocalization, of liberation through delight.

5. ...but the note, entirely pure, that drop, in a perceptible instant made of agglomerated waves, already bears within itself, by the mere fact of its existence, a

potential harmony, a query, an appeal around it for union, sense, commentary, contradiction.

6. Under the impulse of the soul, the sentiment swells up and slackens, it soars through all the notes of the scale up to the most piercing; it descends to the cellar; it coos, it shouts, it bruises, it caresses, it thinks; short-lived but inexhaustible, it listens to itself enjoying, until time without end, a kind of blessed state of which it is, itself, the source. Through sound, silence has become, for us, accessible and usable.

7. But Nature herself is not made to engulf me! I am the master! It is I who make her rise up from that false immobility that I, who know more about it than you, call simply "a sustained note." It is I who explain to her what she is! She is my audience! She is this matter under my orders! I hold inspection! It is I who, amidst all this chaos, utter the name of God!

8. Thus, sound is essentially that which begins and ceases, that which traces the phase from one end to the other. Ear is the instrument thanks to which man can appreciate all the rhythms and aspects of the movement which animates him, using its own flow as a continuous basis. Man is free to create the sonorous image of this pace of life; and this is the origin of music and speech.

9. Number is love, a sharp, omnipotent feeling for conformity, the adherence, serenely, passionately, ecstatically free, to an order, a reason, a justice, a will, to a disposition of an inevitable partner, the lodging of ourselves within a numeral so beautiful that it escapes computation, worthy object of an inexhaustible study.

10. I need nothing less to welcome the prodigious message that I sense all around me than the flapping ears of the orchestra! It is not for my own outcry alone that I must provide, it is the whole Titan, the entire Creation which I must deliver of its potential language and, from now until the end enjoined on it, bring to an understanding with its Creator!

11. There is a certain theme proposed to my art and imposed upon it, for whose development I need the assistance of this inner oracle deep down within me that I must awaken to the sense of its responsibilities.

12. The flute marks out a shining path before him. The cymbals, of their own accord, clash between his two hands, and not the pagan lyre, but the great ten-stringed harp, made of the very rays of Grace and Divine Glory, comes to put itself into his arms for the double, inverted activity of his agile, strumming fingers.

13. This sonorous touch is the sign of a prolonged and detailed commerce which, henceforth, appears realized on the condition that our interior tumult *does not impede the music*. There is, therefore, deep in the ground of our being, the music of a divine harmony, at the same time, the impregnation of our intelligence and the perturbation of our will.

14.   Ah, I am drunk! ah, I am possessed by the god! I hear a
         voice within me, and the measure grows faster, the movement
         of joy...
         What do men matter to me now! I am not made
         for them, but for the
         Delight of this sacred measure...
         What do some of them matter? This rhythm only! What matters
         whether they follow me or not? What does it matter whether they
         understand me or not?

15. It seems that science—scientific reasoning—will go a long way. This is because one believed that the earth was flat. That was true, and it is still true today.... The only thing is that it matters little whether science proves that the earth

is above all round, which no one contests today. Very likely future generations will enlighten us on this interesting subject; then, Science, without displeasuring anyone, will have arrived at some conclusions more or less similar to the words of Christ relative to the other half of existence.

16. Ah, he is without doubt wise, just, moved by the Bible. But modern reality is such that it takes from us those bygone days which we seek to reconstruct in our thoughts. The small events of our life do take us to that same moment, those meditations, and we violently reject our actual existence in our personal sensations—joy, boredom, suffering, anger or laughter.

Conclusion

1. This temple which has taken me for a few precious moments and which Genesis says is terrible, is Bethel, it is God's habitation with man; and this limitless and diverse splendor that surrounds me, this space made up entirely of motes, this silent activity, in full daylight like that of the starry sky—all this is Grace; it is the language God uses with man, Who, in order to make Himself understood, does not consider it proper to employ anything except this light that He is....These panels of colored glass around us are matter that feels, abstract matter, sensitive to the intellectual ray; it is the accidental miraculously isolated from substance; we are enfolded in sensibility, so fine, so fluctuating, so delicate!...Here is Paradise regained. We are enveloped and penetrated by its invisible murmuring, its shimmering shadows, its limitless counsel.

Select Bibliography

General Studies

Albérès, René M. *L'aventure intellectuelle du xxᵉ siècle: Panorama des Littératures européennes, 1900–1963*. Paris: Albin Michel, 1959.

Balakian, Anna E. *Literary Origins of Surrealism: A New Mysticism in French Poetry*. New York: The Gotham Library, [1965].

_____. *The Symbolist Movement: A Critical Appraisal*. New York: Random House, 1967.

Balthasar, Hans Urs von. *Seeing the Form*. Translated by E. Leiva-Merikakis. San Francisco: Ignatius Press, 1983.

Beardsley, Monroe C. *Aesthetics: Problems in the Philosophy of Criticism*. New York: Harcourt, Brace, 1958.

Berchan, Richard. *The Inner Stage*. Ann Arbor: University of Michigan Press, 1966.

Bosanquet, Bernard. *Three Lectures on Aesthetics*. London: Macmillan, 1931.

Cagnon, Maurice. *Ethique et esthétique dans la littérature française du xx siècle*. Saratoga, Calif.: Anma Libri, 1978.

Cassirer, Ernst, *The Philosophy of Symbolic Forms*. New Haven: Yale University Press, 1953.

Chassé, Charles. *The Nabis and Their Period*. Translated by M. Bullock. New York: Praeger, 1969.

Chiari, Joseph. *The Aesthetics of Modernism*. London: Vision, 1970.

_____. *Art and Knowledge*. New York: Gordian, 1977.

_____. *Twentieth-Century French Thought: From Bergson to Lévi-Strauss*. New York: Gordian, 1975.

Chipp, Herschel. *Theories of Modern Art*. Berkeley: University of California Press, 1969.

Chisholm, Roderick. *Perceiving: A Philosophical Study*. Ithaca: Cornell University Press, 1957.

Cohen, Robert Greer. *A Critical Work I: Modes of Art*. Saratoga, Calif. Anma Libri, 1975.

Cornell, Kenneth. *The Post-Symbolist Period: French Poetic Currents, 1900–1920*. New Haven: Yale University Press, 1958.

_____. *The Symbolist Movement*. New Haven: Yale University Press, 1951.

De Bruyne, Edgar. *The Esthetics of the Middle Ages*. Translated by E. B. Hennessy. New York: Ungar, 1969.

Descombes, Vincent. *Modern French Philosophy*. Translated by L. Scott-Fox and J. M. Harding. New York: Cambridge University Press, 1980.

Diéguez, Manuel de. *Essai sur l'avenir poétique de Dieu*. Paris: Plon, 1965.

Dufrenne, Mikel. *Phénoménologie de l'expérience esthétique*. Paris: Presses Universitaires de France, 1953.

Ellis, John. *Theory of Literary Criticism*. Berkeley: University of California Press, 1974.

Focillon, Henri. *La peinture aux xixe et xxe siècles: du réalisme à nos jours*. Paris: Renouard, 1928.

_____. *La vie des formes*. Paris: Alcan, 1947.

Garrelli, Jacques. *La gravitation poétique*. Paris: Mercure de France, 1968.

Geraets, Theodore F. *Vers une nouvelle philosophie transcendentale*. The Hague: Nijhoff, 1971.

Gilbert, Katherine Everett, and Helmut Kuhn. *A History of Aesthetics*. New York: Macmillan, 1939.

Gilson, Etienne. *The Arts of the Beautiful*. New York: Scribner, 1965.

_____. *Painting and Reality*. New York: Pantheon, 1957.

Hatzfeld, Helmut A. *Literature through Art: A New Approach to French Literature*. New York: Oxford University Press, 1952.

Hautecoeur, Louis. *Littérature et peinture en France, du xviie au xxe siècle*. Paris: Colin, 1942.

Hobbs, Richard. *Odilon Redon*. Boston: Little Brown, 1977.

Huyghe, René. *La relève de l'imaginaire*. Paris: Flammarion, 1976.

Jasper, David. *Images of Belief in Literature*. New York: St. Martin's Press, 1984.

Johansen, Sven. *Le Symbolisme: Etude sur le style des symbolistes français*. Copenhagen: Einar Munksgaard, 1945.

Klein, Robert. *La forme et l'intelligible*. Paris: Gallimard, 1970.

Langer, Susanne K. *Feeling and Form: A Theory of Art*. New York: Scribners, 1953.

_____. *Problems of Art*. New York: Scribners, 1957.

_____. *Reflections on Art*. Baltimore: Johns Hopkins University Press, [1958].

Lawler, James. *The Language of French Symbolism*. Princeton: Princeton University Press, 1969.

Lehmann, A. *The Symbolist Aesthetic in France, 1885–1895*. Oxford: Basil Blackwell, 1950.

Lucie-Smith, Edward. *Symbolist Art*. New York: Praeger, 1972.

Malraux, André. *The Voices of Silence*. Translated by Stuart Gilbert. New York: Doubleday, 1953.

Maritain, Jacques. *Creative Intuition in Art and Poetry*. New York: Pantheon, 1953.

Marty, Eric. "La religion ou la repetition imaginaire." *Bulletin des Amis d'André Gide* 11, no. 58 (1983): 199–238.

Michaud, Guy. *Message poétique du symbolisme*. 2 vols. Paris: Nizet, 1947.

Muller, Marcel. *De Descartes à Marcel Proust*. Paris: Baconniere Neuchatel, 1947.

Osborne, Harold. *Aesthetics and Art Theory: An Historical Introduction*. New York: Dutton, 1972.

_____. *Theory of Beauty: An Introduction to Aesthetic*. London: Routledge and Kegan Paul, 1952.

Panofsky, Erwin. *Idea: A Concept in Art Theory*. Translated by Joseph Peake. Columbia: University of South Carolina Press, 1968.

_____. *Meaning in the Visual Arts: Papers in and on Art History*. Garden City, New York: Doubleday, 1955.

Picon, Gaëtan. *Introduction à une esthétique de la littérature*. Paris: Gallimard, 1953.

Pilkington, A. E. *Bergson and His Influence*. Cambridge: Cambridge University Press, 1976.

Poulet, Georges. *Etudes sur le temps humain*. Paris: Plon, 1950.

Raymond, Marcel. *De Baudelaire au Surréalisme*. Paris: Corti, 1963.

Read, Herbert. *The Philosophy of Modern Art: Collected Essays*. London: Faber and Faber, 1952.

Rewald, John. *The History of Impressionism*. New York: The Museum of Modern Art, 1961.

_____. *Post-Impressionism: From Van Gogh to Gauguin*. New York: The Museum of Modern Art, 1962.

Rousset, Jean. *Forme et Signification: Essais sur les structures littéraires de Corneille à Claudel*. Paris: Corti, 1964.

Schmidt, Albert-Marie. *La Littérature symboliste (1870–1900)*. Paris: Presses Universitaires de France, 1963.

Swartz, Robert J. *Perceiving, Sensing and Knowing*. Garden City, New York: Anchor, 1965.

Tison-Braun, Micheline. *L'introuvable origine. Le problème de la personalité au seuil du xxe siècle*. Geneva: Droz, 1981.

Tuzet, Hélène. *Le cosmos et l'imagination*. Paris: Corti, 1965.

Venturi, Lionello. *History of Art Criticism*. Translated by Charles Marriot. New York: Dutton, 1936.

Welsh-Ovcharov, Bogomila. *Van Gogh in Perspective*. The Artist in Perspective Series. Englewood Cliffs, N.J.: Prentice-Hall, 1974.

Whitford, Frank. *Expressionism: Movements of Modern Art*. London: Hamlyn, 1970.

Wölfflin, Heinrich. *Principles of Art History*. New York: Dover, 1950.

_____. *Renaissance and Baroque*. Translated by K. Simon. Ithaca: Cornell University Press, 1966.

Yolton, John W. *Thinking and Perceiving: A Study in the Philosophy of the Mind*. La Salle, Ill.: Open Court, 1962.

Claudel Studies

Andrieu, Jacques. *La foi dans l'oeuvre de Paul Claudel*. Paris: Presses Universitaires de France, 1955.

Barjon, Louis. *Paul Claudel*. Paris: Editions Universitaires, 1953.

Becker, Aimé. "Poésie et mystique: Le thème claudélien des 'sens spirituels.'" *Revue des Sciences Religieuses* 4 (1969): 228–42.

Behr-Sigel, Elisabeth. "Mort et transfiguration: L'expérience transcendée de l'amour humain, (*Partage de Midi*)." *Bulletin de la Société Paul Claudel* 82 (1981): 33–38.

Chaigne, Louis. *Paul Claudel: The Man and the Mystic*. Translated by Pierre de Fontnouvelle. Westport, Conn.: Greenwood Press, 1978.

Chonez, Claudine. *Introduction à Paul Claudel*. Paris: Albin Michel, 1947.

Claudel, Pierre. *Paul Claudel*. Paris: Bloud et Gay, 1965.

Espiau de la Maestre, André. "Claudel et Sartre." *Bulletin de la Société Paul Claudel* 94 (1984): 23–29.

Fowlie, Wallace. *Paul Claudel*. London: Bowes and Bowes, 1957.

Gillet-Maudot, M. J. *Paul Claudel: Documents et images*. Paris: Gallimard, 1966.

Hellerstein, Nina. "Paul Claudel's 'Magnificat': A Structural and Thematic Interpretation." *Dalhousie French Studies* 6 (1984): 23–40.

Houriez, Jacques. "La Bible dans les oeuvres dramatiques et poétiques de Paul Claudel." *Bulletin de la Société Paul Claudel* 96 (1984): 25–28.

Lesort, Paul-André. *Paul Claudel par lui-même*. Paris: Seuil, 1953.

Lioure, Michel. *L'esthétique dramatique de Paul Claudel*. Paris: Colin, 1971.

Morisot, Jean-Claude. *Claudel et Rimbaud: Etude de transformations*. Paris: Lettres Modernes, 1976.

Mouton, Jean. "Claudel et l'espérance. L'espérance de Claudel: De la délivrance du mal à l'annonce du mystère pascal." *Bulletin de la Société Paul Claudel* 84 (1981): 65–75.

Petit, Jacques. *Claudel et l'usurpateur*. Bruges, Belgium: Desclée de Brouwer, 1971.

_____. *Paul Claudel 12: Claudel et l'art*. Paris: Lettres Modernes, 1978.

Plourde, Michel. *Paul Claudel: Une musique du silence*. Montréal: Presses de l'Université de Montréal, 1970.

Roberto, Eugène. *Visions de Claudel*. Marseille: Leconte, 1958.

Starobinski, Jean. "Parole et silence de Claudel." *Nouvelle Revue Française* (September 1955): 523–31.

Tonquedec, Joseph De. *L'oeuvre de Paul Claudel*. Paris: Beauchesne, 1927.

Vachon, André. *Le temps et l'espace dans l'oeuvre de Paul Claudel*. Paris: Seuil, 1965.

Van Hoorn, H. J. W. *Poésie et mystique: Paul Claudel poète chrétien*. Geneva: Droz, 1957.

Waters, Harold A. *Paul Claudel*. New York: Twayne, 1970.

Wood, Michael. "A Study of Fire Imagery in Some Plays by Paul Claudel." *French Studies* (April 1965): 154–58.

Gide Studies

Brée, Germaine. *Gide*. New Brunswick, N. J.: Rutgers University Press, 1963.

Faletti, Heidi. "An Aesthetic Perspective on Gide and Nietzsche." *Revue de Littérature Comparée* 52, no. 1 (1978): 39–59.

Guérard, Albert J. *André Gide*. Cambridge: Harvard University Press, 1951.

Herbart, Pierre. *A la recherche d'André Gide*. Paris: Gallimard, 1952.

Lachasse, Pierre. "La mythologie dans l'oeuvre d'André Gide." *Bulletin des Amis d'André Gide* 11, no. 60 (1983): 562–64.

Martin, Claude. *La maturité d'André Gide: de Paludes à L'immoraliste, 1895–1902*. Paris: Klincksieck, 1977.

Painter, Georges D. *André Gide. A Critical Biography*. London: Weidenfeld and Nicolson, 1968.

Perry, Kenneth I. *The Religious Symbolism of André Gide*. Le Haye-Paris: Mouton, 1969.

Pierre-Quint, Léon. *André Gide: L'homme, sa vie, son oeuvre. Entretiens avec Gide et ses contemporains*. Paris: Stock, 1952.

Rossi, Vinio. *André Gide: The Evolution of an Aesthetic*. New Brunswick, N. J.: Rutgers University Press, 1967.

_____. *André Gide*. New York: Columbia University Press, 1968.

Merleau-Ponty Studies

Bannan, John F. *The Philosophy of Merleau-Ponty*. New York: Harcourt, Brace, 1967.

Barral, Mary Rose. *Merleau-Ponty: The Role of the Body-Subject in Interpersonal Relations*. Pittsburgh, Pa.: Duquesne University Press, 1965.

Heidsieck, Françis. *L'ontologie de Merleau-Ponty*. Paris: Presses Universitaires de France, 1971.

Kwant, Remi C. *The Phenomenological Philosophy of Merleau-Ponty*. Pittsburgh, Pa.: Duquesne University Press, 1963.

Langan, Thomas. *Merleau-Ponty's Critique of Reason*. New Haven: Yale University Press, 1966.

Mallin, Samuel B. *Merleau-Ponty's Philosophy*. New Haven: Yale University Press, 1979.

Proust Studies

Albaret, Céleste. *Monsieur Proust*. Edited by G. Belmont. Paris: Robert Laffont-Opera Mundi, 1973.

Bardèche, Maurice. *Marcel Proust, romancier*. 2 vols. Paris: Sept Couleurs, 1971.

Bell, William Stewart. *Proust's Nocturnal Muse*. New York: Columbia University Press, 1962.

Bersani, Léo. *Marcel Proust: The Fictions of Life and of Art*. New York: Oxford University Press, 1965.

Brée, Germaine. *Marcel Proust*. Translated by C. J. Richard and A. D. Truitt. New Brunswick, N. J.: Rutgers University Press, 1969.

Bucknall, Barbara J. *The Religion of Art in Proust*. Urbana: University of Illinois Press, 1969.

Cazeaux, Jacques. *L'écriture de Proust ou l'art du vitrail*. Cahiers Marcel Proust, no. 4. Paris: Gallimard, 1971.

Champigny, Robert. *Proust.* Englewood Cliffs, N. J.: Prentice-Hall, 1962.

Chernowitz, Maurice E. *Proust and Painting.* New York: International University Press, 1945.

Deleuze, Gilles. *Proust et les signes.* Paris: Presses Universitaires de France, 1971.

Faris, Wendy. "The Poetics of Pleasure: Expansive Images in *Swann's Way.*" *Kentucky Romance Quarterly* 30, no. 4 (1983): 359–72.

Fiser, Emeric. *L'esthétique de Marcel Proust.* Paris: Rieder, 1933.

_____. *Le symbole littéraire, essai sur la signification du symbole chez Wagner, Baudelaire, Mallarmé, Bergson et Proust.* Paris: Corti, 1941.

Graham, Victor E. *The Imagery of Proust.* New York: Barnes and Noble, 1966.

Henry, Anne. *Marcel Proust: Théories pour une esthétique.* Paris: Klincksieck, 1981.

Hewitt, James R. *Marcel Proust.* New York: Ungar, 1975.

Hindus, Milton. *The Proustian Vision.* New York: Columbia University Press, 1954.

Mauriac, Claude. *Proust par Lui-même.* Paris: Seuil, 1959.

Maurois, André. *A la recherche de Marcel Proust.* Paris: Hachette, 1970.

Megay, Joyce N. *Bergson et Proust.* Paris: J. Vrin, 1976.

Monnin-Hornung, Juliette. *Proust et la peinture.* Geneva: Droz, 1951.

Mouton, Jean. *Proust.* Bruges, Belgium: Desclée de Brouwer, 1968.

Painter, Georges D. *Proust: The Early Years.* Boston: Little Brown, 1959.

_____. *Proust: The Later Years.* Boston: Little Brown, 1965.

Pierre-Quint, Léon. *Marcel Proust, sa vie, son oeuvre.* Paris: Sagittaire, 1946.

Rancoeur, René. *Bibliographie de Marcel Proust. Etudes proustiennes 5.* Paris: Gallimard, 1984.

Richard, Jean-Pierre. *Proust et le monde sensible.* Paris: Seuil, 1974.

Sansom, William. *Proust and His World.* New York: Scribners, 1973.

Shattuck, Roger. *Marcel Proust.* New York: Viking, 1974.

Trahard, Pierre. *L'art de Marcel Proust.* Paris: Dervy, 1953.

Vial, André. *Proust: Structures d'une conscience et naissance d'une esthétique.* Paris: Julliard, 1963.

Sartre Studies

Bauer, G. *Sartre and the Artist.* Chicago: University of Chicago Press, 1969.

Fell, J. P. *Emotion in the Thought of Sartre.* New York: Columbia University Press, 1965.

Kaelin, Eugene F. *An Existential Aesthetic. The Theories of Sartre and Merleau-Ponty.* Madison: The University of Wisconsin Press, 1962.

Sartre, Jean-Paul. *Essays in Aesthetics.* Translated by Wade Baskin. New York: Philosophical Library, 1963.

_____. *Situations.* Translated by Benita Eisler. New York: Braziller, 1965.

Schlipp, Paul A. *The Philosophy of Jean-Paul Sartre.* La Salle, Ill.: Open Court, 1981.

Weil Studies

Cabaud, J. *Simone Weil: A Fellowship in Love*. New York: Channel Press, 1964.

Casper, Bernard. "Foi et temporalité dans la pensée de Simone Weil." *Cahiers Simone Weil* 4, no. 4 (1981): 213–25.

Davy, M. M. *Simone Weil*. Paris: Editions Universitaires, 1952.

_____. *Simone Weil, sa vie, son oeuvre avec un exposé de sa philosophie*. Paris: Presses Universitaires de France, 1966.

Kempfner, Gaston. *La philosophie mystique de Simone Weil*. Paris: La Colombe, 1960.

Krebs, Simone. "Simone Weil, souffrance et spiritualité." *Cahiers de l'Archipel* 11 (1984): 23–26.

Narcy, M. *Simone Weil. Malheur et beauté du monde*. Paris: Centurion, 1967.

Ottensmeyer, H. *Le thème de l'amour dans l'oeuvre de Simone Weil*. Paris: Lettres Modernes, 1958.

Rees, R. *Simone Weil: A Sketch for a Portrait*. Carbondale, Ill.: Southern Illinois University Press, 1966.

Vetö, Miklos. *La métaphysique religieuse de Simone Weil*. Paris: J. Vrin, 1971.

Index

Abraham, 65
Abstract, 68, 100
Abstraction, 150
Abyss, 20, 31–32, 40, 81, 63, 96, 101, 122–23, 125, 132, 134, 154, 157–58
Aesthetic (Ecstatic), 20, 34–35, 39, 77, 80, 88, 90, 94, 98, 107, 110, 115, 117, 130, 137, 141, 157–58
A la recherche du temps perdu (Proust), 32
Albertine, 33, 36–37
Allegorical, 100, 121, 127
Allegory of the Faith (Vermeer), 103, 105 (reproduced on 104)
Amalric, 81
"And beyond, the Astral Idol" (Redon), 132
"And He had in his Right Hand Seven Stars" (Redon), 125
"And I Saw in the Right Hand of Him That Sat on the Throne, a Book Written within and Without" (Redon), 128
"And the Searcher was Engaged in an Infinate Search" (Redon), 132
Anny, 90–91, 94
Apocalypse of St. John (Redon), 125–29
Apollo, 85
Apotheosis, 132
Archetypal, 39, 85, 110–11, 134
Architectural, 63, 66, 99
Architecture, 139
Art: and aesthetics of light and darkness, 120–24; baroque, 20, 64–65, 97–98, 119; Christian (Catholic) assimilation of, 63–67; as embodiment of human sentiment, 144–46; Flemish, 20, 99–101, 103, 105, 117–18; French, 114, 117; Italian, 105; as literary, 81–96; as musical, 136–43; as poetical, 27–41, 44, 79, 135; as thought, 125–34

Attention, 29, 100–101, 114, 151; of the body, 30–31; and color, 145; and contemplation, 101, 110; and perception, 51; and prayer, 61, 71–74; of the soul, 30–31
Avenue (Hobbema), 106

Bach, Johann Sebastian, 137
Bacchic, 141
Baudelaire, Charles, 114
Beach (Ruysdaël), 106
Beauty, 17–21; definitions of, 23–41, 95–96; and Christ, 81–88; and color, 143–53; and creation, 99–106; and freedom, 89–95; and grace, 59–78; and harmony, 135–43; and perception, 42–58; as pagan mysticism, 107, 111; as pure images, 125–32; as trace, 134
Beethoven, Luduwig van, 137
Being, 17–22, 24, 40, 42–44, 47–50, 52, 55, 57–58, 62–63, 95, 103
Bergotte, 33
Berma, 33
Bernard, Emile, 153
Birth: and consciousness, 42–50; and love, 31; and sacrifice, 122
"Blossoming" (Redon), 128
Body: closed off to God's image, 61; detached from the soul, 72; and form, 121; and harmony, 138–40; as instrument of birth, 46–56; and the intellect, 124; physiologically considered, 29–30; and the soul, 136; and transfiguration, 85–88
Borch, Gerard ter, 102, 117
Botticelli, 39
Boucher, François, 111
Break at Noon (Claudel), 81
Buddha, 130

Caravaggio, 111, 117
Chardin, Jean Baptiste Siméon, 113

China, 82

Chintreuil, 106–7; *L'Espace* (*Space*), 106

Christ: and the artist, 153; body of, 47, 78, 83, 88; Bride of, 128; and the Church, 64–65, 78; death of, 43, 87, 122–23, 143; and eternity, 50; figure of, 105; form of, 43–44, 123, 125; and humanity, 73–74, 86; and the luminous, 125; mystery of, 118; in the presence of, 67

Church, the, 60, 62–66, 69, 75, 105, 128; of Notre Dame, of Rheims, of Rome, of Rouen, 64

Claesz, Pieter, 117

Claudel, Paul, 17–25, 27, 29, 40–51, 58–68, 70, 78–81, 88, 95–103, 105–6, 114, 117–22, 124–25, 128, 132, 134–40, 143–44, 154, 157–58; *L'art poétique* (*Poetic Art*), 40, 44, 62, 99; *L'oeil écoute* (*The Eye Listens*), 99; *Partage de midi* (*Break at Noon*), 81

Color, 21, 25, 27, 45, 48, 109, 111, 122, 136, 144–46, 148, 150–51, 153–55, 158

Conception, 50

Conception of the Virgin (Murillo), 103

Consciousness: and attention, 51; as dream, 80, 93; of the form, 56; globes of, 128, 132; as nothingness, 52; and the real, 94; and reason, 41; of the self, 55, 122; and the senses, 41; and the soul, 30; state of, 139; as thought, 43, 54; and transformation, 96

Contemplation, 17, 36, 38, 73, 76–77, 80, 93, 97, 101–3, 106–7, 110–11, 115, 117, 121, 123, 158

Contradiction, 73, 76, 78, 157

Conversion, 87

Corneille, Pierre, 113

Correspondence, 48, 54, 67–68, 78, 89, 105–6, 119–20, 124–25, 130, 135, 138–39, 144, 148, 154

Coubert, Gustave, 113–14

Darkness, 45, 49–50, 58, 70, 81–83, 86–87, 95–97, 103, 106, 120–22, 124–25, 128, 132, 158

David (Old Testament), 128

"Day" (Redon), 132 (reproduced on 133)

Debussy, Claude, 137

Delacroix, Eugène, 113

Descartes, René, 110, 113, 115, 117

Detachment, 78; as the good, 76; of the intellect, 71–74; of the will, 87

Discourse, 26

Dou, Gerrit, 102

Doubt, 19, 43, 55, 58, 102

Drama, 63–64, 69, 81, 90, 98, 102, 110–11, 113, 117, 119, 132, 157–58

Dream (Redon), 128, 130–31

Dream(s), 17–18, 20, 30, 38–39, 41, 80, 93–95, 109, 120, 125, 128, 130, 132, 134

Dreams (Redon), 132–33

Ecstasy, 17, 31, 36, 50, 83, 150

El Greco, 102

Elstir, 23, 33, 35–37

Eros, 20, 85

Essence, 17, 20, 25, 35–36, 66–67, 78, 89–90, 94, 109, 120

Eternity, 43–44, 57, 66, 75, 93, 106, 114, 122–24

Existence, 18–21, 23–24, 26–30, 32–33, 41–42, 46–47, 50–51, 53–56, 58, 60–61, 68–70, 73, 75–77, 85, 89–96, 99, 101–3, 105–6, 110, 115, 117, 120–22, 124, 130, 134, 139–40, 142, 146, 150–51, 153–55, 157–58

Exposition of Moses (Poussin), 115

Expression, 17, 26, 28–30, 36, 47, 66, 102, 113, 115, 117, 144, 146, 151, 153–54

Eyes, 20, 25, 32, 40, 45–51, 58, 66–68, 85, 99, 102–3, 109, 111, 122, 125, 138, 144; dazzled, 141; of faith, 58; of the memory, 38–40, 101; metaphysical, 67; of the mind, 18, 40, 130, 132; of the senses, 124; of the soul, 31, 48

Faith, 50, 57–58, 73–74, 76, 105, 121–22, 124, 142, 158

Flemish, 20, 99–101, 103, 105, 117–18

Flesh, 82–83, 85–86, 153

Florence, 34

Form, 17, 22, 24–30, 32, 34, 36–38, 40–45, 48–49, 51, 56, 58, 61–69, 85, 97, 99, 107, 115, 119–22, 124, 127–28, 130, 134–36, 141, 143, 146,

148, 151, 154, 157–58
France, 64, 114, 158
Freedom, 27, 59, 78, 88, 95

Gabrielle, 35
Genesis (Old Testament), 45
"Germination" (Redon), 128
Gide, André, 20, 97–98, 107–11, 113–15, 117–20, 157
Gilberte, 33
Giotto, 135
God, 18–20, 24–26, 40–41, 72–77, 95–98, 117–18, 127–28, 141–43, 154–55, 157–59; as absolute being, 50; in creation, 79–88; and grace, 59–78; in the light, 120–25; object of the soul, 30–32; and perception, 43–57
Gogh, Vincent van, 21, 135–36, 144–55, 157; *The Night Café*, 148 (reproduced on 149); *Pietà* (reproduced on 147); *The Sower* (reproduced on 152)
Good, 67–72, 75–78, 136, 141, 150, 153
Gothic, 63, 65, 99
Goya, Francisco José de, 102
Gozzoli, Benozzo, 91
Grace, 17–20, 36, 68, 82, 85, 88, 97–99, 117–21, 125, 136, 143, 154, 157–58; discussed theologically, 59–78
Gravity, 60, 71, 73–74, 78
Guermantes, 33

Hals, Frans, 102, 117; *Les Régents* (*The Regents*), 102; *Les Régentes* (*The Regents*), 102
Harmony, 19, 21, 27–28, 30–31, 53, 58, 62, 68–69, 100–101, 105, 109, 114, 117, 124, 135–36, 138–42, 144–46, 148, 151, 153, 155
Heart, 48, 50, 63, 76, 83, 103, 111, 115, 124, 136, 139–45, 158
Helst, Bartholomeus van der, 103
Hobbema, 106, 117–18; *Le Chemin* (*The Avenue*), 106
"Holy City, the New Jerusalem" (Redon), 128
Hong, Kong, 82
Hooch, Pieter de, 97, 102, 117
Human: being, 49, 56, 59, 64, 71, 139–40, 148; as humanity, 44, 65, 74,

77, 117, 122–23, 148, 153; as man, 30, 51; nature, 56, 60, 63, 68–69, 74, 102, 124; person, 17, 19, 21, 26, 30, 43, 48, 53, 57–59, 70–71, 74–78, 80, 96, 106–7, 114, 124–25, 138–39, 148

Idea, 17, 19, 21, 24, 28, 36–39, 56, 68, 107
Image, 18–21, 23, 25, 29–31, 34, 40–41, 43–45, 49–51, 53, 56, 58–65, 73, 78–81, 83, 85–86, 88–89, 95–96, 105, 107, 109, 111, 117, 121–22, 124, 132, 134, 139, 142, 158
Imagination, 18, 20, 33, 36, 68, 89, 91, 95, 101, 103, 120, 130, 134, 139, 146
Inspiratioin, 61
Inspiration of the Lyric Poet (Poussin), 107 (reproduced on 108)
Intellect, 31, 39, 49, 70–72, 99, 122, 124
Intentionality, 27–29, 41, 44, 51, 77, 79–80, 95, 101, 103, 124, 140, 143, 158
Inversion, 73, 76–77
Isaiah, 65
Isis, 130
Israel, 63

John (Saint), 125, 127
Joy, 31, 35, 65, 69, 74–75, 85, 92, 98, 110, 141, 143, 145–46, 151, 153–54

La Fontaine, Jean de, 114
La nausée (Sarte), 80, 89
L'art poétique (Claudel), 40, 44, 62, 99
Light, 17–18, 23, 31, 40, 45–51, 58, 60, 63, 68, 79, 81–83, 88, 98, 100, 102, 105–6, 120–25, 127–28, 132, 134, 157–58
Literature, 38, 80, 91, 115
Little Street (Vermeer), 103
L'oeil écoute (Claudel), 99
Longing, 21, 69, 71, 84
Love, 31, 33–36, 40, 61–62, 69, 73–74, 76–78, 81–85, 87–88, 122, 124, 140
Luminosity, 17–18, 20, 32, 81–82, 120, 122, 125, 127

Madeleine, 91
Maes, Nicolaes, 101, 103
Mallarmé, Stéphane, 114, 120

Manet, Edouard, 113
Massacre of the Innocents (Poussin), 110
Matisse, Henri, 114
Melody, 74, 80, 91–93, 114–15, 137, 139–40, 142–43, 146, 154
Memory, 36, 38–39, 74, 99, 101, 114, 142
Merleau-Ponty, Maurice, 18–19, 42–44, 51, 57–58, 157
Mesa, 79, 81–88
Metaphysical, 56, 66–67, 121
Michelangelo, 117
Michelet, Jules, 90
Middle Ages, 65
Mieris, Frans van, 102
Mithouard, Adrien, 114
Molière, Jean-Baptiste, 114
Monet, Claude, 133–14
Motion, 24, 28, 57, 99, 101, 128, 140–41, 154
Movement, 25, 27–28, 32–33, 36, 40, 44, 50, 62, 68, 73, 79, 95, 97, 99–100, 102, 106, 111, 115, 125, 135–38, 140–41, 143, 154, 158
Murillo, Bartholomé Esteban, 103; *Immaculate Conception (The Conception of the Virgin)*, 103
Music, 33, 74, 83, 91–92, 107, 115, 135–44, 148, 151, 154
Mystery, 17–18, 21–22, 32, 40, 50, 56–59, 62–65, 69, 82–83, 85, 87–88, 95, 97, 107, 121, 143, 146, 148
Mystical, 17, 37, 59, 110, 117
Mysticism, 20, 88, 109–10, 113–15, 117–18, 157

Nature, 24, 28, 37–38, 52, 58, 75–78, 97, 99–100, 105–7, 110, 114, 117–18, 120, 130, 138, 144–46, 148, 150–51, 153–54
Nausea (Sartre), 80, 89
New Testament, 64, 78, 99
Night Café (van Gogh), 148 (reproduced on 149)
Night (Redon), 132
Nurture of Jupiter (Poussin), 111

Objective, 18, 20, 23–24, 34–35, 40, 42, 48, 52, 54, 98, 120, 125, 130, 135–36, 139, 143, 151, 154
Odette, 39

Old Testament, 63–65, 76, 78, 99
Ontological, 98, 100, 105–6, 120
Ontology, 18, 95, 120
Origins (Redon), 130
Orpheus, 130
Orpheus and Eurydice (Poussin), 110
Ostade, Isaack van, 103, 117

Parma, 34
Partage de midi (Claudel), 81
Péguy, Charles, 114
Penance, 87
Perception, 18–19, 38, 61, 73, 97, 101, 157; definition of, 42, 51; and the possibility of birth, 46; and the self, 53; and the senses, 56; unity of, 54
Perugino, 48, 105
Phateon, 130
Phenomenal, 17–21, 23, 35, 38, 53–54, 61, 63, 66, 78, 86, 91–93, 96, 98–100, 103, 106, 109, 114–15, 119–22, 124, 127–28, 130, 134–38, 143, 145, 154
Picasso, 114
Pietà (van Gogh), reproduced on 147
"Pilgrim of the Sublunary World" (Redon), 132
Pisa, 34
Poetic Art (Claudel), 40, 44, 62, 99
Poetry, 17, 74, 83, 107, 115, 139, 151, 157
Poussin, Nicolas, 20, 97–99, 107–20, 157; *Inspiration d'Anacréon (The Inspiration of the Lyric Poet)*, 107 (reproduced on 108); *Jupiter et la chèvre amalthée (The Nurture of Jupiter)*, 111; *L'apparition de la Vierge à Saint Jacques (The Virgin Appearing to St. James)*, 111; *L'enfance de Bacchus (The Youth of Bacchus)*, 110; *L'enlèvement des Sabines (The Rape of the Sabines)*, 111; *Le massacre des innocents (The Massacre of the Innocents)*, 110; *Le triumphe de Flore (The Triumph of Flora)*, 111 (reproduced as frontispiece and on 112); *Moïse exposé sur les eaux du Nil (The Exposition of Moses)*, 115; *Orphée et Eurydice (Orpheus and Eurydice)*, 110; *Venus Spied on by Shepherds* (reproduced on 116)
Presence, 27, 43–44, 49–50, 67, 74–75,

93, 105, 123

Proportion, 44, 50, 79, 107, 117, 135, 140–41, 143

Proust, Marcel, 18–19, 23–24, 32–33, 35, 37, 40–41, 157; *A la recherche du temps perdu* (*Remembrance of Things Past*), 32

Racine, Jean Baptiste, 114

Rape of the Sabines (Poussin), 111

Raphael, 111, 115, 117

Rapture, 40, 62, 141, 154

Reason, 29, 47, 56, 69, 101; and conscience, 153–54, 158; and the good, 72–73; harmony of, 79; and the imagination, 68; mystery of, 57; and the senses, 41, 68, 107, 110, 136, 138, 154, 158

Redon, Odilon, 20, 120, 125–34, 157; "A Woman Clothed with the Sun" (*Apocalypse of St. John*), 128 (reproduced on 129); "And He Had in his Right Hand Seven Stars" (*Apocalypse of St. John*), 125; "And beyond, the Astral Idol" (*Dreams*), 132; "And I Saw in the Right Hand of Him That Sat on the Throne, a Book Written within and Without" (*Apocalypse of St. John*), 128; "And the Searcher was Engaged in an Infinite Search" (*The Night*), 132; "And There Fell a Great Star from Heaven" (*Apocalypse of St. John*), 125 (reproduced on 126); *Apocalypse de Saint-Jean* (*Apocalypse of St. John*), 125; "Blossoming" (*In the Dream*), 128; *Dans le rêve* (*In the Dream*), 128; "Germination" (*In the Dream*), 128; *La nuit* (*Night*), 132; *Les origines* (*The Origins*), 130; "Pilgrim of the Sublunary World" (*Dreams*), 132; "Sad Ascent" (*In the Dream*), 130; (reproduced on 131); "The Day" (*Dreams*), 132 (reproduced on 133); "The Holy City, the New Jerusalem" (*Apocalypse of St. John*), 128; "When Life Was Awakening" (*The Origns*), 130

Regents (Hals), 102

Rembrandt, 101, 105–6, 117

Remembrance of Things Past (Proust), 32

Renaissance, 54, 99

Revelation, 110, 121, 123, 127, 134, 157

Rhythm, 21, 28, 31–32, 67, 135–36, 139–41, 154; of images, 79; of reason, senses, and will, 68

Rhythmic, 45, 102, 142

Rollebon, 94

Rome, 64

Roquentin, 80, 89–95

Rubens, Peter Paul, 48, 111

Ruysdaël, Jacob Isaacksz van, 106, 117; *La Plage* (*The Beach*), 106

"Sad Ascent" (Redon), 130 (reproduced on 131)

Sarah (Old Testament), 65

Sartre, Jean-Paul, 20, 79–81, 88–89, 95–96, 157; *La nausée* (*Nausea*), 80, 89

Science, 155

Scripture, 18

Sculpture, 91, 139

Semiotic, 145

Senses, 18–19, 25–26, 38–39, 45, 64, 67, 80, 88, 97, 100, 109, 115, 122, 124, 136, 138–39, 158; and conscience, 79, 124, 154; darkness of, 84, 86; exterior and interior, 47–48, 58, 67; and the intellect, 49, 56; and reason, 41, 79, 107, 110, 136, 154; spiritual, 23, 88, 125

Sensations, 26, 34–35, 42, 44, 50, 52, 60, 67–69, 73, 101, 157

Seurat, Georges Pierre, 114

Sight, 25, 36, 44, 51, 58, 81, 101, 122–23, 158

Sign, 26–27, 64, 77, 100, 125, 127, 139, 145

Silence, 25, 31, 64, 102, 105, 109, 130, 138, 143

Smell, 25, 35, 38, 153, 158

Sorrow, 26, 110, 136, 146, 148, 150–51

Soul, 36–38, 46, 69, 75, 86, 88, 109, 137, 140, 144, 150; birth of, 49; and body, 30–31, 38, 60, 66–67, 136, 154; and God, 68; and grace, 73; harmony of, 139; and intentionality, 158; interior eyes of, 48; and joy, 98; and reason, 110; as spark, 29

Sower (van Gogh), (reproduced on 152

Space (Chintreuil), 106

Speech, 29

Steen, Jan, 117
Subjective, 18, 24, 34, 38, 42, 52, 54–55, 78, 98, 120, 134, 141, 143–44, 151, 153–55
Summer (Poussin), 110
Sumptuous, 98
Symbol, 27, 83–85, 95, 99, 103, 106, 118, 125, 127–28, 130, 134, 141
Symphony, 98, 122, 138

The Eye Listens (Claudel), 99
Theology, 49, 59, 144
Thought, 19–20, 34, 87, 90, 101, 107, 109, 111, 114, 119–20, 125, 128, 134
Time, 57, 69, 98–99, 128; beyond, 148; and ecstasy, 50; and eternity, 43, 75; musical, 135, 138, 140; and space, 52, 106, 128
Tintoretto, 91, 105
Titian, 105, 111, 117
Touch, 25, 35, 38, 100, 110, 123, 141–42, 144, 153, 158
Toulet, Paul-Jean, 114
Transcendence, 17, 23, 26, 57, 63, 80
Transfiguration, 50, 68, 82, 85
Transformation, 32–33, 50, 58, 81–82, 84–85, 87–88, 95, 106, 130
Triumph of Flora (Poussin), 111 (reproduced as frontispiece and on 112)
Truth, 34–36, 72, 77, 144

Ugliness, 39–40
Unconscious, 37, 128, 132
Unity, 18–19, 31, 33–34, 37, 51–53, 58, 60, 95, 106–7, 124, 134, 137, 139, 142

Valéry, Paul, 114, 120
Venice, 34
Venus Spied on by Shepherds (Poussin), (reproduced on 116)

Vermeer, Johannes, 97, 103–5, 117–18; *L'Allegorie evangélique* (*The Allegory of the Faith*), 103 (reproduced on 104); *La Ruelle* (*The Little Street*), 103; *Vue de Delft* (*View of Delft*), 103
Verse, 32, 138
Vibration, 25, 30, 41, 50, 102, 135, 138–39, 154, 157
View of Delft (Vermeer), 103
Virgin Appearing to St. James (Poussin), 111
Vision, 18, 31, 48–50, 52, 58, 69, 78, 90, 106, 110, 122, 125, 132, 144, 146
Void, 60–61, 69–71, 74–75, 77, 127, 132
Voluptuous, 150

Weil, Simone, 19, 60–62, 70–75, 78, 157
"When Life Was Awakening" (Redon), 130
Will, 20, 67–68, 72, 74, 78, 87, 110
"Woman Clothed with the Sun" (Redon); 128 (reproduced on 129)
Word, 140; as circularity, 29, 41; and freedom, 27; and grace, 141; and human action, 63; and human nature, 79, 124; as knowledge, 26; of God, 18, 62–63, 78, 125, 127–28; and the soul, 158
World, 19–21, 24–31, 38, 43–46, 48, 50–51, 53–54, 56–57, 62, 66, 69, 71–75, 78, 80, 83, 86–100, 103, 105–7, 109, 111, 114–15, 119–21, 124, 128, 130, 132, 134–36, 138–42, 144–45, 148, 151, 153, 154, 157

Youth of Bacchus (Poussin), 110
Ysé, 82–88